Media and Violence

Media and Violence

Gendering the Debates

Karen Boyle

SAGE Publications
London • Thousand Oaks • New Delhi

First published 2005

SAGE Publications Ltd
1 Oliver's Yard
55 City Road
London EC1Y 1SP

SAGE Publications Inc.
2455 Teller Road
Thousand Oaks, California 91320

SAGE Publications India Pvt Ltd
B-42, Panchsheel Enclave
Post Box 4109
New Delhi 110 017

British Library Cataloguing in Publication data

A catalogue record for this book is available
from the British Library

ISBN 1-4129-0378-5
ISBN 1-4129-0379-3 (pbk)

Library of Congress Control Number: 2004095882

Typeset by C&M Digitals (P) Ltd., Chennai, India
Printed in Great Britain by Athenaeum Press, Gateshead

Contents

Acknowledgements

So many people have influenced this project along the way, and have supported me during the writing, that it is impossible to name them all here. There are, however, some people I must single out.

Over the last months it has been my pleasure to work with Julia Hall and Jamilah Ahmed at Sage, whose enthusiasm, professionalism and patience have made finishing this book a much easier task.

At an earlier stage, my colleagues and friends in Women's Studies at Wolverhampton – Pauline Anderson, Barbara Crowther, Pat Green and Penny Welch – provided the intellectually stimulating and supportive environment for feminist scholarship within which this project was born. Special thanks to Barbara who has been a great supporter of this book and provided invaluable feedback on individual chapters along the way.

Many colleagues, students and friends have helped clarify my thinking and writing and offered constructive comments on draft chapters: thanks to Eliz Boyle, Rachel Connor, Carole Dodds, Gary Needham, Nik Peasgood, Lisa Price and Paul Sutton, and to all the students on my Screen Violence classes at Wolverhampton (1999–2001) and Glasgow (2002–3).

Thanks also to the anonymous reviewers for their helpful comments on the proposal and individual chapters, and to Michael McCann for technical assistance and good humour in the face of some of my more bizarre requests.

To Helen Wood and Fiona Black I owe a huge debt of gratitude both for their careful reading of the manuscript and for their friendship and support during some of the darkest days. Without the additional support provided by Rachel Jones, Gavin and Carleen Boyle and, in particular, Tracey Coleman, finishing this book would have been a much tougher if not impossible task.

Finally, love and thanks to my parents, Eliz and Sandy Boyle, who have seen me through it all (and there's been a lot of it) and to my nephew, Ryan Boyle, who always lifts my spirits when I need it most.

List of illustrations

Introduction

At the first meeting of my Screen Violence course, students are given a short questionnaire to fill out. In this questionnaire they are asked to give examples of film/television programmes they define as 'violent', say why they define them in this way and describe their own viewing experiences. I invite you to do the same and keep your responses to hand as you negotiate your way through this book.

What is 'screen violence'?

Think of a film or television programme you would define as 'violent'.

- What is it about this film/programme that is 'violent'?
- How does the violence contribute to your decision to watch (or not to watch) it?
- How does the violence contribute to your enjoyment (or lack of enjoyment)?

Write down your answers and come back to them as you read about academic work on media effects and viewing experiences in Chapters 1 and 2.

I find this exercise useful for a number of reasons. First, and perhaps most important, this exercise places all of us in the screen violence debate – a debate more typically focused on 'other' audiences. Instead, I want us to begin by thinking about ourselves – our own investments, experiences and (un)pleasures – and use this to reflect on some of the benefits and limitations of both popular debate and academic research. Second, the exercise challenges us to think about exactly what 'screen violence' is. Again, this is something we will come back to during the course of this book as we reflect on the ways in which our understandings reflect (or do not reflect) popular and academic definitions of the term. Asking a few friends to respond to these questions will give you additional material to draw on here. To what extent are your understandings shared or disputed?

The last couple of times I have used this exercise, the same film titles (*Reservoir Dogs*, *Fight Club*, the *Terminator* films, *Pulp Fiction*,

Natural Born Killers), genres (horror, action, gangster) and directors (Tarantino, Scorsese) have cropped up time and time again. In defining screen violence, then, these movies might seem like an obvious place to start. In many ways they are. These are films – and directors – with a reputation for violence, where the violence is assumed to be part of the pleasure (or unpleasure) that the film offers its viewers, and have often generated considerable controversy for precisely this reason. In defining these films as 'violent' viewers, critics and marketing departments do – to a certain extent – agree. Yet, when the students explain why they think these films are violent, the consensus begins to break down. First, the basis on which they classify the films/ programmes varies widely: **modality**, explicitness, visibility of injury, use of weapons, type of character involved and perceived acceptability of violence in specific generic, cultural or narrative contexts all feature. Moreover, the same films are often described by different students in opposing terms: *Reservoir Dogs* (Tarantino, 1991) is violent because it is realistic and unrealistic, gruesome and moral, it glamorises and critiques violence.

What quickly becomes clear in reviewing the diversity of responses is that there is a range of ideas about what screen violence is. Yet, as academic studies in this field have found (Morrison et al., 1999), there is perhaps a shared sense that screen violence is the explicit representation of physical violence (and injury) that breaks accepted codes of conduct and pushes boundaries of taste, whether it is celebrated or criticised on these grounds.

Confusing things still further, year after year, this exercise also throws up a few apparent anomalies – texts that one student defines as violent in opposition to their peers or the prevailing attitudes about screen violence. These texts tend to fall into three categories: those depicting slapstick physical violence (such as children's cartoons), news and current affairs programming and representations of non-physical violence (verbal aggression, threats, psychological abuse). Certainly, if we count the number of violent acts on screen (as some academic research in this field attempts to do), *Reservoir Dogs* pales into insignificance next to an episode of *Tom and Jerry*. If, on the other hand, we consider the implications of violent actions as being central to our definition, even a movie like *Die Hard 2* (Harlin, 1990), with its notoriously high body count, pales next to the live news broadcasts of the terrorist attacks of September 11th 2001 or the repeated bombing of Iraq in 2003. Thinking about what we don't actually see on screen, it is also, of course, the threat of violence that is truly frightening in many horror movies.

Moreover, the minute we try to come up with a definition of 'screen violence', the difficulty of trying to separate the screen from other media, and the media from life, becomes apparent. To go back to *Reservoir Dogs*, this film has been repeatedly – if contentiously – linked to acts of violence in the real world. In answer to his critics, Tarantino claims that the film is 'realistic' because, 'If someone is hit in the stomach, that's how they die' (quoted in Dargis 1994: 19): the 'real' is here invoked to legitimate the on-screen gore. However, the film has also been linked to viewers' subsequent acts of violence. Perhaps, then, we need to expand our definition of 'media violence' to include real-world violence linked to the media? Of course, most of us only know about these incidents because we read or hear about them in the news media. Are these news stories also media violence?

The title of this book – *Media and Violence* – is thus intended to remind us of some of the difficulties of defining these key terms.[1] This book is not concerned with a definable object called 'media violence' but, rather, with various facets of the relationship between the media and violence. In this respect, it is not only those texts commonly defined as violent that are my concern, as will become apparent in Chapter 6. Further, the subtitle of this book – *Gendering the Debates* – points to the way in which 'violence' is conceptualised throughout this book as a gendered phenomenon. The recognition of the gendered nature of violence is the pre-eminent feminist contribution to our understanding of violence (Price, 1999: 19). To be clear, this does not mean that all men are violent or that women are incapable of violence. What is does mean – simply but crucially – is that our understandings of violence and gender are absolutely interlinked. Stories about violence – including those you yourself have told in response to the questions set at the beginning of this chapter – are, at some level, stories about gender, about what is means to be a man or a woman in the specific social, cultural and political contexts in which the stories are told.

Since at least the 1970s, developing an analysis and understanding of violence (primarily, but not exclusively, men's violence against women) has been central to feminist theory and activism. Feminists have demonstrated that how we define violence – and where we see violence as unjust or criminal – is a reflection of our positioning in other **discourses** about gender, sexuality, justice and society. For example, is a husband who forces his wife to have sex against her will exercising his 'conjugal rights' or is he a rapist? Is a knife attack on an elderly woman outside a shopping centre more violent than a knife attack on a young man outside that same shopping centre? To take a more headline-grabbing example, when Arnold Schwarzenegger allegedly groped and fondled women on movie sets, was he having a bit of fun or was he guilty of **sexual harassment**?

These questions should draw our attention to the fact that violence is not a commonsense category but an ideological one. Moreover, to reduce violence to a series of acts – a punch, a kick, a grope, a stabbing and so on – runs the risk of diverting our attention away from the realities of violence as a behaviour, as something one person (or group of people) does to another person (or group of people) (see Kappeler, 1995: 2). Violence is also a behaviour that takes on particular meanings (for the perpetrator, victim and others) in relation to the specific social, political and cultural context in which it is enacted.

More specifically, making men's violence visible was a crucial aspect of early feminist work. There were two aspects to this:

- making the gendered nature of violence explicit (hence the use of terms such as male violence and **femicide**)
- making 'hidden' violence visible as violence.

Such violence was, and is, 'hidden' because it takes place behind closed doors (as in marital **rape**, child **sexual abuse** and **domestic violence**), because it was (and often still is) culturally and/or legally acceptable – a man's 'conjugal right',[2] a 'bit of fun' – and because we had no words to describe it (terms like domestic violence and sexual harassment entered public discourse as a result of feminism).

In addition to making this violence, its perpetrators and its victims visible, feminists were and are concerned with establishing links between different forms of male violence against women. As Liz Kelly (1988) influentially argues, individual acts of male violence exist on a 'continuum' that encompasses a wide range of criminal and non-criminal behaviour – 'from flashing to rape' as one feminist anti-violence campaign put it. Importantly, then, violence is not the preserve of a few evil or monstrous men. Rather, feminists argue that aggression is a culturally valued and accepted facet of masculinity in Western culture and that violence has to be understood in the context of **patriarchy**. It is a key element in maintaining male power and control over women at a structural as well as an individual level (and over other men, differentiated by class, age, sexuality, race). Seeing and documenting the connections between 'violent' men and 'normal' men can be extremely depressing, as well as challenging and disturbing for those of us who have emotional, practical and erotic investments in dominant constructions of masculinity. However, it is also a far more positive and ultimately hopeful approach than labelling individuals as monsters because, by acknowledging the violent actor's agency and decision to act, we also admit the possibility that he is capable of different decisions and actions. It allows for – and, indeed, requires – the possibility of change and insists that all of us can be involved in this process.

Feminists throughout the world have made significant progress in putting male violence and, in particular, men's violence against women, on political and legislative agendas and in providing services for women victims and survivors. In tandem with this, feminist cultural critics have examined the media's role in the circulation of gendered discourses about violence. Indeed, feminists have long recognised that changes in the way we represent violence do not only follow social change but changes in representation – and interpretation – can also lead the way (Benedict, 1993).

However men's violence against women is not the whole picture. Crime statistics consistently demonstrate that men are the most likely victims – as well as perpetrators – of violence. Yet, precisely because it is so prevalent, male victimisation is undoubtedly under-researched, both in relation to real-life experiences and media representations. Indeed, it is telling that, in this book, male victimisation is most thoroughly considered in relation to screen fictions. Male-on-male violence is simply less newsworthy than men's violence against women or women's violence per se (Surette, 1998; Cavender et al., 1999) and this has been reflected in the critical work. Women's violence – in fact and in representation – has, however, posed more problems for feminist critics. When research and criminal statistics alike consistently demonstrate that women are a small fraction of the perpetrators of all kinds of violence (with the notable exceptions of **infanticide** and female genital mutilation), it is understandable that feminists have often felt that the question of women's violence is a distraction. This is not to say that feminists have completely ignored the issue and, in Chapter 4, I will discuss some of the challenges this work presents. For now, it is sufficient to note that, as women's violence runs counter to cherished notions about femininity, women abusers are always visible as women, while male abusers (whose violence is not in conflict with their gender role) are rarely visible outside of feminist criticism as men.

In this book I, too, am involved in telling stories about violence. While one of my aims is to make the gendered nature of media stories visible, in order to tell these critical stories I have had to consider how best to represent violence in my own text. This has been particularly tricky in relation to the representations of real-world violence discussed in Chapters 1–4. Although I am focusing on representations, it is important to remember that the actual brutalisation of women's (and, less often, men's) bodies and minds lies at their core. This raises difficult questions about how to represent the perpetrators, victims and the acts of violence, not least because a number of contemporary killers – including some of those I discuss in this book – have stated that part of their motivation for killing was a desire to be known. In recognising that their destructive acts have indeed made them known, in naming and discussing them, there is a danger of furthering their cause. Yet, this has to be weighed against a need to hold perpetrators publicly accountable for their crimes. In their excellent examination of **sexual murder**, Deborah Cameron and Elizabeth Frazer (1987) attempt to do this by providing an appendix detailing the 'careers' of the sex murderers referred to in their text. They (Cameron and Frazer, 1987: 178) explain their decision thus:

> The exercise of collating these facts has a function for feminists beyond the mere avoidance of exaggeration and half-truth: it prevents us from forgetting or 'writing out' the victims, both the fact of their suffering and what exactly they have suffered.

Yet, Cameron and Frazer do not provide biographies of the victims killed by these men. Are they, then, guilty of 'writing out' the victims? If what we are interested in is why men (and, rarely in the case of sexual murder, women) commit these atrocities, then this is appropriate: we cannot explain violence by looking at victim behaviour. Yet, to fail to represent the victims at all, or to simply identify them as a 'type' (prostitute, co-ed, mother) robs them of their individuality and, arguably, makes it more difficult to empathise with them. This problem is particularly acute when talking/writing about the victims of **serial killers** as true crime author Ann Rule (1989: 488) notes in her book about Ted Bundy:

> Because Ted murdered so many, many women, he did more than rob them of their lives. He robbed them of their specialness too. It is too easy, and expedient, to present them as a list of names; it is impossible to tell each victim's story within the confines of one book. All those bright, pretty, beloved young women became, of necessity, 'Bundy victims'.
> And only Ted stayed in the spotlight.

How to represent what men like Bundy actually did is also problematic. Here, there is a fine line between registering the horror and turning the victim's violated body into a **voyeuristic** object to be looked at without identification, empathy or a desire for justice. For those of us for whom these scenes are only representations – words on a page, images on a screen – and not lived reality it is, undoubtedly, easier not to think of what men like Bundy did to their victims: women like ourselves, our friends, colleagues, daughters, mothers, lovers, wives. Such knowledge can paralyse us with pain, fear and rage. However, if we lose sight of the victims in these cases, we can all too easily become uncritical consumers of crime and lose the sense of purpose, indeed of urgency, that drives feminist study, research and activism in this field.

I have found negotiating these tensions far from straightforward. Following Cameron and Frazer, I have provided basic information about key cases I discuss in an Appendix at the end of the book. However, I have not included victim biographies. I am still not entirely sure if this is the right decision, although, in the end, it was as much a practical as a political one (as Rule notes, there are simply too many victims and many of them are literally anonymous). Hopefully, the Appendix provides an alternative to the victim-blaming discourse that characterises many of the accounts discussed in Chapter 3 in particular. Yet, I recognise that my approach compounds the invisibility of victims of violence.

As you negotiate your own way through this often difficult material, you will make up your own mind as to whether I have got it right or not. In doing so, I encourage you to think critically about how it could be done differently and to consider the ethical, political and moral – as well as practical – issues in representing the victims of violence in academic work as well as in the media texts investigated in this book.

A brief guide to the contents

As is customary, I want to end this introduction with a few signposts to help you negotiate your way through this book. It brings together a diverse body of new and existing research – conducted within a variety of academic disciplines – concerning representations of violence in the media, their production and consumption. There is a vast amount of critical work in this field and, in this respect, this book should be treated as the starting point for your own studies, rather than the last word on these subjects.

The book provides a series of tasters cooked up in the interdisciplinary context in which I work, and informed by an ongoing commitment to feminist struggles to end men's violence against women. My reading, writing and research is limited to texts in English and I refer mainly (though not exclusively) to the work of Anglo-American critics and draw my examples from mainstream British and American media.

The violence investigated is, primarily, interpersonal violence – the behaviour of individuals. While positioning that behaviour in a wider social, cultural and political context is a vital part of the work undertaken here, equally pressing questions about the representation (and gendering) of state violence, war and terrorism will have to wait for another book. The critics, the media and violence investigated here are all clearly circumscribed, but it is my hope that those of you reading this book in other contexts – or with an interest in other media – will test, adapt, complicate and develop my arguments with your own examples.

The book is organised into three parts, dealing first with the relationship of media to real-world violence (Chapters 1 and 2), second with the representation of real-world violence in fact-based media (Chapters 3 and 4) and, finally, with representations of violence in screen entertainments (Chapters 5 and 6).

Part One kicks off with a critical examination of debates about the effects of violent media on their consumers and asks what is at stake in the attempt to link specific acts of male violence (and it is, overwhelmingly, male violence) to individual media representations. Drawing on an original study of the British press, the first half of this chapter discusses how the press constructs the 'media violence' story. With particular reference to press coverage of the trial of the boys who murdered James Bulger in 1993, and of the 1999 Columbine High School massacre, it explores the gendered social and political functions of media stories about media effects.

The second half of the chapter then moves on to consider how academic research – primarily in the UK and North America – has tackled the question of media effects. Rather than reviewing the findings of these studies – a task undertaken by many others, although with no consensus as to the sum of the evidence[3] – this chapter considers the previously unacknowledged gendered assumptions behind much of the work in this field.

Chapter 2 moves beyond the relatively narrow parameters of the effects debates to explore the complexities of media/violence in relation to production processes as well as consumption practices. The chapter begins with a consideration of anti-pornography feminists' work on abusive production practices and argues that this work offers an important challenge to the effects paradigm. It then moves on to consider how recent work on the gendered consumption of pornographic and horrific media troubles the audience–text relationship assumed by the effects model. The chapter concludes with an evaluation of different approaches to regulating and challenging media/violence.

The two chapters in Part Two are also concerned with the relationship between representation and real-world violence, but here the focus is on the reporting of crimes of violence in fact-based media.

Chapter 3 reviews and analyses a rich body of critical work developing within a variety of disciplinary contexts that both interrogates and challenges the ways in which men's violence against women – in the forms of sexual murder, sexual abuse and domestic violence – is constructed in news and true-crime accounts.

The chapter opens with a discussion of the discourse of sexual murder – its emergence in the late nineteenth century (when the crimes attributed to Jack the Ripper coincided with the rise of the mass media), its use by the press and public and its construction of perpetrators and victims. I then turn to press coverage of non-fatal sex crime, drawing from an original study of 'everyday' sex crime reporting in the British tabloid press as well as from previously published work from Britain and North America. A particular concern here is the way in which female victims of violence are represented. Are they (still) the 'virgins and vamps' Benedict (1992) identified in her study of the US press in the 1980s?

Finally, this chapter deals with representations of domestic violence – a rather neglected issue in writing about gender, violence and the media despite the proliferation of academic, and specifically feminist, studies of domestic violence in recent years.

The representation – in law as well as in the media – of women who kill the men who abuse them has been a key area of feminist intervention and campaigns for justice, as I explore in Chapter 4. More generally, this chapter examines stories about women who kill (or abuse) to argue that they are, essentially, stories about gender conformity and transgression. Three major themes are addressed in this chapter: the relationship between women's victimisation and violence, the linking of women's violent and sexual subjectivity and, finally, motherhood and the female body. Arguments are illustrated with reference to representations of some of the most notorious women in British and North American criminal history.

Against the background of the real-world violence that forms the basis for the stories told in Part Two, the presentation of violence as entertainment has, understandably perhaps, generated particular criticism from feminist critics. Part III considers these screen entertainments, but aims to move beyond simple condemnation (or celebration) to explore how these texts function and the extent to which feminism has impacted on the representations on screen.

Chapter 5 focuses specifically on feature films. However, this chapter is less concerned with the content of filmic representations than with how they work to position their spectators in relation to scenes of gendered violence. With its debt to **psychoanalysis**, feminist film theory has been centrally concerned with the gendered violence of spectatorship – specifically, the controlling and **sadistic** aspects of the **male gaze**. Chapter 5 explores issues of spectatorship in relation to a number of genres – **slasher films**, serial killer thrillers, rape revenge narratives and action films – and ends with a consideration of women's violence on the silver screen.

Clearly, violence in its many forms cuts across genre, period and national cinemas and so my discussion of film is inevitably marked by exclusion as much as inclusion. I have chosen to focus primarily, though not exclusively, on post-1970 US films, as these are the representations that have typically proved most contentious in popular debate as well as in specifically feminist circles and generated some of the most interesting and relevant feminist studies. Again, I encourage you to consider how these theories might be complicated by a study of different texts, genres and national contexts.

In Chapter 6, I turn my attention to the small screen. Television violence is a topic of recurring concern in debates about media effects, censorship and the family. However, much of this work has had little to say about the texts of television violence. In contrast, this chapter examines representations of violence across a range of television genres and texts produced in the US and UK in the last 20 years. My particular focus is once more on those genres that have been of concern to feminist critics and gender theorists – genres such as the soap opera, talk show, made-for-TV movie, cop show and action series. While the concerns of feminist television critics frame this chapter, they are also interrogated and challenged within it as I discuss the ways in which television shows (and feminist television critics) have tackled (or failed to tackle) issues of women's agency and men's violence.

Finally, a few pointers to help you negotiate your way through this book. Introductions and summaries point to the major issues addressed in each chapter, and key questions scattered throughout the book encourage you to think about your own position and to make connections between the critical positions outlined in different chapters. A short list of recommended further reading is provided at the end of each chapter and the extensive bibliography should give those of you who want to take your studies that bit further plenty to go on. Brief definitions of key terms (printed in **bold** the first time they are used in each chapter) can be found in the Glossary and short outlines of the criminal cases I refer to most frequently are provided in the Appendix.

Notes

1 In this I have been influenced by the work of Martin Barker and Julian Petley who similarly argue that the term 'media violence' is both notoriously imprecise and largely meaningless (Barker and Petley, 2001). Instead they refer to 'media/violence', the slash indicating the problematic nature of placing these terms together. I have used this formulation, where appropriate, in this book.
2 In England and Wales, a man could not be charged with raping his wife until the early 1990s.
3 Reviews by Henry (1988), Dworkin and MacKinnon (1988), Cumberbatch and Howitt (1989), Russell (1992), King (1993), Gauntlett (1995) and Miller and Philo (1999) reach a variety of conclusions about the nature and sum of the evidence linking media representation to viewers' subsequent violence.

PART ONE

The media/violence debates

The effects of violence in the media

Chapter outline

This chapter provides an overview and critique of popular and academic debates about the effects of violence in the media. The title is deliberately ambiguous, pointing to 'the media' both as the source of stories about effects (the effects of violence *in the media*) and as the effective agent (the effects of *violence in the media*). The organisation of this chapter mirrors this dual emphasis by, first, examining the ways in which the media (and, in particular, the print media) construct the 'media effects' story and, second, considering what academic research can tell us about the effects of violence in the media:

• Explaining crime or Excusing male violence?	**moral panics**, media effects as gendered **discourse**, agency and accountability
• Academic approaches to media effects	causality and influence, laboratory studies, behavioural effects
• Cultivation and content	television violence, cultivation theory, content analysis.

Explaining crime or excusing male violence?

It has become common practice when faced with apparently inexplicable acts of violence that commentators turn to the question of possible media influence. The judge at the trial of the ten-year-old murderers of James Bulger did it, suggesting that 'exposure to violent videos' might provide a partial explanation for their crime. In the aftermath of the Columbine High School massacre, many reporters did it, suggesting that the killers took their inspiration from the music of Marilyn Manson or *The Matrix* (Wachowski Brothers, 1999) or *The Basketball Diaries* (Kalvert, 1995). However, when we examine the nature of the evidence linking crime and media in these cases, the argument begins to unravel. Which begs the question, what is at stake in blaming the media? In exploring this question, I want to begin by examining these two notorious cases in a bit more detail.

In February 1993, in Liverpool, England, two-year-old James Bulger was kidnapped and murdered by two ten-year-old boys – Robert Thompson and Jon Venables. In his summing up at the boys' trial in November 1993, Justice Morland suggested that 'exposure to violent videos' could provide a partial explanation for their crime. Video violence had not been discussed at all during the trial. In fact, it was a blurred security video and not a commercial **'video nasty'** that had been central to the case – the apparently innocuous image of James Bulger being led out of a shopping centre by his two killers.

Unsurprisingly, the British press seized on the judge's comments and one film in particular – *Child's Play 3* (Bender, 1991) – came to dominate the public debate. The day after the verdict, a front-page editorial in *The Sun* urged readers to burn their video nasties, 'for the sake of ALL our kids' (see Figure 1.1), while inside, the 'chilling links between James' murder and tape rented by killer's dad' were outlined (*The Sun*, 25 November 1993). A cartoon later that week was even more explicit – two boys 'being led away' by Chucky, the demonic doll from the *Child's Play* series, in an apparent pre-play of the security video showing James' abduction (see Figure 1.2). That the cartoon positioned Thompson and Venables in the position occupied by James in the security video functioned to displace the killers' responsibility for their actions. Chucky – an American import – became a convenient scapegoat, diverting attention from the sociocultural environment in which the boys lived and in which kidnapping and killing James became both possible and meaningful to them.

Despite *The Sun*'s certainty that a video bonfire would protect us from future boy killers, there was no evidence that Thompson and Venables had even seen *Child's Play 3* and police investigating the murder consistently denied any link. Indeed, in a thoughtful account

Figure 1.1 *A simple solution to a complex problem:* The Sun *urges readers to burn their video nasties in the wake of the James Bulger murder trial (25 November, 1993).*

of the controversy, David Buckingham (1996: 35) demonstrates that the 'chilling links' *The Sun* reporters perceived between representation and reality were, at best, extremely tenuous and, at worst, completely misrepresented the film. Moreover, tabloid accounts confusingly suggested both that the killers themselves identified with Chucky and that they identified James with Chucky. If Thompson and Venables were indeed acting out the events of *Child's Play 3*, then these reports where far from certain which roles they were playing. Despite (or perhaps

Figure 1.2   *The demonic doll, Chucky, leading the killers of James Bulger to their fate*
(The Sun, *27 November, 1993*).

because of) the lack of evidence connecting James' murder to *Child's Play 3*, the link made by the judge and embellished by the tabloids was to fuel more general concern about video violence. The relationship between text and action was presented with less and less circumspection as the story developed so that, as Buckingham (1996) notes, later news stories referred to this case as unequivocal 'evidence' that violent videos cause violent behaviour.

The stirrings of moral panic in the press were all too familiar to commentators who witnessed similar press-fuelled hysteria over video nasties in Britain in the mid 1980s (Barker, 1984a). Moreover, as with this earlier panic, there was an almost immediate rush to legislate against the living-room menace. This came to a head in April 1994 when a report commissioned by David Alton MP to support proposed far-reaching restrictions to the availability of home videos was published to great fanfare (Newson, 1994). Using the murder of James Bulger as the starting point for her investigation, the author of the report – Elizabeth Newson, a child psychologist with no record of research on media violence – condemned video violence as a form of 'child abuse'. Newson suggested that in films like *Child's Play 3*, the viewer identifies with the perpetrator of violence – an interesting claim in light of the tabloid confusion over the 'chilling links' between original and copy and one that contradicts much of the research on identification processes (see Chapters 2 and 5). Nevertheless, the report received extensive media coverage, dissenting voices were barely heard and the pressure on the Conservative government to 'do something' increased. For those who accepted the link between the murder of James Bulger and *Child's Play 3*, the 'something' to be done was in many ways obvious: these videos must be censored, contained and controlled. In this context of panic and misinformation, an amendment to the Video Recordings Act was passed, stipulating that in awarding certificates to films on video, the British Board of Film Classification (BBFC) must consider the potential for harm to viewers (and to underage viewers in particular) watching in the home.[1]

Six years later and thousands of miles from Liverpool, two teenage boys walked into Columbine High School armed with semi-automatic handguns, shotguns and explosives. After killing 13 people and injuring many more, the boys turned their guns on themselves. As the news media tried to explain the massacre, possible links between (other) media representations and the boys' actions became the focus of much speculation. Films such as *The Matrix* and *The Basketball Diaries* came under attack simply because their characters' long trench coats and choice of weaponry mirrored those adopted by the Columbine killers. However, whether or not the boys had even seen these films was never clear. The killers' enjoyment of the nihilistic music of Marilyn Manson, their Internet usage and interest in computer games also generated considerable debate. Yet, as Michael Moore suggests in the award-winning *Bowling for Columbine* (2002), there is no inherent reason for these particular aspects of the boys' lives to have come under such intense scrutiny. The boys also went bowling on the morning of the murders, but no one suggested that there was a link between these two activities, despite the fact that similar claims are made about contentious media texts on precisely this basis. At most, we might argue that this case suggests there might be a correlation between media and real-world violence – that is, that those who are violent in real life also consume violent media. However, it is important to emphasise that this does not prove a causal relationship between the two terms.

To emphasise this last point, I want to turn to a report in *The Sun* a few months prior to the Columbine massacre. Sensationally headlined 'BOYS KILL FIVE THEN EAT PIZZA' (2 December, 1998), the report describes how two teenage boys, 'massacred five people for kicks after watching video nasties'. While the article goes on to suggest a causal link between 'video nasties' and murder, no one would seriously suggest that there is a causal link between murder and pizza eating. Rather, the juxtaposition of murder and pizza eating is supposed to tell us something about the killers (their lack of remorse, callousness and so on). Yet, on the basis of the evidence offered, the 'murder causes pizza eating' hypothesis is as plausible as the 'viewing video nasties causes murder' hypothesis. All we are told is that one event followed the other, just like killing followed bowling in the Columbine case. However, we are so used to video nasties being linked to murder that this lack of evidence is not glaringly obvious.

Surveying the coverage of the Columbine massacre, contradictory accounts of the relationship between the boys' actions and their media consumption emerge. As in the Bulger trial, some reports attempt to establish a direct causal link between the crime and a specific media text (*The Basketball Diaries, The Matrix*, the music of Marilyn Manson). Many commentators focus particularly on the nihilistic lyrics and gothic, androgynous – and, crucially, different and recognisable – style of Manson and his fans. However, taken as a whole, the sheer variety of potential media influences cited in reports of the Columbine massacre surely demonstrates the impossibility (and absurdity) of trying to identify any one representation as the cause of the boys' actions. Yet, these accounts consistently attempt to distance the shooters from 'normal' boys and adults and isolate these 'dangerous' texts from other cultural products. For example, Senator John McCain, chairing a Senate hearing on 'Marketing Violence to Children' in the wake of the massacre, suggested that a 'rising culture of violence is engulfing our children'.[2] Quite why this culture should engulf only 'our children' – leaving 'us' immune – is unclear, unless we accept that children (unlike adults) are passive, uncritical viewers or that children's and adults' media are entirely separate.

Proposing a rather different model of children's viewing, media scholar Henry Jenkins (1999) suggested at the same hearing that we should be asking 'what our children are doing *with* media' rather than what media texts are doing *to* them. That Jenkins' perspective was infrequently reported is perhaps not surprising as it complicates policy-making no end: if the media are not the violent agents then there are no easy, censorious solutions to the problem of children's violence.

As this brief discussion has shown, in both the Columbine and Bulger cases the evidence linking the crimes to media representations was tenuous at best. Yet it is striking that the legitimacy of the media effects question – whether posed by the judiciary (as in the Bulger case) or the press (as in the aftermath of Columbine) – is commonly accepted. Those who try to respond to the question (like Newson in the Bulger case) often have very little knowledge either of the individual cases or of the huge body of research into media/violence, yet rumour and opinion quickly take on the status of 'truth' and 'authority'. Press coverage thus polarises and over simplifies the debate, as you can either accept that *Child's Play 3* caused Thompson and Venables to kill James Bulger, or be forced into a position of arguing that the media has no influence. A middle ground is hard to find. Yet surely we should be asking how these boys' media consumption – throughout their lives and not just in the immediate run-up to their crimes – reflected and reinforced their conceptions of themselves as boys/men and their understanding of violence. This question, however, demands that we look beyond the 'bad object' (video nasties) to examine texts that we ourselves may invest in and enjoy. It thus demands that we see the connections between those murderous boys and ourselves.

Moreover, these media-blaming accounts routinely ignore the one thing the killers of James Bulger and the Columbine High School shooters really do have in common: they are all male. Can this fact really be incidental or is blaming the media a way of not blaming boys and men? Answering this question requires that we look beyond the Bulger and Columbine cases and, in the remainder of this section, I present the findings of new research into the representation of media effects stories in the British press.

For this study, I examined all reports suggesting a causal link between a real-life act of violence and a specific media representation over a ten-year period (1990–99) in five of the most popular British tabloids and broadsheets.[3] I identified 92 separate cases where one or more of the papers presented an allegedly causal link between 'media' and 'violence'.

Given the import of such cases in shaping public opinion and policy, this may seem like a very slight figure. Certainly, claims about the relationship between media and real-life violence are far more visible than this figure would suggest, with the most high-profile cases – such as the Bulger murder – receiving extensive coverage. However, it is not only these high-profile cases in which such a link is made. During the 1990s, the British press laid the blame for various kinds of violence – spree shootings, armed robbery, **serial killing**, drug-assisted sexual assault and wrestling – on a small range of 'dangerous' texts. As these examples suggest, there is an emphasis on serious violence in these 'effects' stories: more than half of the cases examined involve killings and half of those involve more than one victim. More significantly, perhaps, the vast majority of perpetrators are men – 96% of the murder cases involve at least one male suspect. The 'copycat' profile is also an overwhelmingly young one, the majority of perpetrators for whom racial/ethnic details are available are white and many are explicitly identified as middle class.

Perhaps, then, the media-blaming explanation is particularly likely to be mobilised when the perpetrators of violent crime are so closely identified with the dominant order. Moreover, that so many of the dangerous texts are American both facilitates a certain myopia around the treatment of violence in domestic media and allows us to see extremely violent crimes as 'other' to, or outside of, British society. In Duncan Webster's (1989) words, 'Whodunnit?: America did'.

But how, exactly, does America do it? The two most common models of media influence employed in the British press are 'imitation' and 'addiction'. In relation to 'imitation', the following extract from the *Daily Mail* (30 November, 1996) gives a flavour of the coverage:

> Moore [...] *modelled himself* on Jason Voorhees, central character in the *Friday the 13th* horror films, stabbing his victims with a black-handled double-edged combat knife bought for the purpose. During 20 years of undetected violence culminating in the killings, which took place over a three-month period last year, he also *mimicked* another of his movie heroes, Clint Eastwood's Dirty Harry. In the film, Eastwood stabs a serial killer in the calf. Moore carried out his *copycat* attack on an innocent stranger. (emphasis added.)

The dangerous texts in this example are horror and action films – and, indeed, horror, action and other films aimed primarily at young male audiences come in for particular attack across the decade. In many ways, these films, with their consciously excessive spectacles of violence and their youthful male target audiences, are (like Marilyn Manson or Chucky) easy and obvious targets (see also Barker 1984a, 1984b). Certainly, there are important questions to be asked about these genres (questions I return to in Chapter 5). However, it would be a mistake to ignore their connections with other, more culturally valued, forms of representation – including, for example, news reporting, psychological thrillers, religious texts and sports coverage, all of which also contribute to the dominant cultural construction of violent masculinity. There is also an assumption here – as in the judge's claims in the Bulger case – that the deviant viewer sees the violent act in isolation, ignoring context, character and motive. In the report quoted above, for example, while the *acts* are superficially similar their *meaning* is fundamentally different. In the original, the perpetrator attempts to bring a known serial killer to justice, in the copy, a serial killer attacks an unknown stranger. Blaming the movie does not get us any further forward in understanding the meaning of the act for the real serial killer.

Indeed, if we follow the logic of such news stories, it would seem that boys and young men are the least likely to be able to differentiate between violence in fantasy and reality, and the most likely to 'imitate' what they see on the screen. How might we explain this? We could argue that young viewers are less able to understand the complex moral universe in which screen violence is embedded and, therefore, are more likely to see the violent acts in isolation. However, this developmental model is contested by research that explores how children and young people actually make sense of screen violence (Buckingham, 1996; Bragg, 2001) and does not get us any further forward in terms of explaining why this appears to be a gendered phenomenon. Assuming that we can reject biological essentialism (that boys are biologically less able to differentiate between fantasy and reality than girls), then we could argue that boys and young men are the copycats because it is boys and men who are the violent actors on screen. What this argument leaves unexplained, however, is why one element of the representation – the gender of the perpetrator – should override other factors in structuring identification and engagement. Why assume that a male viewer identifies with a character who is – in every respect other than gender – fundamentally different from them: older, living in a different nation or time, racially or ethnically different, or clearly fantastical (like Chucky the living doll)? And why assume that a female viewer fails to identify with a male character on the basis of gender alone (an issue I'll return to in Chapter 5)? So, once more we have to ask what is to be gained from making these connections?

In a discussion of the relationship between **pornography** and men's sexual violence against women, Deborah Cameron and Elizabeth Frazer (1992: 364) ask:

> Where does a sex killer's account of himself come from? Not, we suggest, from some privileged personal insight, but from a finite repertoire of cultural clichés, which the murderer, like everyone else, has come across in case histories, pop-psychology, newspapers, films and ordinary gossip with family, friends and workmates. At any given time, the clichés available are a heterogeneous and contradictory collection: some may carry more authority than others (for instance, we no longer think much of a killer who tells us he was possessed by the devil [...]); new clichés may enter the repertoire, challenging or providing alternatives to the existing explanations. Porn-blaming is a recent example.

Cameron and Frazer argue that porn-blaming – and, by extension, media-blaming – comes from the culture. They illustrate this point by tracing the development of another popular 'explanation' for men's violence: mother-blaming. Mother-blaming has its origins in psychoanalytic theory but did not enter popular consciousness until the 1950s and 1960s by way of cultural products such as Hitchcock's *Psycho* (1960). As mother-blaming was popularised, violent men – and those who sought to explain their actions – drew on this discourse. In time, the mother-blaming accounts of these violent men and experts – accounts that had only been made possible by the dissemination of the mother-blaming story in mass media forms – were, in turn, cited as concrete evidence that mothers were to blame for the violent actions of their sons.

It can be argued that a similarly cyclical process is in operation in accounts of media effects:

1 the media-blaming explanation enters popular awareness from a variety of sources – moral objections to certain types of representations, academic research, feminist campaigns against pornography and so on
2 real-life killers and abusers of women – as well as those who investigate, defend and prosecute them – use this as a way of explaining their crimes
3 these explanations feed back into the popular discourse as case histories that 'prove' the accuracy of this explanation
4 against this background, media-blaming becomes a commonsense way in which to explain crimes.

An editorial from *The Sun* (3 August, 1995) provides a succinct illustration of this process. This editorial – entitled 'REAL WORLD' – responds to two separate incidents: the publication of an academic book disputing the commonsense 'knowledge' that violent media have demonstrable effects on behaviour and claims by the father of a 14-year-old armed robber that his son was imitating the gangsters in *Reservoir Dogs* (Tarantino, 1991):

> *IF anyone in the country still doubts the link between TV and violence, listen to Chris Richards.*
>
> His 14-year-old son held two newsagents at gunpoint because he wanted to be like the gangsters in the film *Reservoir Dogs*, which he'd seen on video.
>
> So much for the airy-fairy theories of wet-behind-the-ears sociologist David Gauntlett, 24.
>
> 'He's never seen what real life is,' blasts Mr Richards. 'He should come down here to south London.'

Mr Richards draws on the familiar media-blaming discourse to explain his son's actions. *The Sun* casts Mr Richards in the role of expert, his personal testimony challenging 'airy-fairy' academic theories of media influence and reinforcing *The Sun's* established position on media effects. Straightforward enough. Yet, even if we accept that he sought to emulate the screen gangsters, Mr Richards' son could not have held the newsagents at gunpoint without a gun. It is perhaps not difficult to imagine why Mr Richards is more interested in the influence of a movie than in explaining how his son had access to a firearm.

Mr Richards' concluding remarks about 'real life' in south London also bear further scrutiny. Mr Richards (unwittingly, perhaps) suggests that *Reservoir Dogs* has a particular *meaning* for young south Londoners like his son, a meaning that ivory-tower academics have ignored. This reminds us of the important role of interpretation – that is, there is no single meaning of a film/video/book/song that viewers (male or female) uncritically accept and act on. Mr Richards' son might have found the gangsters in *Reservoir Dogs* 'cool', but other interpretations are possible. When I show *Reservoir Dogs* in class, it typically elicits a wide variety of responses, from appreciation of the film's technical qualities, dialogue or humour, to boredom, disgust and outrage. Even those students who agree with Mr Richards' son that *Reservoir Dogs* is cool do not necessarily agree that this makes armed robbery cool – they are able to draw a distinction between armed robbery in a fictional, stylised world and armed robbery in real life. It does not make sense, therefore, to talk of Mr Richards' son acting on *the* message of *Reservoir Dogs* because there is not *one* message.

The other model of media influence commonly employed in the press is 'addiction'. The idea here is that the consumer watches/reads/listens to a violent media text or group of texts repeatedly and becomes so desensitised to these images/words that he no longer realises the enormity of being violent in real life. While there is evidence to suggest that repeated viewing might desensitise viewers to screen violence, it is quite a leap to suggest that viewers are, therefore, desensitised to violence in real life and a bigger leap still to assume that this leads viewers to become violent themselves. The news reports try to get around these leaps of faith by suggesting that those (literally or metaphorically) in the dock are 'abnormal' viewers. Newspapers are definitely not concerned with the effects that viewing such material might have on *their* readers, but with their effects on 'others' – younger, less well-educated, mentally unstable, lower-class others. The problem is always elsewhere and the affected viewers are, once more, conceptualised as passive, uncritically accepting what they see on screen, barely media-literate. The following headlines provide a flavour of such tabloid coverage:

I HEARD VOICE OF VIDEO MICHAEL: KILLER'S **MAD OBSESSION**.

The Sun, 1 May, 1990

FRIDAY THE 13TH MOVIE **NUT** STABS WIFE.

The Sun, 20 July, 1991

BOY KILLER COOKS KID: SCHOOLBOY HORROR FILM **FANATIC** COPIES MOVIE PLOT TO KILL 7-YEAR-OLD.

The Mirror, 20 June, 1996

THE VIDEO KILLINGS **COPYCATS**: LIFE FOR HORROR FILM **ADDICTS** WHO BUTCHERED A FRIEND.

The Mirror, 8 May, 1999 (emphases added)

The addictive, obsessive nature of the killers' media consumption is thus read as a symptom of the (implied) state of their mental health, a condition that is out of their control and, therefore, responsibility. Yet, while the 'addict' is a passive viewer, his addiction only becomes dangerous when he becomes active, both in identifying with the aggressor and in acting out the violence in reality (Bragg, 2001: 19). How we get from one (passive) mode of viewing to the other (active) one is unexplained – further evidence of the theoretical inconsistencies that characterise the popular effects debate. Further, as Cameron and Frazer (1992: 367) pointedly note:

> Why it should be men and not women who (1) become 'addicts' and/or (2) turn to violence as a consequence of addiction remains totally mysterious.

Reservoir Dogs is a case in point. According to the Cinema Advertising Association, 38% of the audience for this film were women (Hill, 1997: 14). Yet, 100% of the crimes linked to the film by the British press – including the armed robbery involving Mr Richards' son – have been committed by young men.

The number of cases linking violence by women or girls to screen violence in my study was too small to enable detailed analysis of how screen violence is made to function in relation to their crimes. However, in an earlier article (Boyle, 2001a), I explored the representation of the male and female halves of murderous couples whose actions were linked to the movie *Natural Born Killers* (Stone, 1994) and this provides a useful starting point for thinking about these issues. In all three of the killer couple cases I examined, the emphasis was on explaining the actions of the female half of the couple and gender was absolutely central to the news story. When women kill, whether they are copycats or not, they are always visible as women – a theme I return to in Chapter 4. The model of influence adopted to explain the women's violence was neither straightforward imitation nor addiction. Rather, the women were presented as being virtually possessed by the movie and so transformed into something/someone else. It is telling that in these accounts the women were transformed from young girls into killers. In the transformation, their femininity was – it is implied – momentarily lost. Nevertheless, the narratives of transformation return, almost obsessively, to the young women's physical transformations, a move that sexualises the female killers. Neither their male partners, nor any of the male copycats considered in this chapter, are subject to equivalent sexualisation. Indeed, the male killers receive relatively little attention in these reports, neither the fact of their violence nor their apparent imitation of the men on screen seem to require explanation. Male violence – in reality and on screen – is normalised. Blaming individual media representations becomes a way of not asking more pressing questions about the construction of masculinity in our culture at large.

Of course, media representations are part of that culture and highlighting the theoretical flaws in the copycat thesis is not to let the media, in all its forms, off the hook. Even though a causal relationship between individual texts and violent actions cannot be conclusively proved (as I further demonstrate in the next section), there is little doubt that media representations of violence do not only reflect real life, but also shape the way we understand and make sense of violence in the contexts of our own lives. If media blaming 'comes from the culture', as I have suggested, then the way in which we make sense of violence or the possibility of violence, whether we are personally involved or not, also comes from that culture. This is precisely why the ways in which the media tackles violence – whether in press reports, feature films, soap operas, talk shows or sports coverage – have been of concern to those interested in ending and challenging violence.

Finally, in this section, I want to briefly consider the issue of responsibility. Responsibility is crucial in debates about media effects and something that feminists have grappled with repeatedly in relation to pornography. In the aftermath of the war in the former Yugoslavia, for example, Catharine MacKinnon (1993: 28) documented the widespread consumption and production of pornography by soldier-rapists, arguing that pornography, 'is the perfect preparation – motivator and instruction manual in one – for the sexual atrocities ordered in this genocide'. If these men were 'following instructions' – if they were 'led away' like the murderers of James Bulger (see Figure 1.2) – then can they be held individually accountable for the **rapes** and murders in which they participated? Lisa Price (2001: 224) makes a convincing argument that the soldier rapist *is* accountable for his actions, an argument that has a resonance for the media effects debate more generally:

> He could have refused the message of pornography, even a message reinforced by government policy, military ethos, and the encouragement of his fellows. If he had a mother, a sister, an aunt, a girlfriend, or a female teacher, he had access to a different message about women than that presented in pornography. If he was raised as a Christian or as a citizen, he had access to a different message about fit social relations and behaviors. To the extent that he chose to heed one message (that of pornography) and not another, he is responsible and should be held accountable.

While we might take issue with Price's suggestion that there is only one message in pornography and that all women necessarily reject that message, this extract usefully reminds us of two crucial issues in the media effects debate. First, it is extremely difficult to isolate the impact that one representation of violence has on any individual when that representation is itself part of a broader culture in which male violence is valued and normalised. After all, one of the central arguments of this book is that when we talk about media violence we are generally talking about representations of male violence and concerns about their impact on male viewers. Second, despite the pervasive nature of male violence in representation and reality, Price also reminds us that there are alternative stories and experiences. In fiction, news reporting and our daily lives, we have access to a variety of stories about violence – its power, the physical and psychological scars it leaves behind, strategies of resistance and survival. Going back to the 14-year-old armed robber, *Reservoir Dogs* was not the only story of armed robbery that he would have come across in his 14 years. There would have been other stories in television dramas and soaps, the press and television news reporting, in reality crime programming and police procedurals. Stories told from the point of view of the investigator or the victim. Stories about what happened after the robbery. Indeed, even in *Reservoir Dogs* the gangsters are hardly left unscathed by the crime – it is implied that all are dead by the film's conclusion. Mr Richards' son chose to accept one version of the story and not others. It was the 14-year-old boy – not the video – who held two newsagents at gunpoint.

This is not to argue that popular culture has no influence on human behaviour – such an argument would be patently absurd. However, the relationship between representation and reality as presented in popular debate is oversimplified, contradictory and frequently illogical. Isolating individual 'dangerous' representations as *the* cause of violent behaviour also diverts attention from the broader context in which these representations and actions are situated and in which we are all implicated.

Academic approaches to media effects

So far, I have focused on popular representations of the media effects debate and my analysis has suggested that the linking of real criminals to their fictional counterparts may be a way of dodging more complex issues, not least those concerning gender and violence. As I have shown, there is a lack of conclusive evidence offered in these attempts to link individual crimes to specific media representations. Can academic research shed any more light on the subject?

Academic research in this area has been dominated by scientific effects studies. Despite over 60 years of effects research, the relationship between representation and reality remains hotly contested and reviews of the findings of this vast body of scientific research are notoriously inconclusive. Whatever your position on media effects, you can find plenty of scientific evidence to support it, and equally plentiful scientific evidence to challenge it. For example, anti-pornography feminists have argued that the evidence clearly points to a causal relationship between pornography and male violence against women (see, for example, Dworkin and MacKinnon, 1988; Russell, 1992; Itzin, 1992a; MacKinnon and Dworkin, 1997). Feminists on the other side of the pornography debates have, however, argued that the cumulative evidence points in the opposite direction, namely to prove that is that there is no link between pornography and violence (Henry, 1988; King, 1993; Segal, 1993).[4] Nevertheless, despite this lack of consensus, effects research has retained a high profile in the media, in policy reviews and even in courtrooms – wherever a simple answer is sought to the question, 'do representations *cause* violence in the real world'?[5]

As Gauntlett (1997) argues, there are two conclusions that can be drawn from any detailed analysis of these contradictory research findings. First, if, despite the decades of studies, direct effects of the media on behaviour have not been conclusively identified, we may conclude that they are simply not there to be found. Certainly, this is the argument advanced in a number of overviews of the field (such as Cumberbatch and Howitt, 1989; Gauntlett, 1995). However, while I too am sceptical about claiming that the media have direct effects on behaviour, I agree with Jenny Kitzinger (1999a) that justifiable scepticism about the effects literature should not lead us to dismiss the question of media influence altogether. Indeed, scholars within cultural studies have demonstrated the myriad ways in which audiences are influenced by media forms. Sut Jhally and Justin Lewis (1992), for example, use data collected from 52 focus groups to argue that *The Cosby Show* diverts attention from the class-based causes of racial inequality and fuels resistance to affirmative action. In different contexts, Gamson (1992) and Kitzinger (2000) both demonstrate the ways in which mass media commentary provides frames or media templates that viewers/ readers recognise and adopt in their own discussions of contemporary issues, including violence. Kitzinger (1999a) makes a case for retaining the language of 'effects' to describe such processes, but I am not entirely convinced by this argument. The effects tradition has been so thoroughly discredited that to hang on to its language – with all its scientific and behaviourist connotations – seems to me to run the risk of diverting attention from more pressing concerns (see Chapter 2).

The reasons for my scepticism regarding the effects tradition are summarised in Gauntlett's (1997) second conclusion, that media effects research has consistently taken the wrong approach to the mass media, its audiences and society in general. In this section, I outline some of the inherent problems with this approach, focusing specifically on the neglected issue of gender in experimental effects research.

For readers unfamiliar with effects research, a short introduction is necessary. The term 'effects research' is generally used to describe experimental research that investigates the relationship between watching and doing violence. As with the popular debates on media violence, effects researchers have mainly been interested in whether or not representations of violence cause people to behave or think in particular ways.

There are several different methods for investigating this question – namely, laboratory experiments, field experiments, natural or 'found' experiments, correlation studies and longitudinal panel studies – all of which have been considered in some detail in reviews of the field (such as Gauntlett, 1995). Of these studies, it is arguably the laboratory experiments that are the most well known and have been the most influential in policy debates concerning the regulation of pornography and violent media (Fuller and Blackley, 1995; Petley, 2003). Gauntlett (1995: 17) describes the process of the laboratory experiment as follows:

> subjects are randomly divided into two comparable groups, and in a specially prepared setting, one (experimental) group is exposed to a particular treatment, whilst the other

(control) group receives a similar but different treatment, or no treatment at all, and then observations of the subjects' subsequent actions or behaviour are made. Differences in these responses are presumed to be attributable to the effects of the treatment given to one group and not the other.

There are various relatively obvious problems with such an approach. First of all, underpinning all effects research is an assumption, derived from the natural sciences, that it is possible to measure and predict the effect of one object (media violence) on another (the behaviour or attitudes of viewers/readers/listeners). This is partly why effects studies are given such weight in the courtroom, where they are argued to provide objective, scientific evidence of patterns of influence and, therefore, to legitimate (or fail to legitimate) censorious measures against individual texts.

However, applying causal explanations to human behaviour is fraught with difficulty, as we have already seen. To see the contentious representation as the cause of future behaviour – as the effects model implicitly does – is to ignore that we are able to make choices about what we say and do and, therefore, that we should be held account-able for those choices. In other words, the effects model conceives of the media audience as passive and uncritical and, further, assumes that all audience groups will respond to the same material in the same way.

In fact, effects research has focused on very specific audience groups, although this work is often used to make unfounded general-isations about all viewers. The majority of effects research is US-based, though the ways in which social, cultural and political contexts influ-ence the studies (and the viewers studied) has rarely been acknowl-edged. In addition, many researchers use their own college students as subjects, a group that is in no way representative of the general adult population in terms of race, class or educational background. Reflecting the concern with male violence identified elsewhere in this chapter, male subjects have been the focus of a vast majority of the research in this field, although gender bias is frequently hidden behind gender-neutral terms such as 'college students' or 'viewers'.[6] An early review of literature on television violence, for example, found that, of 67 studies, there was only 1 that dealt solely with females, while many studies dealt exclusively with males (Andison, 1977). Nearly two decades later, a meta-analysis of some 217 studies found that 40% of research considered male viewers only, while 2% focused solely on female viewers. In only 40% of the studies with both male and female viewers were the results broken down by gender (Paik and Comstock, 1994: 524).

It is also immediately obvious that effects research is interested in a limited range of individual physiological, behavioural and attitudinal responses to media texts. There is a particular emphasis on the violent act, both on and off screen. In seeing the act as an effect, we sidestep the issue of who is doing what to whom. As you might expect, the 'effects' measured in a laboratory have little relation to processes of media consumption in the real world – how and why we read, look, listen, watch and play.

The gap between the laboratory experience and the real world is perhaps most obvious in relation to pornography. Being wired up to a machine measuring physiological aspects of arousal is hardly equivalent to an orgasm in the privacy of your own home. While arousal can be physiologically measured, this tells us nothing about individual affective responses to that arousal (pleasure, fear, shame, distress and so on). Effects research cannot account for how participants make sense of what they see in relation to their own lives and why they choose to engage – or not – with specific media texts.

This criticism applies not only to researching the effects of pornography, but equally to expressions of violence in the laboratory that bear a tangential relationship to real-world behaviour. For example, violent behaviour following exposure to violent media may be measured by the subject's willingness to administer electric shocks or hit a doll. Subjects do not choose this behaviour from a range of possible options as they would in the world outside the laboratory. In the real world, our post-viewing options are not simply to aggress or not to aggress, but to aggress or do something else entirely – change channels, go to the pub, phone a friend and so on. Of course, if we choose to aggress there are many more or less legitimate forms that aggression could take. Hitting a pillow, shouting at a stranger and shooting our spouse are all aggressive acts, but they clearly have different meanings and consequences and require different degrees of prior planning and opportunity. Moreover, the types of illegal violence that inevitably become the focus of popular effects debates – such as armed robbery, murder and rape – have no laboratory equivalent. That a subject is prepared to administer electric shocks or hit a doll in a sanctioned experiment does not tell us anything about whether or not that subject would engage in violence in the real world, where such behaviour has myriad consequences for both perpetrator and victim. It also cannot be ruled out that the subject administers the electric shocks or hits the doll because they think that is what the experimenter (who, remember, may also be their professor) expects of them. For example, commenting on Albert Bandura's Bobo dolls experiments – where children are shown a filmed sequence of someone attacking a Bobo doll, without any critical comment, and then left in a room with a similar doll – Noble (quoted in Gauntlet, 1995: 18) notes:

> ... the very young child is usually anxious to please the experimenter and does what he [or she] expects the experimenter wants him [or her] to do – one four-year-old girl was heard to say on her *first* visit to a Baundura-like laboratory, 'look, Mummy there's the doll we have to hit'.

It is also useful to note that the girl is 'expected' to hit the doll almost immediately after watching a similar act on film – in other words, the effects measured are short-term. While there are clear problems with the focus on short-term behavioural effects, experimental research on longer-term effects is not only practically but ethically problematic. If it is hypothesised that exposure to violent and/or pornographic material may have demonstrable effects, then the ethics of prolonged exposure outside controlled environments must surely be called into question, unless the researchers do not really expect to find anything?

Having considered the realities of concern in this research, it is also important to consider the representations themselves. The nature of the 'violence' shown to research subjects is not always explained in research reports and there is an assumption that researchers and subjects share a common understanding of what is violent. Research with audiences has, however, shown that defining violence is far from straightforward (Sander, 1997; Morrison et al., 1999) – as we saw in the Introduction. For feminists, who have struggled to redefine the meaning of various forms of violence against women over the past 30 years (see Chapter 3), this should be a particular concern. Certainly, it should worry feminist anti-violence campaigners that effects research has been predominately concerned with acts of male-on-male physical violence as both on-screen cause and off-screen effect, although the gender of perpetrator and victim is often considered insignificant (Boyle, 1999). In this way, researchers have perpetuated the 'normality' of male violence – it's not *male* violence, it's just violence – while making much violence against women invisible.

Violence is not the only term left largely undefined in the experimental literature. In the studies most often cited in the pornography debates, for example, the terms 'pornographic', 'erotic', 'obscene', 'sexually arousing' and 'sexually explicit' are used interchangeably to refer to a diverse range of representations, from nudity to sexual activity between consenting adults and scenes of sexualised mutilation (Senn, 1993: 180). Whether or not research subjects share the researchers' perceptions of the material as 'pornographic', 'erotic', 'obscene', 'sexually arousing' and/or 'sexually explicit' is debatable. Presenting this material in an academic setting is also likely to change its meaning and this may impact on the subject's performance in the experiment. Imagine that your previous encounters with pornographic magazines have been furtive, guilty or private and then you are given the same magazines by a university professor in a formal setting. Might this not cause you to reflect on or re-evaluate the cultural value or acceptability of the material? In other words, by taking this material out of its normal consumption contexts, its meaning is altered.

However, effects studies rarely provide a context for representations of violence. Some studies use clips or slide shows of just a couple of minutes' duration – narrative, character, point-of-view and **modality** are all subordinated to individual violent acts. Needless to say, this is not the way that we encounter violence in our everyday media consumption. It is difficult to see what reactions to a two-minute clip screened in a laboratory can tell us about the effects of watching a two-hour battle against aliens on the cinema screen or seeing an abused wife stab her abuser as part of a long-running soap opera featuring well-established characters. Further, while academic studies have considered the effects of violence across a range of media – still photographs, written and spoken texts, short sequences filmed for the experiment, feature films, video games – there is no consideration of the varying processes of media consumption (looking, reading, listening, watching, playing). Reviews of the research tend to draw together the findings of studies using different media to reach generalised conclusions about effects (see for example, Linz, 1989; Allen et al., 1995). In other words, the content or message is assumed to be more important than the medium. With this in mind, do we really know what effects researchers are investigating the effects of?

From effects to audiences?

How would you design a research project to explore audience responses to violence on screen?

Think about the theoretical, ethical and practical implications of your research design. Studies exploring audience responses to violent movies outside of the effects tradition are discussed in more detail in Chapter 2.

Cultivation and content

Although I have criticised the experimental effects literature for failing to differentiate between media, there is a related body of research that focuses specifically on television violence. With its physical location in the home, debates about television – its content, regulation and impact – are inextricably linked with debates about the organisation and regulation of the private sphere, touching on, for example, questions of childrearing and discipline, gendered patterns of leisure and labour and the relationship between family and the State. If children (or, more accurately, working-class boys) are popularly and academically perceived to be the audience most 'at risk' from television's pernicious effects, it is their parents, and especially their mothers, who are supposedly responsible for protecting them from that risk.

However, women's television viewing also emerges as a concern in its own right. Research on television viewing patterns consistently identifies adult women as 'heavier' viewers than men, with those from lower socio-economic groups watching considerably more than those in the highest groups (for example, Gerbner et al., 1994; Cumberbatch et al., 2002). It is telling, however, that researchers concerned with the putative effects of television on its 'heaviest' viewers have been less concerned with behavioural aggression as an effect than with the cultivation of a television worldview. Taken alongside the behavioural studies discussed in the previous section, there seems to be an assumption that male viewers act and female viewers are acted on.

Cultivation theory – most associated with the work of George Gerbner in the US[7] – posits that 'heavy' television viewing cultivates attitudes and beliefs in the viewer that are more consistent with the world of television programmes than with the real world. Of particular relevance here, research in the cultivation tradition has generally found that 'heavy' viewing is associated with what has been dubbed a 'mean world syndrome'. That is, those who watch more television are likely to believe that the world is a nastier place than those who do not, and to overestimate both the incidence of violent crime and their own likelihood of becoming a victim of violent crime (see, for example, Gerbner et al., 1978, 1979, 1994).

In many ways, this might seem like a fairly straightforward and commonsensical claim. After all, a large part of my argument in this book is that media matter because they shape and reflect our understandings of the world, gender relations, violence, crime and justice. However, while – as with effects research more generally – the findings of cultivation studies may seem seductive, there are problems with much of this research that mean we should be extremely cautious about uncritically adopting its findings. For example, we cannot assume that 'heavy' viewers are necessarily 'heavy' viewers of crime and violence (Hirsch, 1980, 1981). This shortcoming is particularly apparent when you consider that many 'heavy' viewers (who, remember, are more likely to be women) are so categorised because they view during the day. However, very few academics interested in television violence have seriously examined the content of daytime television: Gerbner's work, for example, focuses on primetime and Saturday morning programming. In other words, we don't really know an awful lot about what these 'heavy' viewers are actually watching.

The amount of television they watch is not the only – or necessarily the most significant – difference between 'heavy' and 'light' viewers – gender, age, ethnicity, neighbourhood, socio-economic and employment status all come into play here. Some critics have argued, for example, that the apparent relationship between exposure to television violence and fear of crime can actually be explained by the neighbourhood viewers live in. Those who live in high-crime areas are more likely to stay at home and watch television and also (with some justification) likely to believe that they have a greater chance of being attacked than those who live in low-crime areas (for example, Wober, 1978; Doob and MacDonald, 1979; Gunter, 1987). Further, Gerbner's work takes census data as the measure of the real world, suggesting that (for the 1970s when much of his work was produced) there were 0.32 violent crimes per 100 people. This simply does not equate with subsequent feminist work, which has demonstrated that as many as 1 in 4 women may suffer an assault in their own homes at some point in their lives. So, again, we come back to the fact that we cannot divorce television viewing – or any other media consumption – from the complex lived experiences of viewers.

Cultivation analysts also have to determine what television's world view is and, in so doing, work with an assumption that television content can be classified, coded and counted. Content analyses of television violence – such as the Broadcasting Standards Commission's monitoring in the UK or the National Television Violence Study in the US – produce striking statistics with obvious appeal for journalists and policymakers. In a widely reported speech in the aftermath of the Columbine High School massacre, for example, President Clinton drew on this research to claim that, by the time they reach 18, most Americans would have seen 40,000 dramatised murders. What Clinton didn't tell us was how many actual killings most Americans would have seen on television, including those resulting from his own foreign policy. However, it is not only Clinton whose definition of violence is selective. If we examine how content analysts typically define violence, we find an explicit bias towards physical aggression in their working definitions, as illustrated both by Gerbner's classic 'cultural indicators' project and the more recent National Television Violence Study:

> [the definition of violence used in this study is …] only clear, unambiguous, overt physical violence. To be recorded at all, a violent incident must be plausible and credible. It must be

directed against human or human-like beings, and it must hurt or kill, or threaten to do so, as part of the script's plot. No idle threats, verbal abuse, or gestures without credible violent consequences are included.

Gerbner et al., 1978: 178

Violence is defined as any overt depiction of a credible threat of physical force or the actual use of such force intended to physically harm an animate being or a group of beings. Violence also includes certain depictions of physically harmful consequences against an animate being (or group of beings) that occur as a result of unseen violent means. Thus, there are three primary types of violent depictions: credible threats, behavioural acts and harmful consequences.

Wilson et al., 1997: 186

As with many effects studies, both of these definitions exclude non-contact forms of abuse by defining violence as a physical act.[8] It is perhaps inevitable, then, that even when they attempt to address issues of context, content analyses cannot be other than reductive, substituting an analysis of narrative with a focus on individual scenes or sequences. This is particularly pertinent when considering whether or not violence is justified and whether or not its perpetrators are punished – after all, if the villain of an action movie was punished in the movie's first scene there would be no movie. This does not, however, mean that in the movie as a whole the villain goes unpunished. Whatever content analysts would have us believe, studying narrative content is not – and cannot be – an exact science.

Defining violence

Think about the film/television programme you defined as violent in the Introduction.

What would be the benefits and limitations of using content analysis to analyse this film/programme's violence?

Furthermore, if patterns of abuse on screen were to mirror patterns of abuse off screen, a great deal of violence against women would be omitted from these analyses. An example of this is provided in the second of the studies quoted above where stalking is explicitly excluded unless physical contact takes place between the stalker and the victim (Wilson et al., 1997: 194). As we will see in Chapter 5, stalking is one of the central means by which the **slasher** (or stalker) film shows women in peril. Yet, using Wilson et al.'s schema, a content analysis of a film such as *Halloween* (Carpenter, 1978) would find only a few minutes of violence. Other forms of non-contact abuse – from obscene phonecalls, to flashing, threatening behaviour or verbal harassment – are similarly ignored, as are the complex dynamics of prejudice.

Two of the shows I go on to discuss in Chapter 6 illustrate the limitations of these definitions. First, as Lisa Parks (2003) argues, a content analysis of *Buffy the Vampire Slayer* might tell us how many punches were traded, and by whom, but at the expense of any understanding of how these fights function metaphorically. Social alienation and prejudice – themes that are central to the show's treatment of the high school experience – also disappear from view. Second, in excluding talk about violence, these studies ignore the ways in which 'women's genres', such as soap operas, talk shows or made-for-TV movies, typically seek to make sense of gendered violence.[9] For example, when the long-running British soap *EastEnders* (BBC1, 1985–) tackled the issue of child **sexual abuse** in 2001, it did so by focusing on an adult character's disclosure of the abuse she had experienced as a child. This was arguably the most high-profile media story on child sexual abuse of the year, yet, because we didn't *see* anything, it wouldn't 'count'.

Indeed, any detailed reading of individual content studies suggests that the coding of sexual violence remains a particularly thorny area. For example, in Britain, the Broadcasting Standards Council's (BSC) content monitoring of sex, violence and bad language on television, classifies a '*sex* act' as 'intercourse, *abuse* and oral sex' (BSC, 1993: 65, emphasis added). Another British study (Gunter and Harrison, 1998) found no representations of rape in a sample that included the film *Basic Instinct* (Verhoeven, 1992). There is an infamous scene in this film where a female character explicitly – though unsuccessfully – attempts to reject the aggressive sexual advances of her ex-lover. This interaction would certainly fall within a feminist understanding of rape, yet many critics simply refer to it as 'rough sex' – a view to which the content analysts clearly subscribed. This is a further reminder that definitions of violence (on television as in life) are ideological, and violence against women is often invisible as such. Therefore, the findings of content analyses concerning violence against women – and sexual violence in particular – may be especially unreliable. Nevertheless, as we will see in Chapter 6, there is very little academic work outside this tradition that addresses how violence is represented within and across the televisual landscape.

With these provisos in mind, I want to end with some brief notes on the findings of content analyses of contemporary US and UK television.[10] It is significant that, even though these studies typically adopt an extremely conservative definition of violence, more than 50% of programmes are generally found to contain some violence. Television violence, then, is clearly not something we can bracket off from a discussion of television per se. Whether the sample is of prime-time programming, children's shows or all programming, violence on television – as in recorded crime statistics – is an overwhelmingly white, male preserve. Over the three years of the *National Television Violence Study*, for example, at least 70% of perpetrators and victims of violence were white, between 73 and 78% of perpetrators were male and 9 to 10% were female (Wilson et al., 1997, 1998; Smith, 1998). There was a similar ratio of males to females among targets of violence. However, in reality programmes (news, documentaries, talk shows) – where *talk* about violence was also coded – the percentage of women victims was considerably higher at 33% (Whitney et al., 1997: 295).

While these statistics might give us some food for thought, they cannot tell us a great deal about how violence and gender are made meaningful in television programming. Nevertheless, the apparently clear-cut answers of this 'scientific' research – like those offered by the effects studies discussed in the previous section – have an obvious appeal for policymakers and campaign groups alike as 'science', and (the invariably male 'scientists') have been invested with considerable authority in public policy debates (Ross, 1997). In contrast, in an article focusing on the relationship between pornography and rape, Robert Jensen (1998a: 101) makes a convincing argument for moving beyond the demands of 'science' – an argument that has implications for thinking about the relationships between media representations and reality more generally:

> the search for causation demands 'science' while a concern for pornography's role in rape leaves us more open to listening to stories. Because science has no way to answer the question, predictably the search for causation and the use of science leads most everyone to conclude that we just don't know enough to say for sure. But a shift in emphasis and method offers a way to state not The Truth (or conclude that we don't yet know The Truth), but a way to tell true stories and begin to make trustworthy moral and political decisions.

The next chapter will consider some of the 'stories' by means of which a more complex picture of the relationship between representations and reality begins to emerge.

Summary

- It is not possible to prove, conclusively, that a media text, in isolation, causes a human being to behave in a particular way.
- Causal explanations – whether in popular debate or scientific research – simplify both human behaviour and media texts and create a false distinction between 'dangerous' and 'normal' texts and viewers.
- The effects model assumes that the relationship between representation and reality is one-way, measurable and predictable, leaving no room for responsibility and human agency.
- Blaming the media becomes a diversion from the gendered nature of violence and a means for those who choose to act violently to dodge responsibility for their actions and their consequences.
- Definitions of violence – in media research as in real life – are ideological. This must be kept in mind when evaluating the findings of effects research and content studies alike.
- Given the severe limitations of effects research – in particular, the use of men and male violence as normative – we should be extremely cautious in using the findings of these studies in academic and policy debates.

Notes

1 The Video Recordings Act (1984) was itself drawn up in response to the 'video nasties' controversy of the mid 1980s (Barker, 1984a), making it an offence to sell or rent unclassified videos (with exemptions for educational, sports, religious and music videos) and requiring that the video's suitability 'for viewing in the home' be considered during the classification process. Following the Criminal Justice and Public Order Amendment (1994) to the Act made in the wake of the Bulger case, a number of additional factors must now be considered. These include harm to potential viewers (including underage viewers), harm to society as a result of viewers' behaviour, the treatment of criminal, violent and horrific behaviour and human sexual activities. (See www.bbfc.co.uk for more details.) Petley (2003) provides a useful account of the impact of this amendment and raises important questions about the use of the effects model in policymaking.
2 The text of John McCain's opening statement to the hearing is available at http://commerce.senate.gov/hearings/0504jsm.pdf
3 This involved a manual search of back issues of *The Sun* (1990–99), *The Mirror* (1990–91) and the *Daily Mail* (1990–92) and an electronic search of the CD-ROM databases for *The Mirror/Sunday Mirror* (1992–99), the *Daily Mail/Mail on Sunday* (1993–99), *The Guardian/Observer* (1990–99) and *The Times/Sunday Times* (1990–99). All sources consulted in the British Library Newspaper Library.
4 The main positions in the feminist pornography debates are outlined at the beginning of Chapter 2. Using the findings of effects research in feminist debate is a strategy I have been critical of elsewhere (Boyle, 2000).
5 For an illustration of how such 'scientific' discourse is used in the courtroom, see Ross (1997) and Fuller and Blackley (1995: 93–115).

6 The abstracts collected in Signorielli and Gerbner's (1988) annotated bibliography of research on the effects of media violence provide ample evidence of this point.
7 For a useful summary of cultivation theory and its critics, see Chandler (n.d.).
8 Guy Cumberbatch's 1987 study, *The Portrayal of Violence on British Television*, is one of the few studies that deals with verbal as well as physical violence.
9 A companion study to Wilson et al.'s, which also formed part of the *National Television Violence Study*, dealt with talk about violence but only in the context of non-fiction programming (Whitney et al., 1997; Wartella et al., 1998; Whitney et al., 1998).
10 I am drawing on the following studies: Broadcasting Standards Council (1993) and Broadcasting Standards commission (2002), Gunter and Harrison (1998) and the various reports included in the *National Television Violence Study* (1997, 1998a, 1998b).

Further reading

Barker, M. and Petley, J. (eds.) (2001) *Ill Effects: The Media/Violence Debate,* 2nd edn. London: Routledge.

Boyle, K. (2000) 'The pornography debates: beyond cause and effect', *Women's Studies International Forum,* 23 (2): 187–95.

Boyle, K. (2001a) 'What's natural about killing? Gender, copycat violence and *Natural Born Killers', Journal of Gender Studies,* 10 (3): 311–21.

Gauntlett, D. (1997) 'Ten things wrong with the "effects model"', in R. Dickinson, R. Harindranath and O. Linne (eds), *Approaches to Audiences – A Reader.* London: Arnold.

 *Beyond cause and effect*

Chapter outline

Having outlined some of the limitations of the effects model in the previous chapter, here I consider other ways in which to think about the relationship between representation and action. This takes us, first, behind the scenes where feminist work on the abusive production practices of **pornography** raises questions about harm that a linear cause and effect model necessarily excludes. On the other side of the screen, research on audiences also complicates the notion of effects and raises important questions about context, experience and morality.

- Pornography and violence   anti-pornography and anti-censorship feminisms; defining pornography.
- Harmful production practices   abuse of women and children in pornography production; Linda 'Lovelace'; the casting couch.
- Using pornography   arousal; guilt; abuse; homosociality.
- The appeal of violence and horror   managing fears; testing boundaries; performing gender roles.
- The shock of the real   terrorist attacks of 9/11; victims'/survivors' viewing experiences.
- So, what is to be done?   censorship, civil rights, morality, responsibility.

Pornography and violence

Discussing pornography in the context of a book on media and violence is quite contentious. In doing so, you might assume that I am suggesting that pornography is, in itself, violent (explicitly and/or in terms of the oppressive ideologies it enacts) or that it is linked to violence in the real world. These issues are not, however, the substance of this chapter. Rather, what I am interested in doing here is using feminist work on pornography as a starting point to raise questions, not about content or audience, but about production processes. First, however, it is necessary to briefly sketch out the competing definitions of pornography that emerge in feminist work and so shed some light on why pornography features so centrally in debates about violence and the media.

Defining pornography is far from straightforward and, indeed, any review of the literature may well leave you wondering if critics on different sides of the debate simply have different materials in mind when they write about 'pornography'. For anti-pornography feminists, pornography *is* violence against women and it is this assertion that has made pornography central to media/violence debates.

The most well-known anti-pornography feminists, Andrea Dworkin and Catharine MacKinnon, define pornography as the sexually explicit subordination of women that dehumanises, objectifies and degrades women and often sexualises and celebrates their abuse (Dworkin and MacKinnon, 1988; MacKinnon and Dworkin, 1997). This is a textual definition – that is, it defines what pornography *is* – but it extrapolates from this with an implicit argument about what pornography *does* – its impact in the real world. Indeed, anti-pornography feminists see pornography as central to maintaining women's inequality and subordination in all spheres of life (a violent effect) and, therefore, the eradication of pornography is their central goal.

Anti-pornography feminists have largely rejected censorship as an effective means of control, and Dworkin and MacKinnon (1988) famously explored the possibilities of using sex discrimination legislation to allow those harmed by specific pornographic representations to sue the makers and distributors – an approach that I will consider later in this chapter. However, in order to support their argument linking pornography, sexual callousness and **sexual violence**, anti-pornography feminists – particularly those working in a legislative context – have often drawn on the scientific effects literature discussed in Chapter 1 (see for example, Russell 1992, 1993; MacKinnon and Dworkin, 1997). Given the problems with effects research, this has made anti-pornography feminism a sitting duck for criticism and diverted attention away from other key issues – such as abusive production and consumption practices – that have also, as we will see, been central to anti-pornography feminism (Boyle, 2000).

While the anti-pornography position is not universally accepted within the feminist movement, few feminists identify themselves as supporters of the pornography industry and its products in their current form.[1] More commonly, feminist opponents of the anti-pornography position identify themselves as anti-censorship. This has led many commentators to assume that anti-pornography feminists' primary goal is censorship and that anti-censorship feminists are necessarily pro-pornography: neither characterisation is accurate or helpful. Indeed, anti-censorship feminists often agree with anti-pornography feminists that much pornography is both **misogynist** and racist. The emphasis of anti-censorship work, however, is largely on sexual fantasy, arousal, pleasure, freedom of speech and threats to that freedom. In particular, anti-censorship feminists have been concerned with the ways in which the 'pornographic' is defined and 'pornographic' materials are restricted, arguing that this is bound up with broader questions about State control, class and sexual repression. Violence is not central here and anti-censorship writers argue that anti-pornography feminists over-estimate or exaggerate the amount of explicit violence in pornographic media (Rubin, 1993), fail to acknowledge the agency of women performers (Owens, 1993; Royalle, 1993; Williams, 1993) and ignore the complex pleasures pornography offers its consumers (Vance, 1984).

So, the issue for these feminists is not how to legislate against pornography as a form of violence against women, but how to change both what it is and what it means – for example, by increasing women's agency in production, showing women's desires on screen and destigmatising the pleasures of consumption.

In considering abusive production practices, then, I am focusing on only one aspect of the pornography debate and I am certainly not suggesting that all women in pornography are coerced into being there nor that all pornography is explicitly violent in content.[2] Nevertheless, an examination of these practices raises a number of important questions about the relationship between representation and action, questions obscured in the effects debate. Listening to these stories also raises questions about our relationship to these images and our responsibilities as consumers, as we will see at the end of this chapter.

Harmful production practices

Anti-pornography feminists have documented the ways in which women and children have been abused in the making of both commercial and non-commercial pornography. However, the emphasis on proving (or disproving) that a cause and effect relationship exists between pornography and sexual violence (Chapter 1) has enabled critics to sidestep this compelling evidence. If a woman or girl is raped in order for a particular piece of pornography to exist, her reality is obscured if we ask simply whether that representation causes (or might cause) male viewers to commit further violence. In other words, we need to differentiate between pornography as the cause of sexual violence (a relationship impossible to prove) and the prior abuse associated with the production of some pornography.

Nowhere is such a distinction more important than in relation to child pornography. As Liz Kelly (1992: 121) argues, 'Child **sexual abuse** is not "caused" by child pornography, rather the pornography is the record of abuse which has already taken place.' A debate about causality obscures this fundamental fact. However, here too it is necessary to be precise about which pornography provides such a 'record of abuse'. Film, video and pictorial pornography of children, by definition, require the abuse of the children featured (see Danica, 1988; Itzin, 1996). This is not by definition true of written texts, drawings or cartoons that sexualise children. Equating a cartoon and a photograph obscures the fundamental reality of pre-existing abuse.

Turning now to adult pornography, the picture may appear to be less clear-cut. Certainly, film, video and pictorial pornography featuring adults does not by definition require the abuse of the performers. Nevertheless, adult women have testified that they have been abused in the production of both commercial and non-commercial pornography

In discussing the abuses of the adult pornography industry there is one name that stands out. Linda 'Lovelace' (née Linda Boreman) was the star of the 1972 film *Deep Throat* 'the porn movie that made porn movies chic' (Steinem, 1983: 23).[3] *Deep Throat* was a cheap and hugely profitable movie about a young woman whose clitoris is in her throat and can, therefore, only achieve sexual satisfaction via fellatio.

At the height of the film's popularity, 'Lovelace' publicly detailed the pleasures she derived from her hardcore performances (Lovelace, 1974), but has since given a rather different account of her life (Lovelace, with McGrady, 1981). Before this later account – *Ordeal* – was published, Linda went through an 11-hour lie detector test to verify her story. In *Ordeal*, she claims that she was violently coerced into her infamous performances by her pimp/husband, Chuck Traynor, an initially charming man who offered an escape from her repressive home life. However, once she was under his roof, Traynor began to control every aspect of her life. She was physically beaten, mentally abused and sexually violated in prostitution and pornography. People in the industry – including those on the set of *Deep Throat* who witnessed a vicious beating – knew about the abuse but chose to ignore it (Marchiano, 1983: 26).

Linda had considerable difficulty making this story public (Lovelace, with McGrady, 1981: 194–5; Marchiano, 1983). Literally millions of people had seen *Deep Throat* (it is one of the most profitable movies of all time), had witnessed what she subsequently described as **rape**, but had chosen to see her smile, not her bruises. The various attempts to suppress or discredit her account demonstrate the investment of millions in the fiction – investment not only in terms of financial profit, but also in terms of pleasure. Acknowledging the truth of Linda's story means asking uncomfortable questions about the relationship between production and consumption and, therefore, of the complicity of the viewer.

There are obvious parallels between attempts to discredit Linda's account – if she didn't like it or it was that bad than she would/should have left[4] – and the myths surrounding other forms of male violence against women, most notably **domestic violence**, rape and **sexual harassment**. While this could be argued to demonstrate the position of pornography production on the continuum of male violence (Kelly, 1988), some commentators, including some anti-censorship feminists (such as Strossen, 1995: 183–4), have argued that Linda was not, therefore, abused in or through pornography, but that her story is one of spousal abuse. What such an account ignores is that coercion into performing in pornography was an integral part of that abuse. Further, the sexualised representation of that abuse – in *Deep Throat* and other pornographic movies – remains widely available throughout the world.

Moreover, this case raises troubling questions about the relationship between abuse and representation in the eyes of the abuser. Research on **sexual murder** has demonstrated that many sexual murderers record their crimes (in writing or in photographs, on video or audiotape) as a means of extending their control over their victim beyond the moment of her/his death (Cameron and Frazer, 1987). Arguably, pornography functioned similarly – and spectacularly successfully – for Traynor, giving him the power to control Linda's public image long after the woman herself had escaped from him. Traynor is certainly not the only abusive husband to have used pornographic representations in this way (MacKinnon and Dworkin, 1997).

Reflecting on the first time Traynor took pornographic photographs of her, Linda (Lovelace, with McGrady, 1981: 47) writes:

> I was wondering what they were doing with the pictures they were taking. Where would they go? Would my mother and father ever see them? I had an awful feeling that the pictures would someday be used against me. Whether they were or not, they made this part of my life real, part of some record, uneraseable.

Sadly, she was right: such images are both unerasable and often definitive. In articles following her death in 2002 (in a car crash), Linda was routinely referred to by the name given to her by Traynor, as a 'porn star', 'porn queen', 'porn icon' and simply as '*Deep Throat* Linda'. Thus, the controversial film text eclipsed the reality of her life and death.

While Linda's story is undoubtedly the most widely known, there is a depressing familiarity to it. Numerous testimonies collated by anti-pornography feminists reveal a range of abuses linked to the production of commercial and non-commercial film, video and pictorial pornography, including:[5]

- physical and emotional coercion into performances
- defamation through pornography (a strategy frequently used against feminist anti-pornography writers)
- nude photos sold and/or distributed without the consent (or knowledge) of the woman pictured
- discomfort, pain and physical injuries sustained in the posing and performance of pornographic scenarios
- unsafe sexual practices resulting in the spread of sexually transmitted diseases and risk of HIV infection
- the filming or photographing of actual sexual violence – including war rape and spousal abuse – to be used as pornography
- the sexual murder of women on screen in so-called **snuff** movies.[6]

However, to see pornographic films or photographs as a documentary record of abuse distorts the fact that they are also fictionalised representations. As anti-pornography feminists argue that the pleasure in pornographic texts cannot simply be read as 'real' pleasure, so it is important to remember that their representations of rape cannot be assumed to be 'real' rape. Anti-pornography feminists are, often justifiably, criticised for reading evidence of abuse from pornographic images, assuming an uncomplicated relationship between representation and reality (Dworkin's groundbreaking *Pornography*, 1981, is particularly guilty of this). While it is not always possible to distinguish between representation and abuse (such as in the filming of war rape), it is a mistake to collapse the one into the other – that is, to argue that a pornographic rape scenario is always and necessarily the rape of the performer. Such a strategy can be extremely patronising to women performers and actually work to obscure production abuses as, following the logic of this argument, if the woman smiles on screen – as in *Deep Throat* – can we believe that there was really a rape?

Anti-pornography feminists remain unconvinced that any women freely choose to perform in pornography. In a society where the sexual objectification of women is routine, where women are paid less than men and are concentrated in poorly paid professions, anti-pornography feminists argue that it is unsurprising that women are encouraged to think of their bodies as their most valuable commodities. They also point out that women in pornography and other forms of **commercial sexual exploitation** often have few economic alternatives and that, once in the industry, abusive pimps, debt, drug dependence and blackmail can make it very difficult for them to leave. Anti-pornography feminists have also made the link between sexual abuse and women's later involvement in pornography. One study reports that at least 70% of adults involved in the sex industry were sexually abused as children (Leidholdt, 1999: 22), while a review of the literature on prostitution concludes that 60–90% of prostituted women (including those in pornography) were sexually abused as children (Farley, 2003). Such abuse erodes women's sense of ownership of and rights over their own bodies, facilitating their entry into pornography. The public display of the pornography made of these women then reminds other girls and women of their/our lack of rights (Dworkin, 1981). With this in mind, anti-pornography feminist Susan Cole (1989: 137–8) challenges us to think not of our right to watch 'real' sex, but of our relationship to the performers – who are they, how did they get there and would we be prepared to put ourselves in their position?

While the relationship between reality and representation has been a central concern in the pornography debates, there has, to my knowledge, been no equivalent research concerning the reality of more mainstream representations of sex and/or violence. Although the cycle of abuse in and through which women, children and men often become involved in pornography has no direct equivalent in mainstream cultural production, the issue of abuse behind the scenes cannot be so easily dismissed. Cole (1989: 42), for example, notes, 'the casting couch is a fixture everywhere in the entertainment business', adding that, 'many models in the fashion industry or in TV advertisements have had to put up with sexual pressure to land a job'. Where alluded to in popular culture, the 'casting couch' is rarely treated as a serious abuse of power, making it very difficult for women (or men) subjected to this sexual pressure to resist or refuse safely.

It is notable, though hardly surprising, that very few women or men in the industry have been willing to discuss their experiences of sexual harassment or rape in these terms. In 2000, one UK rape case gave a stark example of this. A bogus film director was found guilty of raping a woman at an audition, having previously sexually harassed other women in similar circumstances. Although a number of the women had told their agents about his behaviour, the agents continued to send women to audition for him and he was not reported to the police (*Daily Mail*, 17 July, 2000). That the agents were neither surprised nor outraged by his behaviour reminds us that in cultures where violence is endemic, it is often invisible as such. Here, it would seem, sexual harassment did not amount to violence in the eyes of many agents and auditioning actors, but was an accepted – or, at least, expected – part of the audition.

It is clear that such sexual harassment does not begin and end with the casting process, nor is it restricted to the low-budget end of the market. Take the following quotation from Susan Faludi's (1992: 148) description of life on the set of the movie *9½ Weeks* (Lyne, 1985) for its female star, Kim Basinger:

> During the filming, the humiliation continued between takes. Kim Basinger [...] was cringing not only before her character's lover but also from the ministrations of [director] Lyne, who waged an intimidation campaign against the actress – on the theory that an 'edge of terror' would 'help' her prepare for the role. At one point, heeding Lyne's instructions that 'Kim had to be broken down', co-star Mickey Rourke grabbed and slapped Basinger to get her in the mood.

Clearly, being a highly paid Hollywood actor is no protection against violent **misogyny** in the workplace and Basinger's is far from an isolated case. Consider the allegations of sexually harassing and abusive behaviour made against Arnold Schwarzenegger during his campaign for the California Governor's office. In his public 'apology' for aspects of his past behaviour, Schwarzenegger implicitly suggested that this kind of behaviour was and is unexceptional on what he described as 'rowdy' movie sets. For Schwarzenegger, Lyne and Rourke, it would seem that sexual harassment is not abusive and potentially criminal behaviour but an unremarkable aspect of movie culture.[7]

Moreover, look through any movie magazine and you are likely to find examples of abusive on-set behaviour hailed as a sign of genius, an inevitable part of the process of creating 'serious' films dealing with sex, violence or fear. The on-set abusive behaviour is frequently legitimated by the drive for realism. This raises uncomfortable questions for viewers, both in terms of spectatorship (how does such evidence change our relationship to the image?) and consumption (does our enjoyment of these films legitimate the abuse?). It should also be noted that the sanctioned abusers in all of the cases I have found are male, although the fact that this is a uniquely gendered expression of 'fun' or 'genius' has gone largely unremarked.

The whole question of abusive and unethical production processes in entertainment media is underexplored territory. As feminists and others have tackled sexual harassment and abuse in other workplaces and explicitly addressed questions about the production of pornographic representations, so there are ethical and political questions to be asked – not only about the content of violence on screen, but also about its production. Nevertheless, while violent misogyny behind the scenes of mainstream entertainment media clearly needs to be named and challenged as such, mainstream media forms are not so straightforwardly situated in the cycle of abuse that characterises much of the pornography industry. As Cole (1989: 42) writes, 'The difference between the sexual harassment in the entertainment industry and the rape in pornography is a matter of degree, *but I think the degree matters*' (emphasis added).

The abuses documented here challenge the tendency within debates on pornography and media violence to assume that the message is more important that the medium. Some media (film, video, photography) require the performances of real women, men and children; others (writing, cartoons, drawings) do not. This is not an insignificant difference. Perhaps the time has come for feminists to not only move beyond debates about causality, but also to abandon 'pornography' as a unitary concept (Boyle, 2000). Yet, it is surely worth hanging on to the knowledge gained from anti-pornography feminist work and using this as a springboard for thinking about production processes – and the relationship between production and consumption – more generally.

Using pornography

In attempting to move beyond cause and effect, I have so far concentrated on production. In the remainder of this chapter I will be looking at the other side of the screen, beginning with a brief discussion of research into the consumption of pornography. This research does not focus solely on representations of violence, but, given claims about the relationship between pornography and sexual violence against women, it is worth exploring what we really know about pornography consumption. This is a relatively new field of inquiry, a particular limitation of which is the lack of any sustained comparison of the consumption practices attached to different pornographic media. However, from what we do know about the use and consumption of pornography, five key themes emerge:

- arousal
- education
- male bonding
- male entitlement
- harm to women.

Although often ignored in academic debates, arousal is clearly a primary goal of using pornography. How that arousal is experienced and acted on is, however, far from straightforward or uniform.

Defenders of pornography have noted a number of potentially positive aspects of using pornographic media for sexual arousal: it can enhance sexual fantasy for individuals and couples, give information and ideas about sexual practices and techniques and provide 'safe' sex (for viewers) in the era of HIV and AIDS. Clearly, there are women and men who find specific pornographic texts both arousing and pleasurable and who choose to engage with sexually explicit material on their own, or with partners or peers. In particular, pornography produced by and for lesbians and gay men has been argued to provide a sense of community as well as practical safer sex information and a passionate affirmation of marginalised sexualities in a homophobic culture (see for example, Watney, 1987; Hollibaugh, 1996; Ross, 1997). Of course, material by and for lesbians and gay men is a small fraction of commercial pornography, although this example again raises the question as to whether or not pornograpy (in the singular) is a meaningful category for analysis.

However, it is important to recognise that physical arousal is not, necessarily, experienced as pleasurable. Swedish research has, for example, demonstrated that young women's experiences of being turned on by heterosexual pornography can be accompanied by a variety of contradictory emotions related to their perceptions of heterosexuality and gender roles (Berg, 1999). Similarly, men's accounts of purchasing and using pornography are not entirely pleasurable, revealing feelings of depression, guilt and shame as well as ambivalence and anxiety about sexuality, gender and relationships with both partners and peers (Hardy, 1998; Jensen, 1998a). Whether this is seen as evidence of the dehumanising aspects of the consumption of pornographic media or the stigma attached to pornography in Western (and particularly British) societies does, of course, depend on your position on pornography.

It is also relevant to ask here what pornography users are being aroused by. Feminists on both sides of the pornography debate have generally agreed that the vast majority of commercially produced heterosexual pornography is both misogynist and racist. Further, research on men's use of pornography shows that some men recognise and enjoy the sense of power over women they get from these texts and, indeed, acknowledge that pornography promotes sexual selfishness in men (Hardy, 1998). There are uncomfortable parallels here with sexual murderers' and other abusers' accounts of their own home-made pornography – both action and representation provide an eroticised power and control over the object of desire (an argument developed more fully in Chapter 3). This again points to pornography's position on the continuum of male violence, and anti-pornography feminists have argued that in repeatedly masturbating to these texts and images men (and women) are being conditioned to find such inequalities sexy. The user's orgasm is the proof that these inequalities *are* sexy and, in

Catharine MacKinnon's (1995: 102) words, 'try arguing with an orgasm sometime'.

It is worth reiterating, however, that the sexual objectification and denigration of women is not confined to sexually explicit media. Abusers consume a variety of media/literary texts, not only those we recognise as 'pornography'. Read any true crime anthology and you are as likely to find obsessive Bible-readers among the anthologised sexual murderers as you are to find pornography consumers (for example, Wilson, with Wilson, 1995). The eroticisation of power in the Bible is not an issue I have space to consider here (see Cameron and Frazer, 1987), but the sexual murder/Bible reading connection surely highlights the difficulty of identifying individual representations as causative in a culture steeped in violence. It also, of course, raises questions about effective and appropriate mechanisms for the regulation of texts – would we seriously consider banning the Bible because a serial sex killer took inspiration from its pages?

Another theme emerging from research on the consumption of pornography is education. As Robert Jensen (1998a: 140) argues, there is nothing inherently wrong with learning about sexuality from a sexually explicit publication, the problem is that heterosexual, commercial pornography constructs sexuality in a male-dominant framework and presents women as sexual objects. As sex education, pornography not only teaches certain mechanics of sex, but also teaches attitudes about gender, sexuality, pleasure and resistance – an education that is reflected and reinforced in more mainstream representations of sex and sexuality.

Pornography can serve as sex education in another way. Survivors of child abuse and child abusers alike have testified to the use of pornographic texts to groom children – girls in particular – for abuse. It is important to emphasise that it is not only child pornography that is used in this way. Legal publications that feature adult women are also used to break down the resistance of girls to sexual activity, to confuse them and discourage disclosure of abuse by presenting that behaviour as 'normal' and pleasurable (Brady, 1984; Itzin, 1996). More generally, the sexualisation and commodification of young girls in other sites – such as fashion, art, girls' magazines and music – reinforces the child abuser's sense of the legitimacy of his desire (Silverman and Wilson, 2002: 39–43).

For adult survivors, pornography can reinforce the messages about sex learned from their abusers and further alienate the survivor from her/his own body and desires. Heterosexual, commercial pornography has also been implicated in the abuse of adult women, most commonly in forced consumption (in public and private arenas) and coerced re-enactments of pornographic scenarios (*Everywoman*, 1988; MacKinnon and Dworkin, 1997). Survivors have described how their rapists (strangers, husbands, gangs, pimps) used pornographic videos, magazines and text to pressure and force them into performing specific sexual acts or scenarios.

There may be no linear cause and effect relationship between the consumption of pornography (or other cultural texts) and these acts of abuse, but it is clear that the pornographic texts are integral to the way in which these abusers justify their actions to themselves and their victims. Heterosexual pornography is an intrinsic and powerful part of the rape culture, a culture in which 'masculine sexual entitle-ment is offered to boys as part of their birthright' (Kimmel, 1993: 127). This sense of sexual entitlement is reinforced when porno-graphy is shared and viewed communally and, more generally, is reinforced by the homosocial environs that characterise other forms of commercial sexual exploitation (strip clubs, lapdancing bars and so on). Kimmel (1993: 127–8) asks:

> What is it about groups that seems to bring out the worst in men? I think it is because the animating condition for most American men is a deeply rooted fear of other men – a fear that other men will view us as less than manly. ... Men's fear of being judged as a failure in the eyes of other men leads to a certain homosocial element within the hetero-sexual encounter: men often will use their sexual conquest as a form of currency to gain status among other men.

Homosociality characterises many males' first experiences of porno-graphy (Hardy, 1998; Jensen, 1998a) and makes their subsequent pornography use acceptable – from sharing magazines in the play-ground or pub to viewing pornographic videos in a fraternity house, military base or other working environment. Such public consump-tion is not necessarily linked to masturbation or sex, but is more com-monly an expression of exaggerated adherence to traditional norms of heterosexual masculinity, providing a powerful assertion of the men's (or boys') difference to and power over the women whose bodies they 'consume'. Therefore, the context in which these texts are consumed is central to the meaning they assume for their audience. Entirely private consumption of pornography, for example, remains publicly stigmatised – a pursuit for inadequate men who 'can't get a "real woman"' (Jensen, 1998a: 139). The public acknowledgement of private consumption mitigates against this according to one of the men interviewed by Simon Hardy (1998: 104):

'I mean, basically, it's wanking material, isn't it? I mean that's the reason people [sic] buy it, I mean, they buy it, and they bring it into work, and "This is what I bought today, have a look, chaps", you know, and I imagine they go home and wank over it.'

What is interesting here is the way in which the prior sharing of the material provides, in this man's words, 'a cover-up' – or perhaps a legitimisation – for the private masturbation over the magazine. It is also significant that the man first shows his 'wanking material' to work colleagues. Such display and camaraderie both asserts the men's entitlement to public space and problematises women's occupation of the workspace.

The picture of pornography use and real-world violence that emerges here is far from straightforward. On the one hand, pornography use is pleasurable and positive for some men and women, gay and straight. However, set against this is the evidence of the role of pornography in promoting a rape culture of male sexual entitlement and women's acquiescence. Clearly, pornography does not *cause* rape in any straightforward way, but this does not mean that consumption practices do not raise troubling questions about gender, sexuality, power and control.

The appeal of violence and horror

Like pornography, the horror genre has long been the focus of popular and academic concern about media effects. The parallels between the two are further underlined by Caputi and Russell's (1992: 18) description of the '**slasher**' horror film as '**gorenography**'. The term gorenography highlights what, for many feminists, has been of central concern about this kind of horror: the linking of violence and sex.

For some feminists at least, there has been a temptation to assume – on the basis of textual analysis alone – that male viewers are uncritically accepting of, if not explicitly aroused by, this sexualised violence (see, for example, Caputi, 1988; Caputi and Russell, 1992; Domingo, 1992). While there is certainly a place for examining how media texts attempt to position their audiences (as we will see in Chapter 5), without empirical audience research we can say very little about how audiences actually engage with and make sense of these texts in their own lives.

In the next few pages, the key findings of a number of relevant audience studies are summarised, challenging the assumption that viewers passively consume representations of violence and horror. It is, however, important to remember that audience activity is not in itself evidence of resistance. As Jackie Stacey (1994: 46) notes in the context of a study of female fans of 1950s Hollywood films, 'women may be active viewers in the sense of *actively* investing in oppressive ideologies.'

Viewing horror

Write a short account of the last time you watched a horror movie.

Include in your account the context in which you watched the film, the way you reacted during the screening, the way the reactions of others (if present) shaped your own viewing experience and whether or not the film had any impact on you beyond the moment of viewing.

How does your own experience of viewing horror complicate the effects model outlined in Chapter 1?

While feminists and film marketing departments alike have often assumed that horror and violence appeal primarily, if not exclusively, to young male viewers, the pleasures some female viewers take in horrifying and violent fare have been explored by researchers (Hill, 1997; Cherry, 1999). Indeed, women make up a significant proportion of the audience for certain kinds of horror (vampire movies, occult/ supernatural films, psychological thrillers) and other identifiably violent movies (Hill, 1997; Cherry, 1999).[8] But what do these viewers make of what they see?

Audience research has demonstrated that there is no self-evident definition of 'violence' that viewers share – as we saw in the Introduction. In a study examining viewers' definitions of screen violence, Morrison et al. (1999: 6) found that viewers labelled as 'violent' behaviour that broke the codes of conduct of their own social groups. In other words, their definitions of violence were subjective and relational, depending not on quantity or even explicitness but on the nature and context of the action. So, those programmes labelled as 'violent' by researchers are not necessarily recognised as such by viewers. For example, quantitative content studies of the kind discussed in Chapter 1 show that children's cartoons are among the most violent programmes on television (*National Television Violence Study*, 1997), but they are rarely defined as violent by viewers (Gunter, 1985; Sander, 1997; Morrison et al., 1999).

We should, however, be wary of adopting viewers' definitions uncritically in academic research. Indeed, there are questions to be asked about the conditions in which aggressive behaviour is *not* defined as violent, particularly in the context of this book where the reluctance to see some forms of male violence as violence (and as male) is repeatedly documented.

Moreover, the appeal of violent genres cannot be condensed down to the violent actions alone. For example, for the female horror fans interviewed by Brigid Cherry (1999: 195), 'the pleasures of viewing horror films did *not* include the violence' (emphasis added). Instead, the women took pleasure in the strong heroines, gothic moods and tense, suspenseful narratives. So, while violence was an expected element of the horror films, it was not the reason for these women choosing to view them (or, at least, it was not a reason that they felt comfortable disclosing to the interviewer, which in itself is significant).

Of course, many viewers are attracted to a film because of its violence – or reputation for violence. For many of the men and women interviewed by Annette Hill (1997, 1999), the decision to view notoriously violent movies such as *Reservoir Dogs* (Tarantino, 1991) was about taking a risk, deciding to test their own boundaries by viewing movies others had defined as violent. Such risk-taking has a particular cachet for men and boys, for whom experiences of watching and discussing violence and horror can provide a way of testing and proving their masculinity, a way of differentiating themselves from female or feminised others (Buckingham, 1996; Hill, 1997). Interestingly, in Buckingham's study of children's emotional responses to television violence, the text itself was of less importance than the boys' ability to talk about their responses to it. Similarly, a 20-year-old male student of mine, responding to a class exercise on viewing experiences,[9] wrote of a frightening experience he had as a ten-year-old:

> I watched it with my younger sister (she was about six or seven at the time) and she was really terrified – crying, etc. Although I was just as frightened as her, I did not react in the same way as her (physically). I used the experience against her – mocking her for being so scared and for crying, even though I was really just as scared! I couldn't sleep for days after watching it, but it made me feel cool when I talked about it at school. I'd always talk about horror films (from what I'd read from the box), even though I never watched them.

What the boy had to gain from viewing or pretending to view horror is clear – the power over his sister, social standing among his peers – but the films themselves are of secondary importance. Indeed, he can get enough information from the video box to fake having watched them.

For girls, too, there are pleasures to be gained from gender role conformity, as revealed in this 14-year-old girl's explanation of the appeal of horror movies (quoted in Zillman and Weaver, 1997: 91):

> 'They're fun to watch. You go with your friends and try to get scared and everything. And you can just be rowdy. You can get all rowdy with boys and jump in their lap, and they can comfort you. They say, "Don't worry, I can protect you."'

Indeed, Zillman and Weaver (1997) found that their male respondents enjoyed a horror film twice as much in the presence of a distressed female as when they viewed with a fearless female, and female viewers enjoyed the film least when viewing with a distressed male. In other words, viewing violence and horror is part of the way in which these viewers experience gender, sexuality and power. However, these viewers recognise that they are performing a gender role here and such performances can take different forms. For example, some of the adult women interviewed by Cherry (1999) and Hill (1999) took pleasure in *flouting* those very conventions in their viewing choices and practices.

It is too simplistic, then, to argue that viewing violence and horror always reinforces gender roles as it may also provide opportunities (albeit limited) for conscious gender performance or play. I say that these opportunities are 'limited' because, as the story of the scared ten-year-old reminds us, there is also a lot to lose – particularly, perhaps, for boys – in not fulfilling the expected gender role. Further, we should not forget that the gender performances of others can shape how safe we feel in public and private viewing spaces, as the following examples – taken from very different sources – illustrate:

> 'Shall I tell you something? When I went to see that film [*The Accused*] first, there was about ten of us, five of them were male. After we walked out of that film the women were devastated, one of the five men was, the other four were cracking jokes. That upset me more after that than the film did. Their responses afterwards.'
>
> English Asian woman with no experience of
> violence, in Schlesinger et al., 1992: 153–4

Having read several letters regarding cinema rage, I felt compelled to write and tell you about an experience a friend and I had that was not only intrusive and noisy but downright scary. During a visit to the Odeon in Manchester we became aware of a strange noise coming from the back row. On glancing behind us we discovered that a lone man was cheerfully masturbating. This in itself is quite disturbing, but what made it particularly unsettling was the fact that the film we were watching was *Dog Soldiers* – and that said, the latter part of *Dog Soldiers*.

Letter from Louise Emmerson, *Empire*,
September 2002: 9

Although viewing very different films, both these women found that men's responses to scenes of violence (trivialising rape, masturbating to horror) fundamentally altered their viewing experiences and reminded them of their own vulnerability. That it was not the films per se that had this effect points to the importance of investigating film viewing in social contexts. For example, how do men and women use cinema space? While there has been a considerable amount of feminist research on domestic viewing practices (such as that of Hobson, 1982; Morley, 1986; Gray, 1992), the gendered dynamics of public viewing remain relatively underexplored.

When we examine how we watch horror and violence, the notion that viewers are passive in the face of an onslaught of screen violence becomes even more difficult to sustain. Viewers are not simply 'exposed' to screen violence (as the effects model would have it), we make choices and decisions about whether or not, when and how to view (Hill, 1997; Barker et al., 2001; Austin, 2002).

Before viewing, we will already have a range of preconceptions, for example, about the genre, star, character, censorship and representations of sex and violence. These preconceptions shape the nature of our investment in the film and enable us to develop specific viewing strategies (Barker and Brooks, 1998; Hill, 1997). At the most basic level, if we do not enjoy looking at violence or its effects, we can usually look away, switch channels or walk out. We employ these strategies not only in response to specific scenes or incidents but also in anticipation of them, drawing on our prior knowledge and experience of this and other texts (Hill, 1997; Barker et al., 2001). For example, in discussing their responses to *Reservoir Dogs*, some of the viewers in Hill's study (1997) acknowledged that, having heard of the film's notorious ear-slicing scene before they saw the film, they hid behind their hands during much of the torture sequence. Actually, the camera cuts away before knife and ear connect, but Hill reports that a number of viewers were, nevertheless, convinced that they had seen

Mr Blonde's blade slicing off the cop's ear. That the violence which is often most disturbing to viewers is that which remains unseen – whether because we are hiding behind our hands or the director cuts away at the key moment – makes something of a mockery of a research tradition that focuses on the isolated act (see Chapter 1).

Let's return, now, to the frightened ten-year-old covering up his own fear in front of his sister. Although, as he self-consciously reflects ten years on, he had much to gain by playing out an accepted gender role, the film did disturb him to the extent that he 'couldn't sleep for days'. Indeed, when I ask students to reflect on viewing experiences that have frightened them, they invariably produce a list of the ways in which that fear impacted upon them beyond the moment of viewing, including loss of sleep, nightmares (sometimes recurring for years), film-linked phobias or a dislike of material objects that remind them of that fear.

I am sure most of us have had such experiences at some point and, as Buckingham (1996) notes, the images, situations and characters arousing such fear can be very unpredictable – *Sesame Street*'s Big Bird can be just as terrifying to a child as *Elm Street*'s Freddy Krueger. Certainly, for the parents in Buckingham's study, managing fear was a greater concern than imitative violence – at least when talking about their own children.

For both children and adults, viewing violence and horror can be a way of working through and managing real-world fears (Buckingham, 1996; Hill, 1997). Further, as Carol Clover (1992) argues in relation to horror, films can allow us to identify with positions of both power and powerlessness not available to us – or not safely available to us – in the real world. We should, therefore, be wary of taking the expression of fear as a description of a necessarily negative viewing experience as it is precisely the pleasure of a 'good scare' that attracts many to horror films in the first place. For others, while the immediate viewing experience is not defined as pleasurable, in retrospect it becomes so partly because of its social function. As another student wrote of viewing *The Shining* (Kubrick, 1980) aged 12, 'My brother and a friend knew I was scared and were playing tricks on me. Terrified at time, loved it afterwards.'

Of course, it would be foolish to extrapolate from this that these viewers enjoy being frightened per se – context is all. For these next two viewers – the first, a female student of mine responding to a viewing experiences questionnaire, the second, a woman with experience of violence interviewed in the *Women Viewing Violence* (Schlesinger et al., 1992: 93) study – the heightened sense of fear was far from pleasurable:

I found the violence [in *A Clockwork Orange*, 1971] so extreme that it made me reassess my opinions of men. It made me scared that someone could potentially be capable of this. I watched the film with my boyfriend and I actually felt a little sick afterwards but *not* because of any 'gruesome' factor (which doesn't tend to affect me). After the film I was scared walking on my own at night (which I don't do much anyway) and it did make me think about the male psyche and reassess my 'faith' in it.

When I watch, whatever, and the woman's been battered ... I sit there – 'It's only make-up' ... You have to just say to yourself, 'It's only make-up. It's make-up.' Because ... I'm still frightened to death, because I think, yeah, that was me ...

For both women, the violence on screen fed into existing fears and perceptions of vulnerability and, crucially, to their experiences as women. It is not the explicitness of the violence (the 'gruesome' factor) that is at issue for these viewers but its **modality** – its relationship to their everyday life and experience. It is to this facet of the relationship between representation and reality that I now turn my attention.

The shock of the real

The previous section concentrated on the appeal of fictionalised horror, but what happens when the boundary between fantasy and reality is crossed? For many people witnessing the terrorist attacks of September 11th 2001 on New York and Washington (hereafter referred to as 9/11), the shock was not that these images were unimaginable, but that they were uncannily familiar. As the satirical online magazine *The Onion* put it, 'American life has come to resemble a bad Jerry Bruckheimer-produced action/disaster movie' (26 September, 2001).[10]

The spectacles of destruction in movies such as *Independence Day* (Emmerich, 1996), *Armageddon* (Bay, 1998), *Deep Impact* (Leder, 1998) – all of which imagine the destruction of New York – looked very different in the immediate aftermath of 9/11. Indeed, such spectacles were deemed 'insensitive' and pulled from television networks in the days and weeks following the attacks. On 19 September, an article in *The Guardian* noted that Sky's movie programming 'was virtually gutted', with over 30 films being dropped in the first week. Meanwhile, Hollywood was, we were told, engaged in unprecedented soul-searching and the future of big-budget action movies was in doubt as studios delayed the release of completed pictures, re-edited others and stalled on green-lighting new projects. Predictably, perhaps, this heightened sensitivity was relatively short-lived and, within months, commentators were predicting a return to patriotic action (Kitses, 2002).

The 9/11 terrorist attacks merit comment in the context of this discussion, not least because they engendered a brief period of reflection on the function of violent entertainment.[11] The knee-jerk censoring would suggest that part of the appeal of these images of mass destruction is their apparent unreality, the escapism they provide and the impersonal pleasure of kinetic spectacle. We do not need to think of the human implications of such spectacular destruction. However, while such movies are escapism on one level, they metaphorically engage with real contemporary anxieties and debates and the 'solutions' they provide are highly political. *Independence Day*, for example, externalises the threat posed to the American way of life (alien invasion), while 'America' itself is presented as a unified, multi-ethnic society organised on traditional gender and class lines and headed by a universally respected and benevolent patriarch. In the film, the alien threat, although at first a threat to America (New York and Washington are decimated, Americans are killed) is, more broadly, presented as a threat to the world. Universalising 'American' concerns in this way metaphorically justifies America's role on the world stage: these Americans are not only national heroes but world saviours. In thinking about escapism, therefore, we need to ask what this is an escape from and for whom is it an escape?

While re-viewing spectacles of destruction through the lens of the real events of 9/11 prompted a short-lived sensitivity to the ethics of violent entertainment, the industry is selective in its concern for 'reality'. To put it bluntly, prior to 9/11, the death toll from terrorist attacks outside US borders did not give pause to the ethics of terrorism-as-entertainment. These examples further remind us that definitions of violence and terror are ideological, begging the question, when do we actually see violence as violence and what are the implications of our selective blindness?

The 9/11 example would suggest that when we are encouraged to identify with the victims of atrocity – when, in the words of an article in *The New York Times* (23 September, 2001), it becomes clear that the bodies are real – our position as viewers or consumers is challenged. Clearly, however, for many, many women (and men), representations of interpersonal violence already carry that shock of recognition. In the words of the woman quoted at the end of the previous section, 'I'm still frightened to death, because I think, yeah, that was me ... ' (Schlesinger et al., 1992: 93). Like viewers interviewed by Hill (1997), this woman has quite specific strategies for managing the viewing experience, but her response – like those of many of the women who participated in the *Women Viewing Violence* study – is clearly mediated by her own experience of violence. While the woman reassures herself that it is not real, her own experience demonstrates that it could be real. Similarly, viewing *Independence Day* post-9/11, the shock is partly that we know that the collapse of a skyscraper is possible and partly that we know – or can imagine – what it means for those inside.

The findings of research on victims'/survivors' viewing experiences are particularly important in the context of this chapter as they demonstrate the complex ways in which viewers respond to on screen violence in relation to their off screen experiences of abuse (Schlesinger et al., 1992; Kitzinger, 2001). In the *Women Viewing Violence* study, for example, groups of women with and without known prior experience of violence discussed a variety of representations of men's violence against women, including an episode of the long-running soap *EastEnders* (BBC1, 1985–), the feature film *The Accused* (Kaplan, 1988) and the reality crime programme *Crimewatch* (BBC1, 1984–). While many of the women personally found these representations distressing, they nevertheless stressed the importance of showing male violence against women realistically, arguing that popular representations can provide a lifeline for an abused woman, letting her know that she is not alone. They also noted that films and television programmes can raise awareness about these often hidden crimes and so educate the public.

Indeed, feminist organisations have also found that these popular texts can often be hugely helpful in creating a relatively safe space for women and children to begin talking about men's violence and for analysing and challenging the violence. In Glasgow, where I work, the local Women's Support Project runs an annual screen debate during the month of action on child sexual abuse for precisely these reasons. Similarly, Jenny Kitzinger's (2001) work has shown that media portrayals of child sexual abuse have played important roles in the lives of individual survivors, helping them to recognise and name what is otherwise a very hidden form of abuse. These, we might argue, are potentially pro-social effects.

However, among these survivors there is also concern about balancing the need to make the violence visible with the danger that, in a drive for ratings or box office success, these serious issues are reduced to 'entertainment' (Schlesinger et al., 1992; Alcoff and Gray, 1993; Armstrong, 1994). Specific concerns expressed by the women in these studies include the ways in which entertainment media – from talk shows to feature films – sensationalise the story, sexualise female victims and employ racial and class stereotypes. There is also concern that these representations perpetuate myths about male violence – 'She asked for it', 'It is an individual, personal problem', 'He only does it when he drinks', 'It's his mother's fault he's violent' and so on.

Fact-based representations are also a focus of audience concern. The women interviewed by Schlesinger et al. (1992), for example, revealed a variety of responses to the reality crime programme they viewed – it was educational, a way of contextualising their own fears, the sensational style adopted allowed them to critically distance themselves from its content. For children and parents interviewed by Buckingham (1996), television news frequently caused greater anxiety than fictional violence and the 'need to know' and ability to manage knowledge and fear had to be balanced with the emotional impact of such knowledge at various stages in the child's development. Again, viewers are actively engaging with questions about the representation of violence and attempting to moderate their own – and others' – viewing in light of these concerns.

In her work on child sexual abuse, Kitzinger (2000) has also examined the ways in which the media's framing of violence provides audiences with templates for understanding events, policies and actions. Even when people do not uncritically accept what they see or read, these media templates can shape the ways in which an audience engages with a topic – the themes they identify as important, the questions they ask, the assumptions they make. An example particularly pertinent to our concerns in this chapter comes from Barker et al.'s (2001) study of the controversy surrounding the British release of *Crash* (Cronenberg, 1996). The *Daily Mail* and *Evening Standard* mounted a campaign against this 'sex and car crashes' film that lasted for several months. They defined the film as pornographic and morally corrupt, condemned its likely effects on viewers and called for it to be banned. Barker et al.'s study of responses to the film demonstrated that even those viewers resistant to the *Mail*'s moral campaign nevertheless frequently used the *Mail*'s template to discuss the film – that is, they felt obliged to engage with questions of pornography, morality, violence, censorship and media effects.

Clearly, then, it would be a nonsense to claim that representations of violence in the media have no impact on us. Equally, it is clear that we cannot generalise either about the nature of media violence itself, which, as we have seen, includes such a wide variety of representations under its umbrella that the term is almost meaningless, or about the nature of its influence on viewers. The evaluation of the evidence in this chapter points to the way in which the media shapes and circulates **discourses** of violence and is instrumental in gendering that violence. Interrogating and challenging the nature of these representations is therefore one way in which critics can question – and ultimately change – the meanings and rewards attached to violence in our society.

So, what is to be done?

When I tell people that I am working on media/violence, the two questions I am most often asked are whether or not I think violence in the media causes real-world violence and what I think should be done about it. In these first two chapters, I have, hopefully, answered the first question, but I am still not entirely resolved as to the best way to answer the second, though the two questions are obviously related.

Regulating viewers

In what ways is your own viewing of film and television regulated? Why is it so regulated? Who does the regulating and what are their qualifications for doing so? Are there any conditions in which you think your own (and others') viewing should be regulated?

On the one hand, as this chapter has demonstrated, there is no legislating for what people do with what they see on screen and neither could nor should there be. To take the attitude that viewing violence is necessarily 'bad' or 'immoral' is both profoundly patronising to viewers and distorts the experience of viewing violent acts in a narrative and social context. As we have also seen, in practice, it is certain kinds of viewers (young, male) and their viewing of certain types of representations (pornography, horror) that are most often of concern and these concerns cannot be divorced from broader questions about masculinity, youth, taste and class.

On the other hand, to argue that the relationship between media and real-world violence – in all their various forms – should not be an issue for concern is absurd in light of the evidence presented in this chapter. Some of the research presented here very clearly demonstrates the ways in which screen representations are implicated in real-life abuse and, relatedly, in the perpetuation of gender inequality. This is where the question 'What is to be done?' takes on a particular urgency.

It is safe to say, however, that censorship pure and simple is not a credible option. To cover all the angles in the censorship debate is beyond the scope of this chapter,[12] but, there are a few points worth emphasising. First, censorship only really makes sense if we ask what texts do to viewers, not (as I have done in this chapter) what viewers do with texts. In other words, censorship is a solution only if direct effects are the problem and, even then, as we saw in Chapter 1, isolating individually dangerous texts is a virtually impossible task.

Second, experience has shown that censorship tends to hit feminist and alternative representations hardest – it is a blunt instrument, often wielded by those who have no understanding of the texts that they are asked to censor (Ross, 1997; Petley, 2003).

Further, decisions about censorship – at least in the context of current legislation and guidelines in the UK – are based on extremely subjective and poorly defined criteria. In deciding what we do and do not get to see in cinemas and in our homes, for example, the British Board of Film Classification (BBFC) is bound by the Obscene Publications Act of 1959. This Act defines as **'obscene'** material likely to 'deprave and corrupt persons who are likely, in all circumstances, to read, see or hear the matter contained or embodied in it'. However, we might well ask which persons are of concern here and, further, exactly what constitutes depravity and corruption?

Also governing the BBFC's decision making is the Video Recordings Act (1984) and the Amendment to the Act passed in the wake of the killing of James Bulger (see Chapter 1), which requires that harm to potential viewers, including underage viewers, watching in the home is considered. Problems with this legislation have been fully explored elsewhere (Petley, 2003), but even at a glance there are obvious issues of concern. There is no requirement to prove the existence of harm, simply the potential of harm, 'harm' itself is undefined (are nightmares evidence of harm?) and adults' viewing is circumscribed by the behaviour of potential and underage viewers. However, in the context of the current chapter, what is perhaps most damaging about focusing on censorship is that this approach provides no remedy for those abused in the production of entertainment genres. So, what are the other options?

Since the 1980s, anti-pornography feminists in the US have been arguing for a civil rights approach to legislating against pornography-related harm, using a definition of 'pornography' that is sufficiently broad to include a range of mainstream representations of sexist violence (Dworkin and MacKinnon, 1988; MacKinnon and Dworkin, 1997). They define pornography as 'the graphic sexually explicit subordination of women through pictures and/or words', which also includes one or more of the following: dehumanisation, pleasure in pain, humiliation or rape, physical injury, sexual submission, bestiality, penetration by objects, the sexualisation of degradation, **fetishism** of women's bodies and the representation of women as 'whores by nature' (Dworkin and MacKinnon, 1988).

The civil rights approach to legislation is not simply a call for increased censorship (although it is commonly misrepresented as such), but an attempt to conceive of pornography as a practice of sex discrimination and so give the survivors legal redress in the civil (not criminal) courts. The civil rights approach would allow for the following five circumstances in which women, children and men could take action:

1 having pornography forced on you in any place of employment, education, home or public place
2 coercion into the making of pornography
3 defamation as a result of the unauthorised use in pornography of your image, name or likeness
4 being assaulted because of specific pornography
5 trafficking in pornography: production, distribution or sale of material that meets the definition of pornography in the legislation.

Adapted from Dworkin and MacKinnon, 1988

In the first circumstance, the action would be against the individual/ institution forcing pornography on others. All of the remaining causes for action would allow those harmed to sue the makers and distributors of the pornographic media in question.

This approach has yet to be endorsed by any legislature. Most famously, attempts to introduce this legislation in Minneapolis and Indianapolis were thwarted when it was ruled unconstitutional on First Amendment grounds – that is, freedom of expression. However, it has generated much debate within feminist circles. Supporters have argued that such an approach shifts the emphasis away from censorship and regulation and allows those harmed by pornography – in the five ways outlined above – to hold the pornography industry publicly accountable. It is, they suggest, an approach that dares to put women's rights centre-stage, as the right to freedom from abuse is given higher status than the pornographer's right to freedom of expression. Although it is an approach very much rooted in American political culture, feminists working in other countries have attempted to adapt the Dworkin and MacKinnon approach to their own context (Itzin, 1992b; Busby, 1994), although, again, this has been largely unsuccessful.

Critics, however, have argued that the civil rights approach divorces pornographic images/texts from their broad social and cultural context and that, in practice, it would restrict all forms of sexual expression. Questions have been asked about the power these provisions would hand to State institutions, institutions that, in other contexts, have hardly been sympathetic to feminist politics. In light of this, the support for the anti-pornography approach from right-wing moralists has attracted both concern and derision from anti-censorship feminists and other critics. More importantly, perhaps, anti-censorship feminists have questioned whether or not the civil rights approach would provide a real remedy for abused women compared, for example, to refuge provision, anti-violence initiatives or empowering women by improved job prospects, housing and welfare facilities.[13]

Elsewhere, I have argued that there is also a danger that debates around the Dworkin and MacKinnon proposals – particularly the assault and trafficking provisions, which privilege the effects model critiqued in Chapter 1 – obscure the kind of non-causal abuses discussed in this chapter (Boyle, 2000). Moreover, by extending the claims about pornography's harm to all women, there is a danger that we lose sight of the abuse of specific women by specific men, abnegate these men's responsibility for their actions and simultaneously deny other women's agency, however contingent that agency may be.

The civil rights approach, then, is clearly not without its problems and has yet to be successfully adopted in practice. More generally, discussions of legislative change seem to endlessly return to those 'other' audiences I talked about in Chapter 1 and their viewing practices. Where does this leave our own viewing practices?

At the end of Chapter 1, I quoted Robert Jensen's (1998a: 101) argument that we don't need 'science' to tell us 'The Truth' about pornography, but listening to true stories (note the plural) should enable us to begin to make 'trustworthy moral and political decisions'. Although morality is a much-maligned term within media studies, Jensen is getting at an important point here: as informed viewers (whether of pornographic or mainstream representations), we have choices. With choices come responsibility, responsibility for our own viewing practices and behaviour in place of the relentless concern with 'others' that characterises effects research.

So, where might these choices lead us? First, we might call for localised censorship when our 'right' to view cannot be squared with the rights of others. For example, is our 'right' to watch *Deep Throat* really more important than Linda Boreman's right not to have her rape sold as entertainment? As students and researchers of the media, we are also in a good position to examine, challenge and continue to change the meaning of violence in popular discourse, whether by telling, or promoting, alternative stories or questioning existing stories (including those we enjoy) and the means of their telling. This isn't always easy because, as we will see, it often means unthinking what we have come to accept as obvious or natural and it can raise difficult and uncomfortable questions about our own (conscious and unconscious) investments in violence and power. However, throughout this book, you will find evidence of media critics, cultural producers, activists and academics challenging dominant representations of violence in the press, film and television and offering different and critical ways of thinking about violence, gender and ourselves. In this respect, even textual analysis has a role to play, but so, too, in specific contexts, do boycotts, protests and direct action (see, for example, Asselle and Gandhy, 1982; Craft 1992; Baxter and Craft, 1993). While, for instance, the protests by queer organisations against *Basic Instinct* (Verhoeven, 1992) may have done little to damage the film's box office takings, they gave these marginalised organisations a very public forum for voicing their complaints and concerns about the stigmatising and stereotyping of lesbian and bisexual women. Cultural criticism, in all of these guises, can be a form of political action.

Running through Chapters 1 and 2 has been a concern with the various and complex relationships between representation and action. The conclusion these initial explorations lead to is that, while representations of violence (in all their various forms) cannot be divorced from violence in the real world (in all its various forms), neither should the two be conflated. Having considered the various audiences for violence, in the remainder of this book I will explore the nature of the representations themselves, turning my attention, in the next chapter, to fact-based representations of violence.

Summary

- Anti-pornography feminists have amassed considerable evidence of the ways in which women (and children) are abused in the making of (some) pornography. If we focus only on whether or not pornographic representations cause violence, we risk obscuring these realities.
- Behind-the-scenes accounts of the mainstream entertainment industry suggest that sexual harassment and other forms of gendered violence are rife. This raises troubling questions about the complicity of the spectator and is an area requiring further research.
- Audience studies demonstrate that viewers are far more actively engaged in the viewing process than effects research has allowed. This means that those who use pornographic or other media as part of their justification for abusing others can and should be held responsible for their actions at the same time as we critically investigate and challenge how these texts shape and reflect our understandings of gender, sexuality and violence.
- Media consumption is one way in which gender relations are acted out, but can also provide opportunities for negotiation and opposition.

- We all have moral and political decisions to make about our own consumption of media violence and pornography.

Notes

1 Nadine Strossen (1995), Wendy McElroy (n.d.) and Tuppy Owens (1993) are among the few commentators identifying as both feminist and pro-pornography.

2 For alternative accounts of women's involvement in the industry see essays collected in Segal and McIntosh (1992), Assiter and Carol (1993) and Gibson and Gibson (1993). Annie Sprinkle's one woman show *The Herstory of Porn: Real to Reel* (see www.anniepsrinkle.org for more information) also gives an account of pornography production that emphasises women's agency. It is notable that, despite her generally pro-pornography stance, Sprinkle does acknowledge the abuse and unsafe sexual practices that remain a feature of much pornography production.

3 Born Linda Boreman, the 'star' of *Deep Throat* is most commonly known by the name given to her by her abusive pimp/husband, Chuck Traynor: Linda 'Lovelace'. Linda later remarried and conducted much of her anti-pornography campaigning under her married name, Linda Marchiano. Following her divorce, Linda reverted to her birth name. To avoid confusion, I refer to her in the text as Linda.

4 She *had* tried to escape on a number of occasions but, like many women trying to escape abusive husbands, she was caught and brutally punished by Traynor. On another occasion, Traynor threatened the lives of her family (Lovelace, with McGrady, 1981).

5 Sources: Silbert and Pines (1984); Giobbe (1985); *Everywoman* (1988); MacKinnon (1993); Stoltenberg (1994); MacKinnon and Dworkin (1997); Hughes and Roche (1999).

6 While commercial snuff has not been found (Johnson and Schaefer, 1993), the existence of non-commercial snuff – audio- and videotapes, photographs – made by sexual murderers for their own pleasure is well documented and will be discussed in more detail in Chapter 3.

7 Notably, the allegations did not prevent Schwarzenegger from being elected and, indeed, in an interesting article in *The Guardian* (9 October, 2003), Susan Faludi suggests that the allegations actually reinforced Schwarzenegger's status for male voters.

8 The existence of this audience does not, in itself, challenge the assumption that these movies address or privilege a male viewer, as we will see in Chapter 5.

9 This and other student quotations in this chapter come from responses to the viewing experiences questionnaire partially replicated in the Introduction. These responses are from students in Film Studies/Women's Studies at the Universities of Wolverhampton (October 2001) and Glasgow (January 2002). My thanks to all the students who engaged in this exercise.

10 The article can be found at www.theonion.com/onion3734/american_life_turns_into.html (accessed April, 2004).

11 The representations of the atrocities and the militaristic response to them also merit discussion, although this is beyond the scope of this chapter. For a more detailed analysis of the crisis from the perspective of feminist media scholars, see *Feminist Media Studies*, 2 (1).

12 For a consideration of censorship issues in a British context see Chester and Dickey (1988), Mathews (1994) and Petley (2003).

13 See Dworkin and MacKinnon (1988) for the theory behind the civil rights approach, MacKinnon (1995) and Jensen (1998b) for a critique of the 'freedom of speech' defence, Itzin (1992b) for a discussion of legislative approaches in the UK and Segal (1993) and Strossen (1995) for critiques of the anti-pornography position.

Further reading

Buckingham, D. (1996) *Moving Images: Understanding Children's Emotional Responses to Television*. Manchester: Manchester University Press.

Dines, G., Jensen, R. and Russo, A. (1998) *Pornography: The Production and Consumption of Inequality*. London: Routledge.

Hill, A. (1997) *Shocking Entertainment: Viewer Responses to Violent Movies*. Luton: University of Luton Press.

MacKinnon, C. and Dworkin, A. (eds) (1997) *In Harm's Way: The Pornography Civil Rights Hearings*. Cambridge, MA: Harvard University Press.

Schlesinger, P., Dobash, R., Dobash, R. and Weaver, K. (1992) *Women Viewing Violence*. London: BFI.

PART TWO
Reporting violence

From Jack to O.J. – true crimes of male violence

Chapter outline

This chapter examines the production of male violence against women as news, focusing, as the majority of work in this field has done, on print media. The chapter begins by considering which stories of violence are newsworthy and goes on to explore the construction of three major (if overlapping) stories of men's violence against women: **sexual murder**, non-fatal **sexual abuse** and **domestic violence**:

- Crime and violence
- 'Rippers', their apologists and mythologists
- Reporting sexual abuse
- Virgins and vamps
- Domestic violence and murder

newsworthiness;
the 'law of opposites'
the **discourse** of sexual murder; serial sex killers; seriality and the mass media
sex beasts and paedophiles; racialising the rapist; 'false' accusations
victim culpability; sexual double standards
murder/suicide;
mainstreaming feminism.

Crime and violence

The very different cases of Jack the Ripper and O.J. Simpson, referred to in the title of this chapter, highlight some of the key issues to be addressed here. In 1888, the murders of at least five women were attributed to a never conclusively identified killer who became known in the press at the time as 'Jack the Ripper'. 'Jack' was and is identified both as an everyman (he could be anyone, the threat to women was pervasive) and an invisible man (his identity is unknown, the gendered reality of his crimes downplayed). He also become something of a folk hero, a bogeyman, the subject of countless entertainments – films, television programmes, books, tourist trails.[1]

O.J. Simpson, in contrast, was known as an entertainer but became visible as a perpetrator of domestic violence only when he became a murder suspect. Prior to this, his (alleged) history of domestic violence did nothing to tarnish his celebrity and, indeed, was virtually invisible. After his arrest, competing accounts of the charges against him (of which he was acquitted), sought to frame his story as one of sexism (he was a man who abused his wife) and racism (he was a black man falsely accused of the murder of a white woman and man).[2]

Of course, it is no accident that both these stories also featured female victims. The women in these cases, and the circumstances in which they lived and died, were in many ways very different, yet all had been subject to routinised violence prior to their murder, but only became of interest to the press and the authorities when they were dead. In contrast, even dead, Ronald Goldman – the man murdered alongside Nicole Brown Simpson – generated little coverage: he was simply not a newsworthy victim.

While I am oversimplifying both cases here, they raise important questions about when and how we see violence, gender, race and crime, about the circumstances in which violence becomes newsworthy and about the (un)pleasures to be had from these stories – questions with which this chapter is centrally concerned.

In his by now classic investigation of crime journalism in Britain, Chibnall (1977) identifies eight characteristics of newsworthiness (adapted from Greer, 2003b: 46):

- immediacy (speed, currency)
- dramatisation (drama, action)
- structured access (experts, authority)
- novelty (angle, speculation, twist)
- titillation (revealing the forbidden, **voyeurism**)
- conventionalism (dominant ideology)

- personalisation (culture of personality, celebrity)
- simplification (elimination of shades of grey)

As we will see later in this chapter, many of these factors are key to the fascination with these two stories in their very different contexts. More generally, crime – and crimes of violence in particular – fulfils many of Chibnall's criteria of newsworthiness. Indeed, crime stories make up a substantial proportion of our daily news and the overall percentage of crime stories in the press has increased considerably since the 1960s (Reiner et al., 2003: 17).

Studies of crime reporting in the press, typically, if unsurprisingly, conclude that the crime we read about is, in general, the crime we are least likely to experience. This finding is usefully and succinctly characterised as 'the law of opposites' (Surette, 1998: 47) – in other words, the characteristics of crime, criminals and victims represented in the media are, in most respects, precisely the opposite of those recorded in official crime statistics or in crime and victim surveys, so property crime is generally considered un-newsworthy, while violent crime and sexual offences are disproportionately newsworthy. For example, in a study of crime news in the British press since the Second World War, Robert Reiner et al. (2003: 18–9) found that around two-thirds of crime news stories primarily focused on violent or sexual offences – offences that account for less than 10% of crimes recorded by the police.

In the context of this chapter, two further qualifications are needed. Police reports are themselves produced in specific socio-cultural contexts and cannot be taken to be an unproblematic reflection of actual incidence of crime. Numerous feminist studies have, for example, demonstrated that men's violence against known women is both under-reported and inadequately and inaccurately recorded when it is reported. Second, though not unrelatedly, not all violence is 'crimed', either in practice or in theory. That is, particular types of violence are not seen as illegitimate or criminal.

An area in which 'the law of opposites' does not seem to apply is in relation to gendered patterns of offending and victimisation. Reiner et al. (2003: 19–20) found that, in both official statistics and news stories, the vast majority of offenders are male, although Bronwyn Naylor (2001a: 181–2) suggests that the proportion of stories about violent women is still higher than their appearance in criminal statistics. Reiner et al. (2003: 21–2) also found that men are more likely to be the victims of violent crime in criminal statistics and in newspaper crime stories, though, again, Naylor (2001a: 182) suggests that female victims are more visible in the press than in criminal statistics. However, it is important to emphasise that, whether offender or victim, men are rarely visible as men. For example, Maggie Wykes (2001: 157), found that gendered labelling of perpetrators and victims was and is less available for men than for women in the British press.

The current chapter explores what is at stake in portraying male perpetrators of violence as genderless, in the context of crimes – such as sexual murder, **rape** and domestic violence – which are obviously both 'gendered' (committed by men in the vast majority of cases) and 'sexed' (understood by perpetrators, victims or others as involving a sexual component) (Howe, 1998). For more than 30 years, feminist work on the realities and representations of male violence against women has focused largely (though not exclusively) on interpersonal violence and provided an alternative framework for making sense of and working to end that violence. One of the central concerns of this chapter is, therefore, the ways in which feminist discourse has (or has not) been incorporated, mainstreamed, marginalised. However, as in the Simpson case, the male victims of male violence are largely invisible here. This invisibility – mirrored in the majority of critical studies on fact-based accounts of violence – is, in itself, arguably related to the construction of masculinity as powerful and dominant, with which I am concerned in this chapter (to be a victim is to be powerless, feminine). Nevertheless, more work on the treatment of male-on-male violence in the news media is certainly needed.

'Rippers', their apologists and mythologists

Relative to its presence in official crime statistics, sexual murder attracts a disproportionate amount of attention in national news, true crime writing, reality television and, of course, crime fictions (Chapter 5). This section begins to unpick this fascination by examining sexual murder as a discourse – a group of statements that, together, produce particular types of knowledge within the context of a Western patriarchal society. This is not to deny that sexual murder is also an act – a man's (and it is virtually always a man's) annihilation of another human being for sexual pleasure. However, I want to explore how that act is given meaning, not only by the killer himself but also within society more generally. Deborah Cameron and Elizabeth Frazer, whose excellent book *The Lust to Kill* (1987) provides the framework for this discussion, argue that sexual murder as a distinctive category emerged in the West in the late nineteenth century. This is not to suggest that killing for sexual pleasure did not exist before Jack the Ripper, but that the meaning of such crimes (for experts, lay people, killers) was different. Earlier killers were, for example, allied to the supernatural and occult, represented as witches, Satan worshippers, vampires, rather than as sexual murderers. Cameron and Frazer (1987: 22) argue:

> As well as allowing the production of a history, the emergence of a recognized category of sex-killing provided a self-conscious identity or role for individuals to take up and define their acts by. By the turn of the century a man could set out to be, or be seen as, a 'sex maniac' in a way that would have been impossible fifty years earlier. The coming of a category thus brought with it the possibility of creating a tradition, which established itself in practice both by expanding to encompass the killers of the past and ... by offering a label to those of the future.

In other words, the discourse of sexual murder is productive – it forms the objects of which it speaks (Foucault, 1972: 49). The media and, in particular, the news media, with its status as a purveyor of 'truth', is vitally important in popularising these ideas. It is no accident, then, that the construction of the sexual murderer (in the figure of Jack the Ripper) coincided with the rise of a popular, mass press. While this points to an inextricable relationship between representation and murder, it is not a linear, causal relationship (as we saw in Chapter 1, such a relationship is impossible to prove).

The media plays an important role in circulating and shaping the discourse of sexual murder, but that discourse neither originates in nor exists solely through the media. No one media representation causes the violence, but, rather as Cameron and Frazer, (1987: 142–3) argue:

> Representations help construct and shape people's desires by offering them certain objects, certain channels, certain meanings. What aspirations and pleasures are available, what practices, identities and dreams are even thinkable is determined to a very large extent by the culture. Our culture has violent, pornographic dreams; it has aspirations to (male) freedom and transcendence. Not coincidentally, it has sadistic **serial murder**.

Also, not coincidentally, it is men who have taken on the identity of the sexual murderer, and a specific group of men at that.

The standard profile of the serial sexual killer (based, in part, on the FBI's work with incarcerated men) is of a white male, aged 25–45 – a profile that appears with predictable regularity in true crime writing and crime fictions alike. The position of black men and all women within the history of serial sex crime remains a point of some dispute. It has, for example, been argued that the relative invisibility of black, male serial sexual killers is a reflection not of their rarity in fact but of the racist assumptions underpinning the discourse of sexual and serial murder (Jenkins, 1994). When true crime accounts of murder (of all kinds) are compared with FBI statistics, it becomes clear that black and minority ethnic perpetrators and victims are considerably under-represented in these popular accounts (Durham et al., 1995). There is, however, no such reluctance to represent black or minority ethnic men as the perpetrators of other kinds of violent and sexually violent crimes (Benedict, 1992; Grover and Soothill, 1996b; Oliver and Armstrong, 1998). How can we understand these discrepancies? As we will see, murderers – and serial, sexual murderers in particular – are frequently represented as being 'beyond' simple criminality, elevated to a kind of folk hero status. The heroes of popular representations are rarely black. Further, as the vast majority of serial and sexual murder is intraracial, the exclusion of black men as perpetrators reflects a lack of concern with black women (and men) as victims.

Whether women murderers can be understood as sexual or even serial killers – given the connotations of **sadism** attached to these terms – is even more contentious. Cameron and Frazer argue that 'fairly ordinary' female killers have been labelled sadists simply because they were women who, in the act of killing, transgressed the boundaries of femininity as well as the law of the land. They continue, 'a woman who kills, be her methods ever so mild by male standards of brutality, is sadistic by definition in the eyes of many writers' (Cameron and Frazer, 1987: 23). As we will see in Chapter 4, this double standard is alive and well in representations of violent women, while, as this chapter demonstrates, the simple fact that the vast majority of sexual (and serial) murderers are men is too often overlooked in popular explanations.

In their discussion of male sexual murderers, Cameron and Frazer identify two key themes in mainstream accounts: the representation of the murderer as 'deviant' or 'hero'. The figure of the 'deviant' sexual murderer – sick, deficient, inadequate, traumatised, subcultural – is the most straightforward, emerging in scientific discourses such as criminology, psychiatry, **psychoanalysis**, social theory and anthropology, and permeating popular accounts of sexual murder. Such representations position the killer as deviant from (and not a product of) societal norms and offer no explanation for the fact that sexual murder is an overwhelmingly male preserve. If we ask – as Cameron and Frazer do – why women with similar illnesses, deficiencies, experiences or subcultural affiliations do not also become sexual murderers the inadequacies of the deviance theory become immediately clear.

The 'hero' theme is rather more complex. The sex killer is a 'hero' first and foremost in his positioning at the centre of the sex murder narrative – he is the protagonist, he commits the crimes that drive the story forward and expresses, through murder, his total power and control over another human being. This act of annihilation affirms his own identity – he is subject, his victim is object. In this respect, it is significant that so many sexual murderers make their own representations of their crimes. The personal **snuff** collections enable the sexual murderer to extend his control over the object of his desire even beyond death.

Cameron and Frazer (1987: 66) go on to identify two types of 'heroes' – the sex beast, 'whose terrible desires put him outside the pale of society' and the libertine or rebel, 'whose desires are also outside social norms, but only because society is so repressive and constricting'. Using the term 'hero' in this first sense is to strip it of any positive associations. The sex beast is subhuman, driven by animal urges rather than acting on conscious desires.

While the sex beast is arguably the dominant image of the sexual murderer, at least in the British press, accounts of serial sexual murder tend to present the murderer as a highly intelligent, organised and conscious actor, rebelling against society. Not surprisingly, this is how many serial sexual murderers present themselves. Moors Murderer Ian Brady (2001: 87), for example, suggests that, as a result of his actions, the murderer decisively cuts 'the umbilical connection between himself and *ordinary* mankind' (emphasis added). Such accounts suggest that the meaning of killing for the serial sexual killer lies in the achievement of a kind of transcendence.

Fact and fiction

Is Cameron and Frazer's categorisation of the sexual murderer as 'deviant' or 'hero' useful for analysing representations of sexual murderers in fictional forms?

Whether sex beast or transcendental rebel, the 'heroes' of these narratives are individuals – and apparently genderless individuals – outside of society. In contrast, feminists point to the continuities between the sexual murderer and 'normal' men, between the sexual murderer's pleasure in power and the eroticisation of power and control endemic in patriarchal culture. For feminist critics, the sexual murderer is a product of his society and culture, not its antithesis.

This suggests that **misogyny** is central to any understanding of sexual murder, its representations and its social impact. For example, at the time of the sexual murders attributed to 'Jack the Ripper', Florence Fenwick Miller argued that the murders were not homicides but 'womankilling', part of a 'constant but ever increasing series of cruelties' perpetrated against women (quoted in Walkowitz, 1982: 567).[3] Even a cursory glance through the popular press of 1888 provides ample evidence of Miller's claim, with murders of women by men – and, specifically, by known men – appearing on an almost daily basis. Indeed, the fact that this violence was both pervasive and widely accepted had concrete repercussions for the Ripper investigation as is apparent in the following extract from the *Star*, (1 October, 1888):

> The police have been told that a man, aged between 35 and 40 years of age, and of fair complexion, was seen to throw the murdered in Berner Street to the ground. Those who saw it thought it was a man and his wife and no notice was taken of it.

Nearly 100 years later, the misogynist speech and actions of Peter Sutcliffe – the so-called 'Yorkshire Ripper' – were to be equally unremarkable among his peers. Discussing Sutcliffe's treatment of prostitute women, one of his friends (quoted in Bland, 1992: 251) commented:

> He had a sock and I think there was a small brick or stone in it ... I think [he said] he hit her on the head ... But Peter never showed any hostility towards prostitutes and there was nothing unusual in his attitude towards them.

Men's violence against prostitute women is so pervasive, so normalised, that even this obviously aggressive act – hitting a woman on the head with a small brick – is not recognised as hostile, unusual or illegitimate. A feminist understanding of the crimes of Jack the Ripper and his successors therefore demands that we see the murders not as individual aberrations, but as the extreme end of a continuum of male violence.

While there are countless examples of sexual killing and its representation as expressions of overt misogyny, Cameron and Frazer (1987: 166–7) nevertheless argue that it is a mistake to see sexual murder as necessarily misogynist, due to the simple fact that not all victims are female. What the victims do have in common is their desirability for their killer – he kills what he desires, hence 'the lust to kill'. More importantly, as Cameron and Frazer (1987: 167) point out, the killers themselves are virtually always male:

The common denominator is not misogyny, it is a shared construction of masculine sexuality, or even more broadly, masculinity in general. It is under the banner of masculinity that all the main themes of sexual killing come together: misogyny, transcendence, sadistic sexuality, the basic ingredients of the lust to kill.

The extent to which the sexual murderer's construction of masculine sexuality is shared in the culture at large is immediately apparent when we look at the ways in which the discourse of sexual murder was and is shaped and circulated.

As the original Ripper story became public property – in press reports, true crime broadsides, rhymes and songs – it was no longer a story with one male author and many men actively participated, in more or less explicitly abusive ways, in its construction. For example, the name 'Jack the Ripper' is widely thought to have originated in letters sent to the Central News Agency, letters whose authenticity was disputed by police authorities who suggested that they were the 'creation of an enterprising journalist' (Walkowitz, 1982: 551). However, the 'enterprising journalist' was not the only one to lay claim to the crimes and so shape their telling. Around 230 similar letters were received by news agencies, the police and individual women, while other men carried out their Ripper impersonations on the streets or in pubs. In the words of one contemporaneous news report, 'Every drunken man was more or less liable to seek a temporary notoriety by proclaiming himself the Whitechapel murderer' (*Star,* 2 October, 1888). As Walkowitz (1982: 561) argues:

> the Ripper episode ... covertly sanctioned male antagonism toward women and buttressed male authority over them. It established a common vocabulary and iconography of male violence that permeated the whole society, papering over class differences and obscuring the different material conditions that provoked sexual antagonism in different classes. The Ripper drama invested male domination with a powerful mystique ... enforcing the segregation of social space: women were relegated to the interior of a prayer meeting or their homes, behind locked doors; men were left to patrol the public spaces and the street.

For the men who wrote letters, claimed the crimes as their own or demanded new forms of social control, the Ripper was a mask for various forms of male domination. However, it is important to understand that these men's (inter-)actions in turn contributed to the shaping of the Ripper persona and the emerging discourse of sexual murder. As Jane Caputi (1988: 22) notes, 'the myth of the Ripper – from its very beginnings – was a collective male invention, a product of criminal, press, and public'.

The Yorkshire Ripper case would follow a similar pattern. Men on the terraces at Leeds United football club infamously chanted their approval of the killer's ability to evade the police, while the police received hundreds of 'hoaxes' laying claim to the crimes. Most damaging of these was a tape from a man calling himself 'Jack'. When 'Jack's' handwriting and the recording of his voice were made public, the police received 878,796 calls 'all of them misleading, many of them "larks"' (Ward Jouve, 1986: 201).[4] Without seeking to detract from the reality of Sutcliffe's crimes, we might nevertheless question whether, to paraphrase the football terraces, there was indeed 'one' Yorkshire Ripper, as others' active participation in his story undoubtedly prolonged his killing career. Depressingly, this phenomenon has become part and parcel of the serial sexual murder narrative: serial sexual murder is repeatedly represented as a game of evasion, detection and cunning, effacing the reality of what the killer does.

There remains, in the cases of both Jack the Ripper and the Yorkshire Ripper, dispute over the number of victims claimed by one man and a question over whether other killers have 'got away' with crimes pinned on the Rippers. This question haunts fact-based accounts of many other serial killers' careers. For example, between 28 and 110 **femicides** have been pinned on Ted Bundy, and the number of murders attributed to Henry Lee Lucas varies from 2 to 300-plus (Caputi, 1988: 38). The relentless focus on the sexual murderer as a unique individual thus obscures the continuum of male violence on which his crimes are located and consumed and allows other abuses – and abusers – to hide in his shadows. Sadly, there is rarely (if ever) only one.

I have already discussed some of the ways in which the discourse of sexual murder (and serial sexual murder in particular) blurs fiction and reality, but, of course, it is not only in representations of the sexual murderer himself that such slippage occurs. While Jack the Ripper is a fictional construct, the crimes attributed to him – the murders of at least five women – are not. Establishing the links between these murders at an early stage in the story served a clear commercial purpose for the emergent mass media, promising future attractions for readers, as in the following advertisement from the *Illustrated Police News* (15 September, 1888):

IMPORTANT NOTICE TO NEWSAGENTS. WILL BE PUBLISHED ON MONDAY NEXT, SEPTEMBER 17TH, A new and thrilling Romance entitled: THE WHITECHAPEL MURDERS, OR, The Mysteries of the East End. This Sensational Story fully describes the details connected to these Diabolical Crimes and faithfully pictures the Night Horrors of this portion of the Great City. No. 2 will be Given Away with No. 1 in a Handsome Illuminated Wrapper.

The blurring of news and entertainment is particularly clear here, with the promise of facts (details, crimes, locations), sensations akin to those offered by gothic fiction (thrills, romance, fear) and consumer pleasures (in seeing, feeling, owning). As Walkowitz (1982: 550) notes, in the absence of well-known historical precedents of serial sexual murder, commentators frequently resorted to 'horrifying fictional analogues' in attempts to make sense of the Whitechapel killings and construct an identity for the unknown killer. Of course, the relationship between fiction and reality is not one-way. In the years since the fictional analogues helped to make sense of his crimes, Jack the Ripper has himself become 'a popular folk devil, rather like Dracula or Frankenstein's monster' whose crimes provide a reference point for contemporary atrocities (Cameron and Frazer, 1987: 123).

If, in 1888, the 'horrifying fictional analogue' was the only reference point for the Whitechapel murders, more than 100 years later there are all too many historical precedents. Yet, the 'horrifying fictional analogue' remains central to the sex killer news story. For example, the contemporaneous release of the film *The Silence of the Lambs* (Demme, 1991) with the arrest of cannibalistic serial sexual murderer Jeffrey Dahmer was exploited to full effect in press reports (*The Daily Mirror*, 25 July, 1991):

> For sheer breathtaking horror Anthony Hopkins' chilling portrayal of cannibal killer Hannibal Lecter couldn't be beaten ... until now. Because hard on the heels of the grisly fiction has come the dreadful reality.

To be newsworthy, Dahmer's crimes had to be *more* chilling than the fiction. In this way, fiction, reportage and true crime accounts of sexual murder arguably provide one long serial (killer) narrative in which each new instalment must offer something distinctive, whether it be more or different victims, a new mode of killing or disposing of the bodies, a unique signature. However, the fictional analogue also distorts crucial aspects of the story, such as, in this case, Dahmer's selection of primarily non-white, gay men as his victims. In this respect, the news story mirrors the sexual murderers' perception of his victims, that they are interchangeable objects rather than unique individuals.

As we will see later in this chapter, the female victims of sexual murder and non-fatal sexual abuse are the focus of particularly intense and sexualised scrutiny.

Reporting sexual abuse

There has been a massive increase in the number of rapes and indecent assaults reported to the police in the past 30 years. However, the vast majority of sexual assaults still go unreported. In 1998, only 12% of the 50,000 women contacting the Rape Crisis Federation in England and Wales had reported the crime to the police. This is hardly surprising when only one in five reported rapes ever reaches trial, and the rate of conviction after trial has fallen from one in three (33%) in 1977 to one in 13 (7.5%) in 1999.[5]

Investigations of how these trends have been reflected in and discursively shaped by the news media have taken the form both of quantitative surveys and detailed analyses of the coverage of individual sex crimes.[6] Mirroring the increase in the number of sex crimes reported to the police, studies in both the UK (Soothill and Walby, 1991) and US (Benedict, 1992) have found that the number of published stories about sexual abuse significantly increased in the 1970s and continued to increase throughout the 1980s. Studying the Northern Irish press between 1985 and 1997, Chris Greer (2003a: 97) found that recorded incidents of sexual offences quadrupled in this period, while the number reported in the press trebled. By the 1990s, Cynthia Carter (1998: 220) found that every British tabloid reported at least one sexual abuse case per week and my own study of the *Daily Mail*'s treatment of sexual abuse stories in 2000 identified an average of five stories per week.[7]

However, not all sexual assault stories are equally newsworthy. Quantitative studies have consistently demonstrated that sexual assault stories are case-based (rather than more general stories about trends, legislation, policing and so on) and that – at both the local (Meyers, 1997; Greer, 2003b) and national (Soothill and Walby, 1991) levels – certain kinds of assault, perpetrators and victims appear with exaggerated frequency. These include:

- stranger assaults
- inter-racial assaults
- sexual murder
- serial rape
- assaults on children
- assaults on the elderly

- institutional abuse (e.g. within care homes)
- assaults resulting in criminal proceedings
- assaults resulting in serious physical injury
- cases in which consent is contested
- cases featuring celebrities or persons of high status.[8]

Despite the undue prominence afforded celebrity rape narratives in this list, there is no tradition of representing the 'everyday' sexual abuser as a libertine or rebel, transcending societal constraints in a heroic pursuit of self-actualisation and pleasure like his murdering counterpart. However, the sex beast is a stock figure in news reports of non-fatal sexual abuse, as Soothill and Walby (1991: 36) note:

> in the best of all possible media worlds, all rapes and sexual
> assaults would be committed by just a few sexual maniacs
> and the press could then help to orchestrate the national
> search against these declared aliens in our midst. The focus
> of media coverage in the popular press is implicitly working
> towards this chimera.

The 'aliens in our midst' are, unsurprisingly, rarely known to their victims either and it is striking that this holds across a range of media forms and contexts. For example, in an analysis of the reality crime show *America's Most Wanted*, Cavender et al. (1999) found that 75% of the adult rape victims featured were the victims of stranger rape. In my own study of the *Daily Mail*, nearly 60% of all sexual abuse stories reported involved stranger assault, and Greer's (2003a, 2003b) study of the Northern Irish press between 1985 and 1997 arrived at similar findings. Compare this with the British Crime Survey, which found only 23% of sexual assaults on women were by unknown men (Myhill and Allen, 2002).

As the 'sex beast' is irrevocably 'other' (someone not like 'us', against whose difference we can define ourselves), the casting of black and minority ethnic men in this role should not be surprising, despite their relative invisibility in accounts of sexual murder. In her discussion of rape reporting in the US press, Helen Benedict (1992) discusses two highly contentious cases – the Big Dan's and Central Park Jogger rapes (see Appendix for details) – in which race, ethnicity and rape were linked in complex and sometimes contradictory ways. Both cases were thought to feature gangs of minority ethnic perpetrators and press coverage consistently allied the perpetrators with their ethnic or racial group (Portuguese rapists, black and Hispanic youths) and attempted to explain the crimes by examining the men's communities. Thus, the perpetrators were not presented as individuals – and as men – but as representatives of their racial or ethnic group.

In the Big Dan's case, the Portuguese community was repeatedly characterised as sexist and juxtaposed with the 'American' people whose belief in the victim was presented as evidence of 'progress' in the public understanding of rape. The sexism of press coverage was displaced by the insistent suggestions that it was the Portuguese community, and only the Portuguese community, that was sexist. When members of the community responded angrily, accusing the media of racism, the media response was to ignore this complaint and present the controversy in terms of feminists (and liberals) *vs* locals. The victim's Portuguese heritage was rarely mentioned and, partly as a result of this, she was denied the support of her community.[9] Against such a background, it is not surprising that, for minority ethnic women, speaking out about abuse remains a doubly daunting prospect (Razack, 1994).

The victim in the Central Park Jogger case was a white businesswoman who was repeatedly raped and brutally assaulted while out jogging in New York's Central Park. In this case, the perpetrators were (allegedly) a gang of young, black and Hispanic youths[10] and the exceptional brutality of this crime seemed to give the media licence to describe the attackers in animalistic terms, which would be deemed racist in any other context. Whether or not the attack itself was racially motivated became a contentious issue, filling many column inches as reporters tried to untangle race and (gang) rape while themselves reproducing racist stereotypes about rape and, particularly, about black men's rape of white women. In contrast, news coverage of the contemporaneous rape of a black female student by six white male students consistently sought to explain the crime in terms of male ethos while completely ignoring the possibility of racial motivation (Benedict, 1992: 220; Moorti, 2002). Few reports kept race (and racism) *and* gender (and sexism) in the frame.

The failure to consider the intersectionality of gender and race in the experience of rape is not unique to the US context, nor to the reporting of these high-profile cases. My own year-long study of sexual assault reporting in the *Daily Mail* similarly identified a disproportionate interest in inter-racial attacks by black and minority ethnic men (nearly 20% of all reported cases featured this statistically unusual scenario) and an emphasis on race and ethnicity in these reports. Moreover, the victims in these stories of inter-racial assault were, without exception, presented as innocent, even when aspects of their behaviour could have opened up a complicit victim narrative. For example, in a short report on the sentencing of Benarsko Gaisley for three counts of rape (*Daily Mail*, 8 March, 2000), the convicted rapist is immediately positioned as 'an illegal immigrant' and the report is concerned with his ability to evade detection as a rapist and as an immigrant. In contrast, his victims are first identified by occupation (student, literary agent, marketing executive), emphasising their respectability and their difference from Gaisley. The Italian nationality of one of his victims is mentioned twice, providing another point of differentiation between victim (a white European in Britain legally) and rapist (a racially 'other' illegal immigrant). Finally, while his victims went to Gaisley's flat willingly, this information is held back until late in the article and the emphasis is on the after-effects of their rape (physical and psychological injuries), rather than on their behaviour prior to the attacks. This is striking when, as we will see, women's behaviour is so frequently interrogated in press reports of sexual assault. This is not to suggest that these women were in any way complicit, but that these aspects of their behaviour are more likely to have been used against them had their attackers been of the same racial and ethnic group.

In the *Daily Mail*'s worldview, black and minority ethnic perpetrators not only consistently target white women, they are also more likely than their white counterparts to be stranger and gang rapists. This both generalises the threat of the 'other' and renders invisible black and ethnic minority women as victims (there was only one intraracial assault on a black woman reported in the *Daily Mail* during the period of my study). The focus on black and minority ethnic men as representatives of their racial or ethnic group – rather than as individuals and as men – is particularly striking in a report focusing on a series of attacks in New York's Central Park. This report (*Daily Mail*, 15 June, 2000) has obvious echoes of the Central Park Jogger case, discussed by Benedict, and is worth quoting at some length:

> Evidence suggests that the police's inaction, after the first woman came to them battered and in tears, was caused by a culture of political correctness within the NYPD. Most of the officers on duty around Central Park were white.
>
> The Puerto Rican parade is overwhelmingly Black and Hispanic. PREVIOUSLY the parade has become extremely rowdy but police have been slow to break it up for fear they will be accused of harassing a minority.
>
> The famous St Patrick's Day parade is much more heavily policed and public drunkenness is not tolerated.
>
> By contrast the Puerto Ricans march in a much more permissive atmosphere, and once the official parade is over it is common to see cars racing along Manhattan's avenues ... loaded with men who are both drunk and flaunting their aggressive machismo. ... Many of the men who join the parade are from a macho society that has little respect for women.

As in the earlier case, the ethnicity of the perpetrators is used to draw a line between the gang rapist and American values. However, the racist implications of these characterisations are disavowed with the suggestion that it is precisely the fear of accusations of racism that has led to the ineffectual policing of these groups. The language used to describe these men is strikingly similar to that identified in Benedict's study more than a decade earlier: they are a 'wolf-pack posse', 'wilding pack' or 'vicious animals' who 'pounced' on their victims' 'howling their approval' and 'swirling like sexually demented wolves'. This work by Benedict, Moorti and myself suggests a tendency within mainstream news media to position sex crime as outside of the dominant society and culture, the preserve of racial and ethnic 'others' who are out of control.

While the figure of the black rapist is politically contentious, the paedophile is the sex beast *par excellence*, a folk devil for our times. Although child abuse within the family is contested terrain (as we will see shortly), the threat posed by strangers is routinely exaggerated (Kelly, 1996a; McCollum, 1998; Kitzinger, 1999b) and, since the mid 1990s, there has been 'an explosion of interest' in paedophilia in the British press (Soothill et al., 1998). As popularly constructed, the paedophile is sexually inadequate, cannot form adult relationships or focus his sexual energies on appropriate sexual partners and, therefore, by definition, cannot be a husband, lover or father. As Liz Kelly (1996a: 45) notes:

> Immediately the word *paedophile* appears we have moved away from recognition of abusers as 'ordinary men' – fathers, brothers, uncles, colleagues – and are returned to the more comfortable view of them as 'other', a small minority who are fundamentally different from most men. The fact that they have *lives*, kinship links and jobs disappears from view in the desire to focus on their difference. Attention shifts immediately from the centrality of power and control to notions of sexual deviance, obsession and 'addiction'. Paedophilia returns us to the medical and individualised explanations which we have spent too much time and energy attempting to deconstruct and challenge. Rather than sexual abuse demanding that we look critically at the social construction of masculinity, male sexuality and the family, the safer terrain of 'abnormality' beckons.

There is an assumption, then, that these 'abnormal' individuals can be identified – or 'named and shamed' to use the language of the *News of the World*'s notorious campaign of 2000 (see Silverman and Wilson, 2002).

This process, based on the assumption 'once a paedophile, always a paedophile', dangerously ignores the paedophile's *agency* – his decision to abuse and the possibility of arriving at (or learning to arrive at) different decisions. As a number of commentators have noted, by driving paedophiles underground and away from the networks set up to monitor their behaviour, such campaigns may actually increase the risk to children.

Naming and shaming?

What do you think are the benefits and limitations of campaigns – such as that run by the *News of the World* in 2000 – to 'name and shame' paedophiles?

Recall the concerns that I expressed in the Introduction about how we tell critical stories about violence and its representation. Are we, as critics, involved in 'naming' and/or 'shaming'? Should we be?

The abduction and murder of ten-year-olds Holly Wells and Jessica Chapman – a story that dominated all sectors of the British news media throughout August 2002 and again in November–December 2003 – provides a clear example of some of the problems with the dominant construction of the paedophile. Even before there was a suspect and before the girls' bodies had been found, there was a sex beast – the paedophile who had purportedly snatched the girls. This fit an existing media template (Kitzinger, 2001), provided immediate points of reference (most notably, the abduction and murder of Sarah Payne two years previously, which gave rise to the *News of the World* campaign), and fit into pre-existing debates on policy issues (sentencing for sex offenders, public access to the Sex Offenders Register). Juxtaposed with the unknown beast were the girls and their distraught families, and, indeed, the family was repeatedly invoked throughout this initial phase.

When the chief suspects were named – Ian Huntley and Maxine Carr, a young, heterosexual couple known to the girls – they did not obviously fit the paedophile stereotype. As a friend of mine commented, 'they don't *look* like paedophiles' and we can only speculate as to how this might have impacted upon the willingness of possible witnesses to come forward with their suspicions. The picture of Huntley emerging in the press in the days after his arrest (and more strikingly after his conviction) was of a man with a history of trying to control young women – his was not a genderless crime, yet the paedophilia frame obscured this fact.

As this brief discussion of paedophilia suggests, child sexual abuse is not necessarily newsworthy in and of itself. While feminist texts and testimonies began the work of exposing the secret of the sexual abuse of girls by men known to them (see, for example, Armstrong, 1978; Nelson, 1982; Ward, 1984), broader public recognition followed the take-up of the issue by the media in the mid 1980s. However, as Jenny Kitzinger (1996, 1998) notes, 'child abuse fatigue' quickly set in and, in the search for new ways to tell this unappealing story, families – and fathers within them – were recast as the group at risk from overzealous social workers, doctors and feminists. This was, perhaps, most obvious in the coverage of the Cleveland child abuse scandal in Britain (Nava, 1988; Kitzinger, 2000), but Chris Atmore (1998) observes a broadly similar pattern of 'discovery' and 'dispute' in child sexual abuse coverage in the Australian press. In the British context, Kitzinger (1996, 1998) argues that, post-Cleveland, 'false memory syndrome' similarly focused attention away from the routine, mundane and un-newsworthy realities of child sexual abuse, to concentrate attention, first, on the possibility that men were being falsely accused and, later, on the 'science' of false memory.

The child sexual abuse scandals are not the only cases where the perpetrators of abuse appear to be those who are trying to end it. Even when feminist social workers are not represented as the active agents snatching children in dawn raids, feminism is the context within which, in numerous accounts, 'normal' men find themselves accused of **'date' rape**, **sexual harassment** and child sexual abuse. These 'normal' men are represented not as conscious violent and sexual agents, but as confused casualties of the sex war, disorientated by changing gender roles and societal expectations (Faludi, 1992; Lees, 1995; Gavey and Gow, 2001; Moorti, 2002). Thus 'date' rape, marital rape and sexual harassment are popularly explained as miscommunications between men and women who must take joint responsibility for sorting out the confusion. For example, during the 1993 British 'date' rape controversy, the press consistently minimised the violence of this kind of rape and gave a distorted picture of rape conviction rates (Lees, 1995). While such reports acknowledge that there was once a problem with rape, they suggest (often explicitly) that the pendulum has now swung too far in women's favour.

Similar arguments are put forward in Katie Roiphe's *The Morning After* (1994) and Christina Hoff Sommers' *Who Stole Feminism?* (1994), both of which generated considerable publicity and controversy in the US and UK. Positioning themselves as feminists concerned with equality, both women argue that feminism has victimised women and demonised men. Their arguments unsurprisingly generated considerable press coverage and debates about male violence were thus recast as debates between women, with victim feminists on the one side and Roiphe, Sommers et al., on the other. This is a pattern regularly repeated in tabloid treatment of apparently false accusations and 'date' rape as women are called to comment on and dispute other women's allegations of rape. It is not enough that these women support an individual man, this support is used to render the entire feminist project shameful and suspect, as the following headline from the British *Daily Mail* (8 September, 2000) makes clear:

WHY I, AS A WOMAN, FEEL SO UTTERLY ASHAMED BY THIS RAPE CASE.

A wilful distortion of the feminist slogan 'the personal is political', such reports use the experiences and desires of one woman to cast doubt on the politics of feminism, fundamentally distorting feminism in the process.

More generally, as Gavey and Gow (2001: 354) note in their discussion of false rape allegations in the New Zealand press, the language of rape victimisation is used to make sense of the psychological costs to men of false accusation. In so doing, such accounts obscure the way in which men's rape of women is embedded in patriarchal culture and perpetuate a (**post-feminist**) myth that rape claims so routinely result in conviction that men are sitting ducks for false accusations (Lees, 1995). This is underlined by the fact that so many rape narratives – whether presented as genuine or false cases – focus on the competing stories of individual men and women ('he said/she said') and fail to connect these individual stories to social inequalities and structural supports for rape (Moorti, 2002). Rape, then, emerges as a problem of (mis)communication rather than a violent crime.

To illustrate some of these points, I want to turn to a fairly typical report from the *Daily Mail* (29 July, 2000) following the acquittal of a young man on rape charges. In the report, entitled 'THE REAL DATE RAPE VICTIM', we learn that the young man prefers serious relationships to casual flings, had a brilliant future ahead of him and is from a 'secure middle-class home'. All of this, we are told, was jeopardised by the false accusation, the emotional impact of which is described in detail. Meanwhile, his accuser continued with her studies, in contrast both to the accused's forced withdrawal from university and the 'ruined life' discourse, which, we will see, marks 'genuine' rape cases. Her 'emotional disturbance' and mental health problems are read not as the after-effects of rape, but as evidence of hysteria and unreliability. It is further suggested that the accuser only made the accusation because it was 'culturally more acceptable' to her Iranian boyfriend that she had been raped than had consensually lost her virginity. The boyfriend – whose domineering nature is in marked contrast to the 'naïve, shy and rather innocent' accused – is repeatedly marked by his ethnicity and it is suggested that their relationship was the root cause of her mental health problems.

For the *Mail*, then, what is patently false about this claim – and others that similarly focus on brilliant men cut down in their prime by silly or vicious women – is the idea that such a man would need to rape such a woman. Rape is constructed as sex and not violence, an alien concept in white, middle-class suburbia, whose inhabitants are simply too nice, too attractive, too respectable to ever resort to rape.

These media narratives of supposed false memories, false accusations and miscommunciation are constructed in such a way as to reinforce familiar myths about the nature of sexual abuse, its perpetrators and victims. In this respect, it is hardly insignificant that these media narratives repeatedly focus on accusations against white, middle-class men whose class, education, family status and ability to express themselves emotionally are offered by the press as evidence that they cannot be guilty (Lees, 1995; Kitzinger, 1998; Gavey and Gow, 2001).

To be clear, I am not suggesting that these accused and acquitted men are guilty of rape. However, their race, class, sexual/familial relationships and educational background do not prove their innocence – just as race, class, sexual/familial relationships and educational background do not prove the guilt of those constructed as sex beasts or paedophiles.

Virgins and vamps

So far, I have focused primarily on the representation of male perpetrators of **sexual violence**, but what of the victims?

In addition to the distortions already observed, sexual assault reporting betrays a depressingly familiar sexual double standard. As Benedict (1992: 152) argues, when a sex crime victim is labelled as attractive, she usually receives less sympathy. This is so ingrained that even when sympathies are overwhelmingly with the victim, descriptions of her physical appearance invoke the myth that she provoked it. In contrast, when a sex crime perpetrator is labelled as attractive he receives more sympathy as the implication is that he did not need to rape a woman in order to have sex. Sexual history functions similarly: Thus, if a woman has previously consented to sex with this man or a similar man, then her charge is weakened. Equally, if the accused has

Figure 3.1 *Stories about rape, stories about sex (Daily Star, 2 October, 2003).*

had consensual sexual relationships with this woman or any woman, then his defence is strengthened (Lees, 1995).

This underlines the extent to which sex crime is both gendered and 'sexed' (Howe, 1998). Indeed, a number of studies of the UK tabloid press have pointed to the sexualisation of sex crime. Soothill and Walby (1991: 19), for example, suggest that the increasing visibility of sex crime in the 1970s was not simply a reflection of official crime statistics, but of increasing sexual licence. Sex crime, they argue, functioned for tabloids like *The Sun* as part of a 'soft porn package' – also including sexual gossip and photographs of topless models – designed to carve a niche for the paper during circulation warfare.

More recently, Carter's study (1998: 225–6) of sex crime reporting in the 1990s suggests that readers of British tabloids are still encouraged to make sense of sex crime in the context of sex and Figure 3.1 provides a clear illustration of this. Here we have a story from the *Star* of alleged gang rape by eight footballers packaged alongside football success ('GERS GO TOP') and sexual display to produce a reading of rape as sex and/or sport. The model's pose – the look to camera, the smile, the promise of striptease – is an invitation to male readers and she is constructed as a shared possession (*'our* Lucy'), undermining the seriousness of the alleged gang rape.

That the football rape story hit the headlines before any charges had been brought is also significant and this story is far from unique in this respect. Not only does this have potential implications for the investigation and successful prosecution of the cases, but – as with the stories of false allegations – this also works to construct rape and sexual assault as stories about the vulnerability of men rather than men's abuse of women. In the football rape story, for example, questions were repeatedly raised about the naming of the alleged rapists, the sexual availability of women to these men and their vulnerability to false accusations because of the legal anonymity afforded to women in rape trials.

Consistent with the argument that sex crime is frequently framed as a story about sex, the representation of the female victims of sexual murder, rape and sexual assault frequently emphasises the women's desirability in conventional terms. For example, in her renowned account of the Ted Bundy case, true crime writer Ann Rule (1989: 50, 55) describes one of Bundy's victims in the following terms:

> Lynda was as beautiful as she sounded, tall, slender, with chestnut hair that fell almost to her waist, clear blue eyes fringed with dark lashes.

> Just two more quarters and Lynda would have graduated from the University, would have taken a job where she would have been of infinite help to the retarded children whose lives had not been blessed as hers with brains, beauty, a loving and nurturing home.

Desirability and personality are never an issue in representing male victims of sexual killers (Benedict, 1993). Just substitute the name 'Lynda' with 'John' in the above quotations and this becomes obvious. Clearly, the emphasis on female victims' desirability is 'intended to provide a degree of sexual excitement' (Jenkins, 1994: 105). As a journalist covering the 1986 sexual murder of Jennifer Levin in New York's Central Park told Helen Benedict (1992: 147):

> 'We heard the words, "Central Park, young, white teenager, gorgeous and strangled," and it was like TNT was planted under our rear ends – everyone flew out of here like bats out of hell. It was sex, tits and ass, and a strangling – we knew it would sell'.

Levin is here reduced to sexualised body parts ('tits and ass') and the story of her murder is framed as a story about sex. Although the coverage of this case generated considerable public outcry for precisely these reasons, the treatment of Jennifer Levin is sadly not unique. Indeed, Benedict argues that press coverage tends to place women victims of sexual murder or abuse in one of two categories: they are 'virgins' (metaphorically if not literally) or they are 'vamps'.

Women – and, indeed, children – who do not fit the 'virginal' mould are often simply invisible as victims to law enforcement and criminal justice agencies as well as to the news media. For example, the murder of an individual prostitute woman typically generates little media interest or sympathy. Notoriously, in the Yorkshire Ripper case the press, public and police alike seemed singularly uninterested until Sutcliffe murdered a woman who was not a prostitute (Hollway, 1981; Ward Jouve, 1986; Bland, 1992). However, whether women are portrayed as virgins or vamps, innocent or complicit victims, depends not only on the perception of their sexual morality but on interrelated variables such as class, education, race and ethnicity (Caputi, 1988; Benedict, 1992). A female victim is most likely to be sympathetically portrayed if:

- she was attacked by a stranger
- her attacker was of a different race, class and/or ethnic group
- she is very young or very old
- she conforms to conventional sex roles
- a weapon was used in the attack
- she was murdered
- she committed suicide
- her attacker is a serial offender.[11]

As we have already seen, she is not likely to be portrayed at all if she is black (Moorti, 2002).

Moreover, feminist analyses of sexual abuse news coverage have demonstrated that it is the guilt or innocence of the female victim – rather than of her (alleged) attacker – that is most consistently explored in reports of crimes, legal proceedings and verdicts. This is by no means a new phenomenon. As Walkowitz (1982) notes in her discussion of press coverage of the crimes attributed to Jack the Ripper, news reports focused repeatedly on the murdered women's failed marriages, sexual relationships, prostitution, drunkenness and poverty. The stories of their murder thus served – as have so many subsequent prostitute murders – as a warning to 'respectable' women. Indeed, in Victorian England, the Ripper case was influential in debates about the regulation of women's sexuality and place within society. Nearly 100 years later, Peter Sutcliffe's killing spree in Yorkshire led to calls for women to observe a curfew and accept male escorts, flying in the face of contemporaneous demands for equality and women's liberation. In the same period in the US, convicted killer Henry Lee Lucas used a television interview to underline the pervasive nature of the threat to women, as Jane Caputi (1998: 117–18) notes:

> [he] told the vast nationwide audience that he had tracked women across the entire United States, following them persistently, getting gas when they did etc. Whether or not Lucas had actually done this, his message went out to millions. He concluded: 'A woman alone ain't safe at all'. At this juncture, Chase [the female interviewer] responds: 'Mr Lucas, what you say sends a chill through my bones; I do nothing but travel alone.' He replies: 'Yeah, but just think if I was out there. What if somebody like me was out there.'

Lucas confessed to the murder of men as well as women, but in this interview he demonstrates that the discourse of serial murder has specifically gendered functions – to keep women in a state of fear and to consolidate patriarchal control. As Caputi (1988: 117) notes, 'Although some groups of women are branded as especially expendable, *all* women are meant to internalize the threat and message of sexual terrorism.'

This pattern is not unique to the reporting of sexual murder. As Lees (2002: 85–6) argues, the central question explored in press reports of rape is not 'What kind of man?' but 'What kind of woman?' She continues, 'The result is that the positions of assailant and victim are subtly reversed – the suspect becomes the victim and the complainant, who has spoken out about male violence, becomes the culprit.' This is reflected in the attention devoted to the victim's behaviour prior to the attack and, also, in the emphasis placed on personal safety advice directed at women readers in news reports of stranger danger (Greer, 2003a: 100). Two rather different examples from the *Daily Mail* will serve to illustrate these points. Unlike the football rape story or those cases analysed by Benedict, neither of these cases were ground-breaking, they did not involve celebrities and did not achieve widespread national or international coverage. That an analysis of these stories identifies similar concerns therefore suggests something of the pervasive nature of sexual double standards in reporting sex crime.

The first story – 'THE GIRL WHO DIED OF SHAME' (*Daily Mail*, 16 December, 2000) – concerns the drug rape and subsequent suicide of an 18-year-old woman. At first glance, the story is extremely sympathetic to the victim. The rapist is a slightly older 'stranger' (the victim's difference in age and status emphasised by the use of the word 'girl') and the victim is a young woman positioned in relation to her family and friends. Her sexual respectability, fragile femininity and love of life are repeatedly emphasised, adding weight to the devastating effect of the rape and her subsequent suicide. Nevertheless, the story is framed as a warning to other young women – a 'hauntingly tragic tale of our times' about the twin dangers of drugs and dating. It is claimed that the woman is 'the latest victim of a date rape drug', positioning the drug (and not the rapist) as the active agent, while the victim's very ordinariness is used to generalise the threat, in that if it could happen to this young woman, it could happen to any young woman. The attention devoted to the young woman's behaviour on the night of the attack encourages female readers to identify ways to avoid rape by regulating their own behaviour – not accepting drinks from strangers, going to night clubs, drinking alcohol or taking drugs – while men's behaviour goes unexamined and unchallenged.

The use of the term 'date' rape is also extremely problematic here. As Lees (2002: 77–8) notes, in the British press this term is used to refer to rapes by acquaintances of all kinds and is not restricted to situations where the man and woman have made a date to go out together. In this particular story, there is no evidence that the young woman ever consented to 'date' or have any kind of sexual or romantic encounter with the man who raped her. Labelling this a 'date' rape, therefore, fundamentally distorts the nature of the relationship between perpetrator and victim and suggests that this crime is somehow less serious (and more preventable) than 'real' rape (Estrich, 1987). Indeed, some feminists have suggested that 'date' rape is itself a media construct, designed to subtly cast doubt on the sexual assault charge. As Moorti (2002: 48) notes, 'The media focus on the "date" aspect facilitates a narrative that presents women as sexual objects.'

The second story I want to consider – headlined, 'WOMAN OFFICER WAS RAPED BY SOLDIER AS SHE LAY IN BED DRUNK' (*Daily Mail*, 5 May, 2000) – is far less sympathetic to the rape victim. This report focuses on the court martial and sentencing of the first soldier ever to be found guilty of raping a superior in the British Army. However, here, too, it is the behaviour of the victim that is scrutinised:

> A FEMALE Army officer wept yesterday as she told how she was raped in her bed by a soldier.
>
> The woman had been to her commanding officer's house for a dinner party and admitted consuming at least two bottles of wine and several Martinis.
>
> She claims she was attacked by Lance Corporal John Schofield when she returned to her quarters in the German town of Guetersloh.

In beginning with the weeping victim's account the article may appear sympathetic, but, by immediately highlighting her sex, weeping and excessive drinking, doubt is cast over her reliability and her position within the Army itself. The phrasing ('she was raped' rather than 'he raped her') casts further doubt and her own 'admission' suggests her complicity and undermines the reliability of her 'claims'. Although Schofield's defence hinges on consent, the fact that he is married with children and was drunk on the night in question is not mentioned until much later in the report, thus placing his morality beyond scrutiny. In contrast, his victim is positioned as a deviant woman (a drunk, an Army officer) and a deviant Army officer (a drunk, a woman, an accuser who has broken ranks).

The emphasis on the victim's behaviour in both these reports is consistent with a number of rape myths – that sexual abuse is a question of men 'misreading the signals', women provoke attack and their testimony cannot be trusted. Moreover, these women are presented in ways consistent with the rapist's perception – that is, as objects of his desire whose expressions of sexuality (in dress or behaviour, for example) can only be understood in relation to what they mean to him.

The mirroring of the abuser's perception of his victims in the reporting of his crimes is perhaps even more explicit in the voyeuristic examination of the corpse of the victim of sexual murder. Like the sexual murderer, the reader/viewer is invited to transgress, to see what is taboo – the naked body of an unknown woman, her injuries (external and internal), her bodily fluids, the moment of her murder. This is particularly explicit in representations of the original Ripper case, where popular publications, such as the *Illustrated Police News*, provided sketches showing scenes from the victims' lives and deaths, including before and after death portraits, reconstructions of the crime scenes and even sketches of the women in their coffins (see Figures 3.2 and 3.3). There is a suggestion here that, by investigating the victim and her life, we can both identify the perpetrator and (more contentiously) understand the crime, but this subtly removes the perpetrator as agent and obscures the reality of his decision to act.

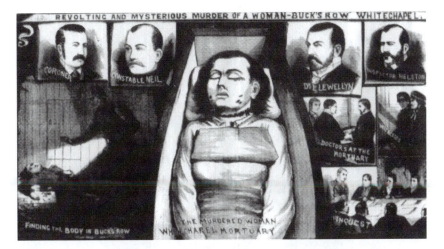

Figure 3.2 *The spectacle of the female victim. Mary Ann Nichols, generally thought to be the first of the 'Ripper's' victims* (Illustrated Police News, 8 September, 1888).

In more contemporary accounts, there remains an emphasis on reconstructing the attack and many true crime publications and programmes use actual crime scene and autopsy photographs, while forensic science fictions – from the novels of Patricia Cornwell to the crime labs of *CSI* – place considerable emphasis on the body as crime scene/seen. This is not to argue that the reader/viewer necessarily identifies with the sexual murderer (an issue I will return to in Chapter 5), but to note the ways in which these representations tread a thin line between showing and replicating the sexual murderers' lusts.

Despite the decidedly anti-feminist emphasis of the coverage discussed thus far, it is important to acknowledge that contemporary news representations do repeatedly acknowledge feminist anti-rape discourses, albeit in contradictory ways. The repeated focus on the devastating consequences of sexual assault and the emphasis placed on the experiences of the victim could, for example, be read in this light. Reports describe medium- and long-term injuries in detail – scarring, disfigurement, physical impairment, sleeplessness, depression, (hetero)sexual dysfunction, distrust of men, loss of job and failure of relationships. In presenting the consequences of rape for the victim, such reports arguably acknowledge feminist discourse, but it is notable that rape generally remains an individualised experience in these reports. The idea that rape is the worst thing that could happen to a woman is ubiquitous and there are few stories that mention women's survival or collective responses to male violence. In my study of the *Daily Mail* articles, for example, the rare references to

Figure 3.3 *The spectacle of the female victim. Catherine Eddowes before and after death* (Illustrated Police News, *12 October, 1888*).

feminism present an aggressive, irrational, man-hating ideology that harms rather than helps individual rape victims.[12] The *Daily Mail* is not alone in marginalising feminist analysis in rape reporting. As Benedict (1997: 267) notes in a US context, feminists are routinely portrayed as extremists, likely to introduce bias to rape stories or, as we have already seen, create the context in which men are falsely accused and families destroyed. Instead, it is commonly suggested that the family, police and the press themselves are women's best supporters and protectors.

Domestic violence and murder

In concluding this chapter, I want to turn my attention to domestic violence. In exploring the treatment of domestic violence in the press, we find condensed and replicated many of the themes that have been of concern in this chapter, namely, invisibility, racism, sensationalism, victim-blaming and – perhaps most significantly – the mainstreaming of feminist discourse.

It is important to note at the outset that domestic violence (against women and children) and even domestic murder are rarely considered newsworthy precisely because they are so common (Meyers, 1994;

McCollum, 1998). For example, in 2000, a quantitative study on the impact of domestic violence in the UK found that at least half a million of the calls made to the police each year relate to domestic violence. This means that one in four crimes of violence reported to the police are domestic and, of these, 88% involve male perpetrators (Stanko, 2000). British Crime Surveys (which consider experiences of assault not reported to the police as well as official crime statistics) consistently demonstrate that women, unlike men, are at a considerably greater risk of assault from acquaintances and intimates than from strangers (Gadd et al., 2002).

In terms of news coverage, the pattern is similar to that observed in relation to sexual abuse and follows Surette's 'law of opposites'. In other words, the cases receiving attention tend to be the most severe and unusual – such as domestic murder and murder suicides – and/or to have other newsworthy elements, such as a celebrity perpetrator or victim. There are other striking similarities – notably, that violence is represented as individual aberrance when the perpetrator is white, but minority ethnic perpetrators (or alleged perpetrators) are represented as emblematic of their communities (Kozol, 1995) as, indeed, was the case in the widespread coverage of O.J. Simpson's criminal trial (Morrison, 1997).

The assumption of Simpson's guilt in the white news media – based, ostensibly, on Simpson's previous admissions of battery and so tied to a pseudo-feminist discourse – can also be linked to the distortion of the everyday nature of domestic violence in the press. As domestic violence is only likely to make the headlines when it results in murder, once Simpson was publicly named as an abuser, it was easier to imagine that he must also be a killer. While there is clearly a link between domestic violence and femicide – for example, between 1991 and 2000, more than 40% of Scottish female murder victims were killed by their (ex-)partners (Scottish Executive, 2001a) – the two are clearly not synonymous. As Stahly and Walker (1997: 428–9) point out in the context of the Simpson case, these domestic murders account for a very small percentage of the women who are abused by their (ex-)partners every year. The news media's emphasis on domestic murder thus disguises the nature of the majority of domestic violence that does not result in death or life-threatening injury. Further, by making the assumption that the domestic abuser was necessarily guilty of murder, the mainstream coverage of the Simpson case maintained a safe distance between domestic abusers (murderers) and 'ordinary' men, who, whatever else they may do to their wives, do not murder them.

It is not only in the emphasis on serious violence that coverage of domestic violence mirrors fact-based accounts of sex crime. Similar devices are used to deny the agency of the perpetrator. For example, the use of the passive voice ('she was beaten', not 'he beat her'), the portrayal of the perpetrator as out of control, drunk, drugged or otherwise not responsible for his actions, or suggestions of culpability on the victim's part (Meyers, 1994; Lamb and Keon, 1995; McDonald, 1999). However, the out-of-control domestic abuser is treated rather more sympathetically than the pathological stranger.

Such sympathy for the abuser arguably reflects the minimisation of domestic violence in society more generally, but the identity of the abuser is another factor here. As we have seen, non-fatal domestic violence is more likely to be deemed newsworthy – particularly at the national level – if it involves celebrity or high-status perpetrators or victims. Where the (alleged) perpetrator is already well known, it is the conflation of private violence with celebrity, rather than the abusive behaviour itself, that merits coverage (Greer, 2003b: 49–51). In such cases, our assumed prior familiarity with aspects of the abuser's story allows for a more complex – and potentially sympathetic – portrait of the abuser to emerge as, unlike the sex beast, the domestic abuser is likely to be known both to his victim and to the reader. As McDonald (1999) notes, celebrity white men who publicly admit their abuse are slotted within a sin and redemption narrative, with extraordinary faith being placed in counselling – rather than the criminal justice system – as an appropriate route to redemption. The focus on counselling – now largely rejected as an appropriate approach for programmes working with domestic violence perpetrators (Boyle, 2001b) – is consistent with the news media's construction of domestic violence as a symptom of individualised pathology rather than as a social problem (Kozol, 1995) and with the emphasis on reconstructing (rather than deconstructing) the family.

In the celebrity cases discussed by McDonald (1999), counselling is also presented as an option for the couple. By presenting domestic violence as a problem for couples, to be solved by couples, the reality of who is doing what to whom gets lost and so men's position within the family is protected. Indeed, domestic violence reporting frequently presents us with two victims. So, for example, news reports mention the couple's fights or arguments or present the abuser as victim of a fatal attraction – an obsessive love for the woman he abuses (Finn, 1989/90; Meyers, 1994). The representation of domestic murder and suicide as a family tragedy is a particularly striking example of the two-victim story, obscuring the man's violent agency and equating his decision to murder with his decision to kill himself: 'he did to her what he did to himself. She suffered no more than he' (Meyers, 1994: 58). In domestic murder cases where the murderer does not subsequently kill himself, feminists have repeatedly noted the ways in which the law – and the press – excuse male violence on the grounds of infidelity, insubordination and nagging. In contrast, women who kill the men who abuse them are rarely – in the courtroom or the press – seen as having been provoked to murder (Lees, 1992; McNeill, 1992; Radford, 1993). In both scenarios, as we will see in Chapter 4, it is the woman's behaviour that comes under scrutiny as reports look at the legitimacy of her complaint of abuse in light of her failure to leave prior to the murder.

To explore some of these arguments, I now want to turn to the long-running story of English footballer Paul 'Gazza' Gascoigne's alleged abuse of his now ex-wife, Sheryl. When the story first broke – in a five page article in the best-selling Sunday tabloid the *News of the World* (3 July, 1994) – the sin and redemption/confession and counselling narratives were employed. The story was billed as 'Gazza's Amazing Confession', told in the first person and peppered with the interviewer's italicised notes on Gazza's emotional state: *'Gazza stops, consumed with grief'*, *'Gazza is convulsed with emotion and sobs unashamedly'*. Paul's distress positions him as victim and this distress is presented as evidence of his sincerity, recalling his spontaneous tears during the 1990 World Cup (a photograph accompanying the article underlines this connection). The 'amazing confession' is presented as an act of bravery and a plea for help from a 'tormented soccer idol', referred to throughout by his nickname, Gazza, which is both familiar and affectionate. Yet, Gazza tells us he is obsessive, jealous, insecure and unable to control his behaviour. Again, this focus on individual pathology does nothing to explain or contextualise his sense of entitlement regarding Sheryl. The *News of the World*'s agony aunt confirms that Gazza is really a 'child who cried for love', deflecting the issue of responsibility and presenting psychiatric counselling as 'cure'. There is no gender analysis.

Sheryl and Paul subsequently reunited, had a son and married. Two months after their wedding, a vicious attack by Paul reportedly left Sheryl requiring hospital treatment and the press returned to the story. The couple separated. I want to pick up the story again in 1999, when Sheryl spoke publicly about their relationship for the first time.

Sheryl's story – which received a week (22–26 November, 1999) of intensive coverage in Britain's biggest-selling tabloid, *The Sun* – can be partly understood as a celebrity confession, though here it is Sheryl and not Paul who 'confesses'. Importantly, however, Sheryl's story is immediately positioned within a broader context by her alliance with Refuge – a charity providing support for women fleeing abusive men. The image of Sheryl used throughout the week shows her wearing a black and white ribbon in support of Refuge and standing in front of a Refuge poster showing statistics on the prevalence of domestic murder

Figure 3.4 *Sheryl Gascoigne's experience becomes the centrepoint of a* The Sun/Refuge *campaign against domestic violence (*The Sun, *24 November, 1999).*

and domestic violence in the UK. Other women's – and children's – narratives support and embellish Sheryl's story (see Figure 3.4), statistics continually remind readers of the broader picture and Sandra Horley, the Chief Executive of Refuge, contributes an article. There is, throughout, evidence of survival. For example, Sheryl's story begins with her new-found freedom from abuse: 'Each morning, Sheryl Gascoigne switches on her mobile phone to be greeted by the words: "Free and Happy."' (22 November) – and ends with a statement about the importance of collective and public action: 'Together we can turn around the image of domestic violence and together we can break the silence' (26 November). Throughout the week, Sheryl acknowledges the role Refuge has played in her understanding of abuse and in her achievement of freedom. So, not only is Sheryl presented as a survivor, but as a woman learning to survive with the support of other women. Unlike the rape narratives discussed earlier, her story is used to establish solidarity with other women, not to warn and regulate. Throughout, *The Sun* explicitly addresses readers who are also being abused, listing the Refuge helpline number, urging women to seek support and reminding them that they are not alone.

There is also a challenge to the ethos of the sports world as columnist Jane Moore explicitly criticises the footballing establishment for their apparent failure to support Sheryl (25 November).[13] Paul's family come in for similar criticism and, taken together, this highlights the ways in which abused women are both isolated and silenced in public and private.

Paul's attempt to prevent the publication of Sheryl's story is also read as part of his continuing control of her, incorporating the feminist understanding that domestic violence is not only physical abuse but also part of broader structures of male control over women (23 November). Thus, within this notoriously misogynist paper, elements of the feminist analysis of domestic violence as a systematic and widely condoned abuse of male power begin to emerge. Indeed, *The Sun* has periodically run anti-domestic violence campaigns in conjunction with Refuge ever since (for example, the week beginning 22 September, 2003; and week beginning 12 January, 2004).

However, *The Sun*'s coverage is not without limitations. For example, while abused readers are explicitly addressed, there is no challenge to male readers/abusers and the emphasis is therefore on women's responsibility to end/escape the violence (notably, Paul is only explicitly challenged when he tries to stop the publication of the story). The focus on serious physical injury and murder in the collected stories of domestic violence underlines the difference between 'normal' men (*The Sun* readers) and abusers (murderous others). The emphasis on charity (wear a ribbon, send a donation) arguably encourages a focus on victimisation and protection, rather than asking more troubling questions about justice and prevention. Further, while Moore offers a limited critique of the family, much of the ongoing narrative is concerned with domestic violence as a dereliction of men's paternalist and protectionist duties – duties *The Sun* is willing to fulfil. The emphasis on abused women as mothers is also used to suggest that when their children are affected, it is morally imperative that women leave. Pitting the 'deviant' family against the 'ideal' family, the final major story of the week focuses on Cherie Blair's backing of *The Sun*'s campaign (26 November). The family is foregrounded here with the first picture of the Prime Minister's wife since the announcement of her pregnancy. Cherie Blair's personal backing of the campaign also evades thorny issues about State funding of domestic violence support services and the prosecution of domestic violence perpetrators. More seriously, of course, the anti-domestic violence campaign sits uneasily with the paper's routine sexual objectification of women for male readers' enjoyment, most obviously, though not exclusively, in the photographs of topless models on 'page 3'.

This brief analysis demonstrates that the dominant press narratives of domestic violence identified by previous researchers (individual pathology, sin and redemption, confession and counselling, the couple's problem) are neither natural nor inevitable. Although anchored by a public figure, *The Sun's*/Refuge's campaign was not simply a celebrity narrative. However, to end on a cautionary note, when TV presenter Anthea Turner went public, alleging that she had been abused by her previous partner, Radio 1 DJ Bruno Brookes, the response from some papers was to challenge her account and condone Brookes' abuse. *The Mirror*, for example – which later that week ran an exclusive on TV actress Lynda Bellingham's 'LIFE AS A BATTERED WIFE' (28 October, 2000) – took up half its front page with the headline 'ZIPPED: WE GAG ANTHEA ON BEHALF OF THE NATION' (26 October, 2000) (see Figure 3.5). Inside, columnist Brian Reade poured scorn on her allegations and concluded that women seriously abused should 'queue up and give her a bloody good smack'. The treatment of Anthea Turner suggests that, as with the virgins and vamps of sex crime narratives, domestic violence victims can be divided into the 'deserving' and 'undeserving'. While this division is obvious to feminist activists, social scientists and legal scholars, its deployment in media narratives has received little sustained discussion.

Even a cursory comparison of *The Mirror*'s Bellingham and Turner stories reveals that what is at stake here is adherence to or deviance from feminine ideals. Bellingham is positioned in relation to her on- and off-screen roles as wife and mother. Her ex-husband – 'a fiery macho Neopolitan' – is marked as ethnically 'other' and Bellingham's use of both civil and criminal actions legitimates her account. In contrast, Turner was not seriously injured, had not reported the abuse and only told her story publicly when a newspaper approached her with the intention to publish the details. Further, *The Mirror* reminds us that Turner is newly married, her new husband having very publicly left his wife and children because of their affair. It would seem that Turner's sexualised role (as the other woman), her high-profile

Figure 3.5 *Asking for it? Anthea Turner as 'culpable' domestic violence victim,* (The Mirror, 26 October, 2000).

relationships and her role in her husband's family break-up, makes her claim to previous victimisation moot. The presentation of Turner as ambitious, opportunistic and a relentless self-publicist – always there, always talking – has similarities with the treatment of supposedly nagging wives, both by the press and in courts (Kennedy, 1992; Lees, 1992). While there are clearly other issues at stake here – Bellingham told her story to *The Mirror*, Turner spoke to a rival newspaper – this nevertheless reveals how myths about domestic violence remain in circulation despite the apparent mainstreaming of feminist analysis suggested by my earlier discussion.

Here, too, there is still a long way to go.

Summary

- Feminist analyses of men's violence against women have made some impact on the way in which these crimes are represented, making certain kinds of male violence visible and challenging some (though not all) of the myths surrounding men's entitlement over women.
- The everyday violence by men against women (and children) known to them remains infrequently represented, while stranger danger, sexual murder and inter-racial assault receive disproportionate attention.

- Male violence is continually represented as individualised and decontextualised – unless, that is, the perpetrator is from a racially or ethnically marginal group.
- The behaviour of female victims of all kinds of male violence is regularly scrutinised in press reports and only certain women (those who conform to patriarchal ideals of femininity) are consistently sympathetically treated.
- The gendered reality of male violence against women is obscured and the press representation of victims of male violence too often mirrors the perpetrators' own perceptions.
- These representations shape the ways in which it is possible to think about men's violence against women. This should be clearly differentiated from the effects research discussed in Chapter 1. What is of concern is not a specific causal relationship, but the more complex ways in which myths about violence against women are circulated, confirmed and also challenged in these public discourses.

Notes

1 See Jakubowski and Braund (1999) for a list of texts focusing on the Ripper case, and Cameron (1992) for a feminist critique of the 'Ripper' industry. Many of the original press reports discussed in this chapter can be found online in the *Casebook: Jack the Ripper* at www.casebook.org. Brief details of the major criminal cases discussed in this chapter are provided in the Appendix.
2 See the essays collected in Morrison and Lacour (1997) for a variety of perspectives on this case and its media representation.
3 Miller's term 'womankilling' prefigures **second-wave** feminist concerns with accurately naming and making visible the phenomenon of violence *against women,* a concern taken up in Radford and Russell's (1992) volume on femicide.
4 In addition to these 'larks', hundreds of women came forward suspecting that their husbands, boyfriends, fathers were the Ripper (Cameron and Frazer, 1987: 33). These claims – which emerge with depressing regularity in serial killer investigations – are of a different order to men's interactive engagement with the emerging narrative as cheerleaders, impersonators and hoaxers. The women calling clearly recognised that the Ripper's crimes were embedded in a culture of male violence that impacted their own lives and also demonstrated the extent to which the Ripper, his apologists and mythologists kept women in a state of fear.
5 Figures from HM Crown Prosecution Service Inspectorate and HM Inspectorate of Constabulary (2002: 1).
6 Although I refer mainly to work on print media in this chapter, there is a small but growing literature on the reporting of men's violence against women on television news, primarily in a US context. See, in particular, work by Marian Meyers (1997, Chapter 4) and Sujata Moorti (2002, Chapter 3).
7 In this previously unpublished study – which I draw on throughout this chapter – I examined all stories centrally concerned with sexual assault in the British *Daily Mail* and its sister Sunday paper the *Mail on Sunday.* In order to identify stories for analysis, the words 'rape', 'sexual assault' and 'indecent assault' were entered into the *Daily Mail/Mail on Sunday* searchable database.

8 Sources: Soothill and Walby (1991), Soothill and Soothill (1993), Grover and Soothill (1996a, 1996b), Cuklanz (1996), Meyers (1997), McCollum (1998), Greer (2003a, 2003b). Although there are obvious similarities in the determination of 'newsworthiness' at a local and national level, Greer usefully highlights the extent to which features such as 'celebrity' and 'status' are locally determined. So, for example, an abusive priest or teacher may be more newsworthy at a local level than a distant film star.

9 In addition to Benedict's work, I am drawing here on Chancer's (1987) and Cuklanz's (1995, 1996) analyses of the press coverage of this case.

10 Although the young men were convicted and served their sentences, the safety of their original convictions was subsequently cast into doubt. See Appendix for details.

11 Sources: Benedict (1992: 19), Meyers (1997: 57).

12 See, for example, Jill Saward's article on 4 July, 2000.

13 *The Sun's* willingness to challenge the sporting establishment on this occasion is in direct contrast to US press coverage of similar stories analysed in earlier feminist work (Messner and Solomon, 1993; McDonald, 1999).

Further reading

Benedict, H. (1992) *Virgin or Vamp: How the Press Covers Sex Crimes.* Oxford: Oxford University Press.

Cameron, D., and Frazer, E. (1987) *The Lust to Kill: A Feminist Investigation of Sexual Murder.* Cambridge: Polity.

Greer, C. (2003b) *Sex Crime and the Media: Sex Offending and the Press in a Divided Society.* Cullompton: Willan.

Kelly, L. (1996a) 'Weasel words: paedophiles and the cycle of abuse', *Trouble and Strife,* 33: 44–9.

Kitzinger, J. (2001) 'Transformations of public and private knowledge: audience reception, feminism and the experience of childhood sexual abuse', *Feminist Media Studies,* 1(1): 91–104.

Meyers, M. (1997) *News Coverage of Violence Against Women: Engendering Blame.* London: Sage.

Soothill, K. and Walby, S. (1991) *Sex Crime in the News.* London: Routledge.

Deadlier than the males? True crimes of women's violence

Chapter outline

While, as we saw in Chapter 3, male perpetrators of violence are rarely visible as men, news stories about women's violence are very explicitly stories about gender. This chapter explores how such stories are told, examining the emphasis placed on explaining women's violence with reference to feminism, sexuality, maternity and biology. As crimes of violence by women are comparatively rare, a relatively small number of sensational cases – such as those of Rosemary West and Myra Hindley in Britain, Karla Homolka in Canada and Aileen Wuornos in the US – have generated attention on an international scale and they are revisited here.

- Deadlier than the male   the myth of equal opportunity violence.
- The cycle of violence   victimisation, agency and **sexual murder**.
- Women who kill   battered women's syndrome; provocation;
  their abusers   diminished responsibility.
- Doing it   sexual subjectivity; bisexuality, lesbianism
  and criminality.
- The maternal instinct   maternity; child-killing; disciplining the
  and the bleeding mad   female body; PMS.

Deadlier than the male?

In August 2002, one story dominated the British news media – the disappearance of ten-year-olds Jessica Chapman and Holly Wells.[1] Two weeks after they disappeared, their bodies were found and a man and a woman were arrested in connection with their murders. The woman's apparent involvement was, in the words of a columnist for *The Scotsman*, an 'extra horror' (19 August, 2002). Why a woman's involvement should add an extra layer to the horror of crimes of violence, and how the press negotiate that horror, is the focus of this chapter. First, though, I want to briefly consider why women's violence attracts such intense media attention in the first place and, relatedly, why feminists in particular have at times seemed reluctant to engage with the issue.

Violence and aggression are intrinsic to our conceptualisation of masculinity. Femininity, however, is associated with nurturing and caring for others, with emotion, passivity and vulnerability. All of this is thrown into crisis when a woman chooses to attack, hurt or kill another human being (or allows someone else to do so). Violent women are thus guilty both of breaking the criminal law and violating gender norms. It is this double deviance that is made explicit in accounts of their violence. For example, in a study of reports of violence between intimates in the British press, Maggie Wykes (1995: 69) found that women perpetrators were three times more likely than males to be depicted as having violated gender norms. Moreover, a woman who kills, or acts violently, is always visible as a woman – she is a damsel or angel of death, a black widow, a *femme fatale*, a female **serial killer**. These labels thus draw attention both to the criminal act and the gender transgression. We do not have equivalent labels for men because their actions are not gender-transgressive but normative: so, for example, media reports did not refer to Peter Sutcliffe as a male serial killer, he was just a serial killer. One aspect of the 'extra' horror alluded to in the opening paragraph above is, therefore, that women's violence threatens to expose the constructed nature of gender.

It is no accident, then, that popular and pseudo-scientific concerns about women's violence periodically surface during times of profound unease about women's place in society, times when women's demands for rights, votes or equality threaten the **patriarchal** order (Jones, 1991: xxii). While the prevalence of women's violence has remained remarkably consistent from one historical epoch to another (Jones, 1991: xv), the increased visibility of women's violence at times of crisis functions as part of a broader **backlash** against women and feminism. In the most recent period of backlash, popular accounts of women's violence have, indeed, adopted the language of **second-wave feminism** to explain (and often distort the prevalence of) women's violence. At its crassest, the thought behind this pseudo-feminist **discourse** of equal opportunity violence can be expressed as, 'if we accept that women can be airline pilots, we should also accept that they can be rapists' (Cameron, 1996: 24–5). So, for example, in a volume on female serial killers, Kelleher and Kelleher (1998) repeatedly claim that 'social bias' has historically impeded our understanding and that, as a result, female serial killers have been able to kill undetected for many years. On the surface, this might look like a feminist argument – that women's violence challenges ideas about what it means to be a woman and so it is only with the advent of feminism that we have been able to acknowledge and study the phenomenon. However, there are serious problems with this formulation.

Most important of these is that the equal opportunity argument distorts what is actually known about women's violence – that is, that it is comparatively rare. For example, Federal Bureau of Investigation (2002) statistics show that women made up 9.7% of known offenders in US murder cases in 2001 and Ann Jones (1991: xv) argues that the percentage of US homicides committed by women has remained virtually consistent (at about 10–15%) throughout history. On the other side of the Atlantic, Scottish crime statistics show that 8% of those guilty of homicide and 7.1% of those guilty of serious assault in 2000 were women (Scottish Executive, 2001b). In Britain as a whole, research suggests that women are responsible for 12% of all recorded **domestic violence** incidents (Stanko, 2000) and 5–7% of child **sexual abuse** (Kelly, 1996b: 43). In Britain, the US, Australia and Canada, there are three times as many partner homicides against women as against men (Gadd et al., 2002). To be clear, I am not suggesting that these statistics reflect women's innate incapacity for violence (nor am I suggesting that men are innately predisposed to **rape** or murder). Rather, this chapter considers the different meanings and possibilities attached to violence in a patriarchal culture.

Despite the comparative rarity of women's violence, there is a willingness – in popular, academic and therapeutic accounts – to define a broad range of women's behaviour as violent and abhorrent. In the Holly Wells and Jessica Chapman murder case, for example, the charges against Maxine Carr (perverting the course of justice and aiding an offender) were, in many popular accounts, equated with the charges of abduction and murder laid against her partner, Ian Huntley. Liz Kelly (1996a: 41–2) similarly notes that women's 'failure to protect' their children is frequently equated with their partner's sexual abuse of those children. While such complicity can clearly have a devastating impact on victims and survivors, and in many cases is itself criminal, there is a danger here of diverting attention away from men's physical and sexual abuse.

So, both official crime statistics and academic research fail to support popular claims of equality in this arena. In Kelly's (1996b: 43) words:

> One has to ask … why so many people want the prevalence [of sexual abuse by women] to be greater than research findings, why they insist that there has to be far more than we are currently aware of, and why the iceberg of hidden cases is always gender-specific.

The 'hidden iceberg' theory will be familiar to any of you who have ever spoken publicly on the issue of violence against women and faced the inevitable question, 'What about men battered/raped/ murdered by women?'. Answering this question is tricky. Certainly, such abuses do occur and we should not condone them. However, it is difficult not to think that the question is designed to be a distraction from dealing with those difficult questions posed by the systematic and institutionalised abuse of women by men. In a patriarchal society, women's violence simply does not mean the same thing as men's violence, as is demonstrated throughout this chapter. The discourse of equal opportunity violence, however, works to make gender invisible, irrelevant. As Cameron (1996: 26) writes:

> One response to feminism ... has been an urgent desire ... to frame all kinds of phenomenon [sic] in gender-neutral terms, as if differences in the positioning of men and women had now been totally eliminated. Battered husbands, male anorexics and violent female street gangs have all made their appearance under this regime of equal opportunities, and deliberately genderless terms like 'parenting', 'spousal abuse' and 'family violence' have proliferated. The result is to mystify the unequal relations which still exist between the sexes.

To claim that men and women are now equal in this sphere is also, of course, to present women's violence as the cost of feminism – that feminists demanded equality and got it in the shape of female serial killers, girl gangs and battered husbands. While equality was indeed the buzzword in **liberal feminist** circles in the 1970s, **radical feminists** – who developed the practical, political and theoretical responses to male violence – have always been far more interested in transforming patriarchy than gaining equality for women within it. As Cameron (1999: 80) reminds us, gendered violence is only possible within the context of patriarchy: 'a system in which social hierarchies are constructed and maintained by means of sexual exploitation and sexual terrorism'.

Against this background, it is hardly surprising that some feminists have felt ambivalent about publicly tackling the issue of women's violence (Kelly, 1991; 1996b). Those violent women who have been the focus of sustained feminist activism and commentary are, typically, those whose stories of violent agency are inextricably linked to accounts of victimisation (and who are considered later in this chapter). By remaining virtually silent about more troubling cases of female violence – such as the sexual murders in which Myra Hindley or Rosemary West participated – the dominant construction of these women as evil and incomprehensible has been allowed to stand unchallenged. Let me be clear at the outset that I am not interested in excusing what these women did. However, labelling them evil doesn't get us anywhere. As Belinda Morrissey (2003) notes, such labelling works to create a mythic, non-human (and, therefore, non-female) figure and points to the difficulty of resolving the identities of woman and violent agent. Acknowledging Hindley's and West's gender and agency provides us with a way both of holding them accountable for their actions and of challenging the naturalness of gender. To my mind, this is a fundamentally feminist project. Indeed, as Kelly notes, it is possible to tackle women's violence (and the representations of that violence) in the context of feminist theory. Women's violence is only a threat to an essentialist feminism – that is, a feminism that views men and women, masculinity and femininity, as fixed, unchanging, biologically based categories – which is an approach now largely rejected in feminist circles. Kelly (1996b: 36–7) continues:

> A feminism which begins from understanding gender as a social construct, which recognizes the variability with which gendered selves and individual biography combine, can locate women's use of violence within its existing framework

We can – and should – be sensitive to the social contexts in which men's and women's violence is possible and meaningful without condoning women's violence, denying its existence or exaggerating its prevalence (Renzetti, 1999). One thing we can say for sure: in a patriarchal society, women are never going to be deadlier than men, whatever lurid true crime titles might have us believe.

The cycle of violence

Rose West – who, in 1995, was found guilty of murdering ten young women – was both an abuser and a victim. Before she met husband Fred, there is evidence that she was sexually abused by both her father and grandfather and raped twice by unknown men. Her life with Fred involved prostitution and **pornography** as well as their joint participation in sexual abuse and murder (Burn, 1998). Rose's defence made little of this history and it garnered little public discussion. Cameron (1999: 70) notes that, while feminists were reluctant to speak publicly about the case (for reasons already discussed), privately many feminists believed that the relationship between what was done to Rose and what she went on to do deserved more attention than it got.

To try to raise this question was, however, to be accused of trying to excuse what Rose did. Why was it so difficult to represent Rose as both abuser and victim without falling into this trap?

The relationship between women's experiences of victimisation and their acts of violence is a complex one that feminists and other theorists have grappled with in a variety of contexts. The idea that abusive behaviour can be explained by prior experience of being abused is not a new one. The so-called 'cycle of abuse' has been a popular means of explaining (and excusing) male violence and has been challenged by feminist critics on a number of grounds. First, the idea of a cycle is problematic: the abused child who becomes a child abuser is not repeating their experience but reversing it. Further, if the original abuser was male, how can we explain it if, as an adult, that child goes on to abuse girls or women (the most common scenario)? The cycle also tends to lump all forms of violence together. How can this help us to understand why a physically abused boy, for example, goes on to sexually abuse others? At a more basic level, the cycle of abuse just doesn't add up as most abused children do not go on to abuse and females are over-represented as victims of abuse but under-represented as perpetrators (Kelly, 1996a).

While the idea of a cycle of abuse is clearly flawed, prior experience of abuse is a part of many male abusers' pasts. For example, FBI research suggests that up to 70% of male sexual murderers have themselves been abused (cited by Cameron, 1999: 75). The association of masculinity with power, control and autonomy in our culture (established in Chapter 3) does, however, open up another way of understanding the relationship between men's victimisation and violence. Is it not possible that the abused-boy-turned-abuser does not seek revenge on others, but sees violence as a means of asserting himself and, specifically of seeing himself as a man – powerful, in control (Cameron, 1999: 77–8)? As Cameron (1999: 79) points out, that so few abused girls follow this path can be at least partly explained by the fact that the imaginative identifications possible for abused girls and boys are different:

> Women and men are not in the same position, even when both are suffering the most hideous abuse; for they live in a world that treats their suffering differently. It is both more important, culturally speaking, for men to transcend it, and more conceivable that they could. Masculinity is by cultural convention incompatible with victim status, whereas femininity is not. Women in patriarchal society are given little or no sense of entitlement and power, and are thus less likely than most men to feel trapped in the victim position.

Thus, Cameron (1999: 79) concludes:

> if the most pertinent answer to the question 'why do so many men abuse?' is 'because they can', at least part of the answer to the corresponding question, 'why do so few women abuse?' may be, 'because they usually can't'.

This might then explain why the cycle of abuse is so problematic in explaining women's violence. Accounts of male perpetrators transcending the abuse in their own lives do not trouble gender categories as the abused boy moves from a position of subjection to one of subjectivity – man's proper place in a patriarchal society. For Rose West to make a similar shift is problematic not only in terms of her violation of criminal law but also in terms of her illegitimate usurption of the male (subject) position. This may help us to understand why there have not been more Rose Wests and it also takes us some way towards explaining why so few popular accounts are prepared to see Rose as both abuser and victim.

As already argued, women's violence is profoundly threatening for patriarchal society because it challenges the naturalness of the gender binarism on which that society depends. Nicole Ward Jouve (1993: 20), in her analysis of representations of an infamous French murder case, further suggests that mainstream representations work to contain this threat either by denying the woman's agency or denying her gender. In West's case, her failures as a woman, her deviance from feminine norms, were continually reiterated in popular accounts. To be a victim is to be feminine. To see Rose as feminine is to acknowledge that gender is not a fixed or essential category. Rose, therefore, could not be seen as a victim.

Morrissey's (2003: 25) examination of media and press discourses about violent women takes the troubled question of women's agency a step further. For Morrissey, the characterisation of women like Rose West as monsters or almost mythical figures of evil is not only a denial of gender but also an agency denial. Morrissey (2003: 25) writes, 'The agency denial which takes place in this technique is specifically that of *human* agency. The murderess is considered to have acted, but not as a human woman'. In rendering Rose West (and others like her) monstrous, by labelling her evil, we absolve her of agency and responsibility by denying her decision to act. Representing Rose as inherently evil and suppressing the knowledge of her own victimisation also, crucially, allows us to separate Rose from the broader social context in which her actions became meaningful. In contrast, to admit the possibility that Rose could also be (or have been) a victim requires an acknowledgement of the broader abusive culture of which

Rose and Fred were a part and their 25 Cromwell Street home the centre. As Cameron (1999: 71) notes, this was 'a culture which concentrated on every conceivable form of **sexual violence** against women and children: pornography, prostitution, rape and murder'. This culture of violence thrived because so many men participated in it – the men who used Rose and the girls in prostitution, the men who bought or used Fred's home-made pornography, the men who took pleasure in Fred's tales of sex and sexual violence and the men who took their turn in sexually assaulting other women living at 25 Cromwell Street. To see Rose as a victim (as well as an abuser) would require acknowledgement of these men's complicity. Instead, these men became witnesses to Rose's sexual perversion in a number of tabloid and true crime accounts, while Rose's girlhood victimisation was recast as evidence of her burgeoning sexual deviance. For example, Gordon Burn (1998: 118), in an otherwise thoughtful account, writes that Rose:

> had been having a sexual relationship with her father for two years at least before leaving [home]. Her father had started having sex with Rose when she was only thirteen.

Contrast this with a later passage from the same book (pp. 226–7) dealing with Rose and her father's sexual abuse of Fred's daughter:

> Rose started to force Anna-Marie to have sex with her and Bill Letts [Rose's father] started to sleep with Anna-Marie at Cromwell Street when she was twelve.

The language used to describe Bill's incestuous abuse disguises the abusive nature of his acts and amplifies Rose's deviance. His actions – including his abuse of Rose – are represented as sex not violence, while she is cast as a deviant (violent and not violated) woman – a seductive daughter and abusive stepmother.

If there was much at stake in denying Rose West's victimisation (and thus her femininity), representations of other violent women work equally hard to deny their agency by focusing on their gender. The account of Karla Homolka provided by Terry Manners in his true crime volume *Deadlier Than the Male* (1995) illustrates this point very clearly. Homolka, like West, acted alongside her husband (Paul Bernardo) in sexually torturing and murdering young girls. Homolka was also a victim of her husband's violence. For Manners at least, Homolka is a credible victim. He prefaces his chapter (1995: 333) with a quotation from Homolka's yearbook, which paints a picture of a young, romantic woman depending on her lover/abuser for her sense of self:

'Paul is the greatest influence in my life. My wildest dream
is to marry him and see him more than twice a week.'

Manners then positions Homolka alongside those traumatised by the
crimes – noting that reporters, mothers of the victims, hardened
police officers and Homolka herself all broke down in tears as the
details of the killings emerged at her trial.

While Manners does not go as far as to excuse Homolka, she is
clearly placed from the outset as a romantic, a witness and a victim.
Manners goes on to detail Homolka's meticulous care over her physical
appearance, her middle-class family, her dream wedding, her devo-
tion to her husband, her pride in their home and her love of animals.
In other words, her conformity to gender norms makes her claims of
victimisation more credible and her involvement in sexual murder
incredible. In describing the crimes and the trial, Manners positions
Homolka as constantly reacting to the behaviour of others. She never
emerges as a conscious agent. She may have an 'evil secret' (p. 337),
but she herself is not evil – rather, she is 'completely in her husband's
power ... almost zombie-like in his company' (p. 356).

Manners' is not the only version of Homolka's involvement.
Indeed, there are other accounts that paint Homolka in a very different light. What is significant for our purposes here is how the victimisation and victimising narratives are made mutually exclusive. As
Morrissey (2003: Chapter 5) notes in a detailed discussion of representations of Homolka, her involvement in these horrendous crimes
is literally incomprehensible to many commentators. Those, like
Manners, who attempt to fit her into the 'victim' frame must ignore
or distort crucial evidence in the case to do so. In contrast, Bernardo
remained comprehensible throughout the investigation and trial, not
least because there was (as we saw in Chapter 3) an existing language
to describe him and a tradition of male sexual murder (and its representation) into which he could be placed. As a result, Bernardo's
crimes were naturalised – there was no need to explain his crimes and
certainly no need to explain why a man behaved in this way.

My purpose here is not to debate the facts of these cases or the accuracy of individual reports, but to illustrate the way in which women's
credibility as perpetrators and as victims of violence are absolutely
intertwined in popular accounts. There is a pronounced reluctance to
see women as both and simultaneously victims and perpetrators. If
the victim story predominates, their agency as perpetrators – however
contingent that may be – seems to be incomprehensible (Homolka
the zombie),[2] but if the perpetrator story predominates, then they
cannot simultaneously be positioned as victims (13-year-old Rose had
'sex' with her father). Such representations certainly illustrate the

enduring anxiety around women's capacity for violence, but do little to help us understand why these women become involved with abusive men and why they themselves sexually abuse other women and may, indeed, take pleasure in that abuse.

Women who kill their abusers

Women's involvement in sexual murder is rare. However, the gendered constructions of victimisation and violence observed in these accounts of the West and Homolka cases can also be observed in the representation of women who kill (or harm) the men who abuse them.

Clearly, women who kill (or harm) the men who abuse them are morally a million miles away from Rose West or Karla Homolka. Feminist campaigners have explicitly linked women's killing of abusive men to their histories of victimisation and have fought – often successfully – for justice for these women (Radford, 1993; Stanko and Scully, 1996). Campaign groups such as Justice for Women and Southall Black Sisters in Britain have long recognised that strategic use of the news media has concrete benefits in raising awareness both about individual cases and the ways in which the legal system fails women (MacNeill, 1991; Bindel et al., 1995).

However, as they acknowledge, while the media are often sympathetic in individual cases (Morrissey, 2003: 90), working with the media does not always ensure that a feminist analysis emerges in print. In particular, there remains a tendency to see the women as either victims or conscious agents, and to focus on extreme cases where a woman has killed while demonstrating a reluctance to enter into more complex debates about domestic violence (Bindel et al., 1995: 74–5). We saw a similar reluctance to represent the everyday nature of domestic violence in Chapter 3 and the focus on stories resulting in extreme physical injury and/or death ensures that these cases are seen as bizarre stories of individual deviance and desperation (Morrissey, 2003: 92).

Moreover, women who kill or otherwise harm those who abuse them (or their children) are – like the female victims of murder, rape and domestic violence discussed in Chapter 3 – most likely to be sympathetically treated if, in other ways, they occupy (or can be made to occupy) their proper feminine place. Noting how 'battered women's syndrome' works – or does not – in defending women who kill, Jean Filetti (2001) compares four US women who attempted to use the defence. Where the defence was successfully employed – that is, where it was accepted in court and by the press – the accused were primarily associated with the domestic, their appearances were described as extremely feminine and their otherwise exemplary conduct as wives was stressed. Where the defence was not successful, the women did not 'look like victims' and had, in various ways, refused the 'protection' of men, marriage and the domestic sphere. One of the women in this latter category was Aileen Wuornos – dubbed, by many, as the 'first female serial killer'. That Wuornos was a prostitute and a lesbian was used, in many popular accounts, to render implausible her claim that she was acting in self-defence following actual or attempted rapes (Hart, 1994; Filetti, 2001). Although feminists were, on the whole, slow to take up Wuornos' case, Giobbe (in Hart, 1994: 142) notes that her claims of prior assault are perfectly credible in the context of the sexual abuse, rape and battery that characterise prostitutes' lives. Again, there are echoes here of the construction of rape victims as virgins and vamps (Benedict, 1992) – their credibility and right not to be raped judged according to their appearance, sexual history and class or economic status.

Even in those cases where the accused woman does fit the victim stereotype, there is an obvious tension. If the woman was so helpless, then how can we explain her decisive action? This apparent contradiction has been central to feminist debates about the use of diminished responsibility and so-called 'battered women's syndrome' in defending women accused of murdering the men who abused them (see, for example, Browne, 1987; Radford, 1993; Bindel et al., 1995; Justice for Women, n.d.; Morrissey, 2003). Feminists have been wary of medicalising women's responses to male violence, arguing that to do so disguises the social contexts in which violence appears to be their only option. Moreover, the 'syndrome' attempts to universalise battered women's experiences, with the result that those women whose experiences don't fit are rendered doubly incomprehensible (as victims and as agents). As Jones (1991: 363) argues:

> [battered women who kill] may be acquitted, but not because reasonable women, like reasonable men, are *justified* in defending themselves from attack. Rather, like women acquitted of husband-killing in the nineteenth-century by reason of insanity, women supposedly afflicted with the battered woman's syndrome may be 'let off' because they're 'sick'. Their 'crime' is psychologized and their defense becomes a kind of special pleading centered not in their social conditions but in their impaired psyche and their sex.

Yet, medicalising and individualising her actions is, in numerous mainstream accounts, the favoured way to reconcile the apparent incompatibility of the helpless victim's momentary agency. This focus on the woman's psychology marginalises the man's abusive behaviour and denies the legitimacy of women's self-defence and the existence of women's rage, containing the more general threat that such violence might be held to represent. The most important point to grasp here is that while, as we have seen, accounts of men's violence may seek to abnegate their responsibility for their actions by focusing on the culpability of their victims, women's responsibility for violence is determined primarily by their own behaviour and character. In other words, whether victim, perpetrator or both, women are the objects of media (and criminal) investigation and they are judged first and foremost as women.

To illustrate some of these issues, I want to examine an article published in the regional daily the *Yorkshire Post* in 2002. As noted in Chapter 3, domestic violence cases receive little attention in the national press and this case only received sustained coverage in the regional press where its proximity guaranteed its newsworthiness (Greer, 2003b). It is important to emphasise here that I am not attempting a comprehensive review of the coverage of this case. Rather, I am interested in exploring how women's violence is explained and contained in the context of one specific report. The article I am going to focus on (*Yorkshire Post*, 28 May, 2002) is a post-verdict account of the trial of Janet Charlton, who killed her lover, Daniel O'Brien, with an axe. Charlton, was cleared of murder but convicted of manslaughter on the grounds of provocation, stating in her defence that O'Brien had abused her and threatened to abuse her daughter. On the one hand, then, the verdict reflects an awareness and acceptance of feminist arguments about the impact of sustained domestic violence on a woman's decision to kill her abuser. However, the report relies on age-old stereotypes to undermine Charlton's credibility as a victim and, arguably, suggest that she was getting away with murder:

> MYSTERY OF WHAT TURNED COOL BLONDE INTO A RAGING KILLER
>
> OUTSIDE court she looked picture perfect. With her dark suit, starched shirt, silver-rimmed glasses and blonde ponytail tied smartly back from her carefully made-up face, Jan Charlton cut a cool persona.
>
> Before her earlier court appearances she had smiled and joked with photographers, never rattled, always controlled. Yet a jury was to hear in shocking detail how Charlton lost that control to devastating effect.
>
> This was the woman, the former escort girl, who, while her three-year-old daughter Amy played in the sunshine downstairs, brutally hacked her lover Daniel O'Brien to

death with a fireman's axe as he knelt naked, gagged, and blindfolded on the bedroom floor – and then resumed her normal life as if nothing had happened.

Unlike the accounts of male killers examined in Chapter 3, Charlton's guilt (or innocence) seems to be 'read off' her appearance. The 'cool blonde', as Helen Birch (1993b: 50–4) argues, has long been linked to both sex and violence – from the filmic *femme fatale* to the Nazi Irma Geese or the notorious Myra Hindley. The *Yorkshire Post's* 'cool blonde' carries this symbolic weight – she is a sexual, mysterious, unemotional woman using her sexuality to get what she wants. Her image is further manipulated to emphasise her guilt (and, hence, her agency) at the expense of her femininity: she is cold ('dark', 'silver', 'blonde', 'cool'), masculine ('dark suit', 'starched shirt') and calculating (the 'carefully made-up' face). The control she appears to exert over her image is, of course, in sharp contrast to the loss of control she claims to have experienced when she killed her lover.

There are two related issues here. First, if Charlton was a man, we simply wouldn't be discussing his appearance at all – switch the names and genders in the above extract and this becomes clear. Second, the description of her appearance serves a clear purpose in marking Charlton's gender and legal transgressions – even using different adjectives to describe Charlton would fundamentally change the tone of this piece. As Jean Filetti (2001) and others have observed, women in the dock are frequently judged – both by juries and by the press – according to their appearance and demeanour, according, in other words, to the extent to which they are made to seem characteristically feminine.

Telling a different story

Without changing any significant details relating to the criminal case, rewrite the extract from the *Yorkshire Post* to make it:

- appear more sympathetic to Charlton
- neither favourable nor unfavourable in its description of Charlton.

What aspects of the report do you have to change in order to achieve these different effects?

Charlton's mystery is, from the outset, constructed around a series of apparent oppositions: controlled/out of control; mother/escort; respectable/sexual; sex object/killer. This unstable characterisation has much in common with the *femme fatale* of **film noir** (see Chapter 5) and, like her celluloid predecessors, Charlton is portrayed as being able to control and manipulate others by means of her performances of femininity (changing her appearance, taking on different roles). Further, it is implicit that these performances disguise her violence (from the photographers, her blindfolded lover, her daughter and, ultimately, from the jury) and so the most obvious opposition – that of victim and perpetrator – is missing. Charlton's claim that she acted in fear of her life is not presented until much later in the article, by which point her apparent instability and unreliability has rendered suspect her claims of victimisation.

In contrast, O'Brien's helplessness is emphasised in this article – he is naked, gagged and blindfolded – while Charlton's claims that he was a 'controlling monster' are held over to the end of the article. Her claim that he brought the axe to the bedroom (central to her defence) is not reported. Rather, we simply learn that he would 'sulk' and 'complain' if he didn't get his own way and that Charlton was 'unhappy'. 'Sulking', with its childish connotations, hardly makes O'Brien a credible threat. Nor is being 'unhappy' an adequate provocation for murder. In this respect, the report mirrors the inadequacies of the criminal justice system itself in failing to place Charlton's actions in a meaningful context – that is, in the history of the abusive relationship (Lees, 1992; Radford, 1993; Bindel et al., 1995). This provides a stark contrast to reports of men's violence against women, which – as we saw in Chapter 3 – endlessly revolve around the guilt or innocence of the victim. Indeed, a comparison of the Charlton report with another story carried in the same edition of the *Yorkshire Post* exemplifies the difference. In an article headlined, 'TRAGEDY FOR "BEAUTIFUL FAMILY" AS MAN STRANGLES WIFE AND THEN HANGS HIMSELF', the murder of a woman by her estranged husband is presented as a two victim story (see Chapter 3). The emphasis is on the murdered woman's culpability (her decision to leave her husband of many years, their children and their home to begin a new relationship), while the killer's behaviour is decriminalised – described as a 'tragedy' and 'terrible domestic incident'.

In contrast to the passive 'estranged husband', the emphasis placed on Charlton's choices – from her carefully constructed appearance to her decision to divorce her husband and have sex for money – means that killing O'Brien is never credibly presented as her only option. Rather, the killing is represented as one of a series of unconventional, selfish and unfeminine choices that she makes. Her gender transgressions, combined with her agency in other aspects of her life, mean that Charlton cannot be seen as a credible victim, but is, rather, shown to be a cold killer and an unnatural woman.

Finally, it is notable that three of the women I have discussed in this chapter – Rose West, Aileen Wuornos and Janet Charlton – were involved in the sex industry and this involvement is frequently referred to in reports of their, otherwise very different, murder trials. However, in all three cases, the link between prostitution and violence against women is downplayed, although the abuse of women in the form of prostitution has been extensively documented (see Farley, 2003). Rather, it is implied that the double life of the prostitute woman renders her criminally and morally suspect. Here, too, it is the woman who is the focus of investigation.

Doing it

In the *Yorkshire Post*'s coverage of Janet Charlton's trial, the two labels most consistently and prominently applied to Charlton are 'former escort girl' and 'axe killer'. It is the apparent connection between these two roles – one sexual, one violent – with which this section is concerned.

Women's sexuality has long been linked – in both popular and scientific discourses – to their potential for violence. Lynda Hart, in *Fatal Women: Lesbian Sexuality and the Mark of Aggression* (1994), argues that to desire – as to commit acts of violence – requires a subjectivity that women in a patriarchal society have traditionally been denied. Women are supposed to be desired objects (a passive position), not desiring subjects (an active position). While any expression of women's active desire can disrupt this equation – as we saw in relation to Charlton – lesbianism is, by definition, disruptive as lesbian desire positions women in both roles (desired object and desiring subject).

Tracing the linking of lesbianism with aggression through medical, criminological and **psychoanalytic** discourses from the late nineteenth and early twentieth centuries, Hart notes that the lesbian was marked as deviant not because of her object choice, but because of her (masculine) subjectivity. Further, Hart (1994: 9) argues, 'Lesbian identity has served many functions, among them as a site where women's aggression has been displaced.'

The figure of the lesbian haunts representations of women's violence. This is not to argue that violent women are necessarily represented as women who desire other women (although such narratives are certainly exploited), but that they are connotatively associated with patriarchal constructions of lesbianism. That is, the violent woman (like the lesbian) wants what men have – subjectivity, desire, aggression. The violent woman and the lesbian are also linked by the equation of their desire with death – that is, both are non-procreative, non-functional in hetero-patriarchal terms.

Bisexuality carries an additional range of connotations. The bisexual occupies a space between boundaries. If lesbian desire is often masculinised, bisexual desire slips between binary oppositions of both gender and sexuality. The fluidity of desire is popularly assumed to be both promiscuous (masculine) and a sign of instability (feminine). Further, as Marjorie Garber (1995) notes, since the advent of the AIDS crisis, bisexuality has increasingly been associated in popular representations with danger and death – the bisexual as 'polluter' of the heterosexual world, 'murdering' by stealth, deception and promiscuous sexual practice.

In practical terms, this means that women who are (or appear to be) lesbian or bisexual are more likely to be marked as criminal than conventionally heterosexual women. So, for example, in the early 1990s, 90% of the women on Death Row in the US were lesbians (Scholder, 1993: 41). In the UK, Ann Lloyd (1995) has demonstrated how the rehabilitation of criminal women detained in high-security hospitals is measured in terms of their successful deployment of heterosexual feminine behaviour. Curing these women of any traces of lesbianism or bisexuality is believed to cure them of violence. In contrast, women who fit (or can be made to fit) conventional notions of heterosexual femininity may be more likely to be treated with leniency (Jones, 1991; Kennedy, 1992; Filetti, 2001).

To illustrate how the linking of women's sexuality with criminality functions in news discourse, I turn once more to the British *Daily Mail* and a report published shortly after the conclusion of Rose West's trial (23 November, 1995):

HAND IN HAND WITH HINDLEY: ROSE WEST'S AMAZING FRIENDSHIP WITH MOORS MURDERESS
ROSE WEST and Myra Hindley have formed a macabre friendship in jail, it was revealed last night.

The two most evil women in Britain – both openly bisexual – have been seen holding hands in Durham prison.

They were drawn together by shared religion, and the 51-year-old Moors Murderess became West's confidante and adviser. They have made unsupervised visits to each other's cell, and prayed together in the jail chapel.

Hindley even sent a 'Good Luck' card before the start of the 31-day trial at Wincester Crown Court which has appalled the nation.

Are they the 'most evil women' in Britain because they are 'openly bisexual' and physically intimate? That representations of Hindley and West – as individuals as well as in the *Mail*'s fantasy of their coupling – endlessly revolve around questions of sex, sexuality and gender points to what is symbolically at stake: their violation of heterosexual femininity.

Hindley's relationships with women in prison were tabloid fodder for three decades. Her bisexuality was implicitly linked with her criminality to provide evidence that she had not changed and was still a threat. Reports of Hindley's prison relationships tended to use a heterosexist frame to position her in a male or masculinised role *vis-à-vis* her lover: she was predatory, manipulative; her lovers, weak and naïve (Birch, 1993b). Rose West, of course, hardly qualifies as weak or naïve, but in the *Mail* article she is nevertheless presented as Hindley's younger *protégé*. Indeed, as Cameron notes (1996), reports of West's trial continually positioned her in relation to Hindley in attempts to construct a category of female sex murderer from which to make sense of West's crimes and, we might add, to make sense of her desire. Their bisexuality is key here. As both Hindley and West were criminally linked with their male lovers, their relationships with women are portrayed as opportunistic and manipulative – they are not real lesbians. Bisexuality is thus made to symbolise instability, insatiable sexual appetites and an ability to deceive (Garber, 1995; Newitz and Sandell, 1994).

While Hindley's relationships with women post-incarceration functioned as evidence of continued evil, West's sexual practices prior to her arrest were the focus of much of the press coverage of her trial. You could be forgiven for thinking that Rose was on trial for sex not sexual murder as her activities with consenting partners (lesbian orgies, inter-racial sex, noisy lovemaking) were routinely presented as evidence of her depravity. Rose's ex-lovers and clients gave interviews to the tabloids, commenting on her love of sex and her satisfying and varied sexual performances (*The Sun* (*Crime of the Century Special*), 25 November, 1995):

> Rose was pleased to oblige when white travelling salesman Charlie Murphy, 33, telephoned.
>
> Charlie called round to see her at No. 25. He explained: 'She said it was £10 for everything. Rose was wearing a flimsy pink outfit fastened at the crotch.'
>
> 'She was plump with full breasts and knew how to sexually excite a man. That first time she undressed me slowly, then we had oral sex.'

> *'I was there for three quarters of an hour and loved every minute.'*
>
> 'It was impossible for two human beings to copulate in more ways. She was brilliant. The best sex ever.' (emphasis in original)

In contrast, Fred was routinely presented as a sexual inadequate. In a companion piece to *The Sun*'s profile of Rose, quoted above, women who were sexually abused by Fred were called on to comment on his sexual performance:

> West was obsessed by sex but was not an accomplished lover. One victim spoke of the act being over very quickly – with West in tears.

There are several points to make about this. First, the evidence of Rose's sexual depravity comes from the men who used her in prostitution, while the evidence of Fred's sexual depravity is taken from women who were sexually abused by him. This works to make the abuse of women by men invisible on both counts as prostitution is represented as fulfilling women's sexual needs, while the testimony of women survivors is presented as a sexual narrative. Second, in representing Rose, there is no need to be explicit about her involvement in sexual abuse – her sexual agency, promiscuity and bisexuality are confirmation enough of her criminality. Further underlining her deviance, Rose's lusts are later reported to have tainted family life – spoiling Sunday dinner, wrecking a family holiday, embarrassing the in-laws – and these disruptions (as much as her actual abuse of her children) mark her as deviant. Quite obviously, then, there is a sexual double standard in operation as Rose's depravity is in her sexual activity and pleasure, while Fred's in his inability to live up to a virile masculine ideal.

This is by no means unique to the West case. A more recent example of these sexual double standards can be found in the representation of Ian Huntley and Maxine Carr, both at the time of their arrest and, later, during their trial in relation to the murders of Jessica Chapman and Holly Wells. In companion pieces in *The Sun* (19 August, 2002), published before the couple were individually charged, Huntley and Carr's sexual behaviour comes under scrutiny. Like Fred, Huntley is portrayed as a poor lover, 'ordinary' and 'less interested in sex than in being control [sic].' In contrast, Carr's ex-boyfriend makes claims about her sexual performance that echo Charlie Murphy's boast about his experience with Rose West:

'She was a good-looking girl and knew how to tease the lads. The sex was great. She was very adventurous in bed and out of it. We had sex in every position. It was anything goes in the bedroom.'

As in the West case, the problem here is not the (in)accuracy of the accounts, but the gendered construction of sexual deviance. This, remember, is before any charges were made against the couple and it is possible to argue that their gender-inappropriate sexual roles functioned here as a substitute for concrete evidence of their guilt. Importantly, from the moment of their arrest, the couple was also continually marked as being different from, or outside of, the family, community and nation so repeatedly invoked in the extensive coverage of the girls' abduction and murder. So, numerous accounts reminded us that the couple was new to the area, that Huntley's ex-wife married his brother, that his mother had a lesbian relationship while estranged from her husband and that Carr was brought up by her mother and estranged from her father. These details worked as further evidence of the couple's otherness and likely guilt and fit a familiar pattern in attempting to explain male violence by focusing on women's behaviour as Carr, Huntley's ex-wife, ex-girlfriends, mother and her lover all came under intense scrutiny.

Huntley was subsequently found guilty of the abduction and murder of the girls. Carr was found guilty of perverting the course of justice but not of the more serious charge of aiding an offender. Nevertheless, during the trial, tabloid coverage made sensational links between Maxine and Myra (Hindley) and, after the trial, Carr's infidelity was presented as a motive for the murders as she was pictured kissing another man in a nightclub in another town the night Huntley murdered the girls. Indeed, headlines such as 'KISS OF DEATH' (see Figure 4.1), positioned Carr as the agent of death. Moreover, here, too, Carr's consensual sexual practice is equated with Huntley's history of sexual abuse – she kissed, he raped and killed – and also arguably works to position Huntley's prior crimes of sexual violence within a sexual frame (see Figure 4.2, and Chapter 3).

So far I have concentrated primarily on linguistic analysis, but the violent woman's rejection of appropriate object status can also be rendered visually. There is, for example, an infamous photograph of Myra Hindley, taken upon her arrest, that, for many commentators, has become 'synonymous with the idea of feminine evil' (Birch, 1993b: 32). In the photograph – endlessly reproduced since – Hindley is a young woman with chiselled features, a square jaw and bleached blonde hair, staring with dark eyes from beneath a heavy fringe (see Figure 4.3). Birch (1993b: 32) argues:

Figure 4.1 *Female sexuality as criminal – Maxine Carr as the agent of death* (Daily Star, *18 December, 2003*).

that image has become symbolic of the threat of femininity unleashed from its traditional bonds of goodness, tenderness, nurturance. It strikes at the heart of our fears about unruly women, about criminality, and about the way gender is constructed.

Figure 4.2   *Female sexuality as criminal – she kissed, he raped and killed (*The Mirror, *18 December, 2003).*

Both in this photograph and in written descriptions of her appearance in court, Hindley (like Charlton) is the inscrutable blonde, a *femme fatale* who wears femininity like a mask. In the photograph – taken, according to Hindley, after four sleepless nights (Birch, 1993b: 53) – that 'mask' is slipping – she has bags under her eyes, the roots of her bleached blonde hair are showing, the lighting emphasises the hard

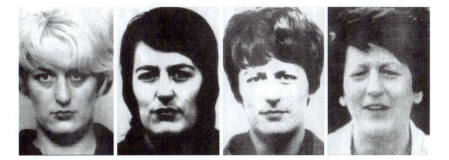

Figure 4.3 *The changing faces of Myra Hindley (*The Observer, *17 November, 2002). The photograph on the far left is the infamous shot taken just after Hindley's arrest in 1966.*

angles of her face and she is staring directly into the camera. The physical imperfections, the lighting, the pose are most often associated with photographs of men (Dyer, 1982). Thus, we could argue that the fascination with this image lies in Hindley's apparent usurption of the male role – she is both violent and specular subject, challenging ideas of female (hetero-)sexual objectification.

This mugshot remained the dominant image of Hindley throughout the 36 years of her imprisonment. Later photographs released to the press by her supporters were published but interpreted by the tabloids as further evidence of her ability to deceive. Indeed, on her death in 2002, a number of papers presented photographs of Hindley through the ages and drew attention to her 'changing faces' (see Figure 4.3). Even behind bars, the implication is that Hindley retained her ability to produce herself as subject, attempting to manipulate, deceive and seduce in image and argument.

Hindley and West were, without doubt, involved in horrendous crimes. Our critical analysis of the ways in which they have subsequently been represented should do nothing to detract from this. However, it can provide us with some sense of why these crimes, by these women, have retained such a powerful hold on the public imagination. As Soothill and Walby (1991) found in their study of sex crime in the news, Hindley continued to attract more attention than contemporary murderers convicted of equally heinous crimes and – nearly four decades after her crimes – Hindley's death was front-page news across Britain. Inherent in these intense reactions to Hindley (as to West) is a revulsion that a woman should be involved in the murder of children. This, more than any other aspect of women's violence, seems to turn the natural order on its head.

The maternal instinct and the bleeding mad

Although Myra Hindley was not literally a mother, Cameron (1996: 25) argues that 'she was treated as a "crypto-mother" because of the unquestioned cultural tendency to conflate femininity and maternity'. The greater repugnance felt towards Hindley than towards Brady thus arose from the conviction that women have a natural instinct to protect and nurture children. That Hindley – in the infamous taperecording of the torture and murder of ten-year-old Lesley Ann Downey – can be heard threatening a girl who is begging for her mother, led many commentators to explicitly argue that Hindley's crime was worse than Brady's. The juxtaposition of the bad pseudo-mother with the good mother of the children she killed remained a feature of the Hindley story throughout her incarceration.[3] As Birch (1993b: 54), writing prior to the death of Downey's mother and of Hindley herself, notes:

> The public duel between Myra Hindley and Ann West, mother of Lesley Ann Downey, that has raged in the tabloid press has become a kind of modern morality play, starring the 'bad' mother ... who killed children, and the 'good' mother, whose 'innocent' fantasy of cosy family life has been destroyed by the brutal murder of her daughter. Horribly exploitative as these excavations into Mrs West's personal tragedy are, none the less, each time the press seizes on a new Hindley story – particularly if it pertains to the possibility of her eventual release – Ann West is drafted in on the flimsiest of pretexts, to give the public the condemnation it wants ...[4] the spectacle of the grieving mother pitted against the 'devil's daughter', as West has called Hindley, serves the purpose of reminding us of what 'natural' femininity is – and, significantly, what it is not. In this black-and-white drama there is no space for a third term; as woman terrorizes woman, the man is written out.

Ann West publicly and repeatedly stated that if Hindley was ever freed from prison, she herself would kill her. This mother's threat, of course, was understandable within a discourse of femininity – that is, denied the opportunity to protect her own child, she would protect others and ensure justice for her daughter. This is the one area in which women's rage and violence is popularly accepted – from the avenging mother in Hollywood films such as *The Hand That Rocks the Cradle* (Hanson, 1992) to mothers venting their anger outside the trials of paedophiles and murderers of children. However, mothers concerned about the abuse of children within their own families are rarely publicly heard (although mothers who do nothing to prevent such abuse are roundly vilified). In other words, mothers' rage is culturally acceptable when it can be used to bolster the (nuclear) family.

Unlike Hindley, Rose West was literally a mother, a mother who murdered one of her daughters and sexually abused and tortured her other children. In coverage of the case, Rose's involvement in the murder of her eldest daughter, Heather, seems to eclipse all the other horrors in which she and Fred are implicated (Cameron, 1996; 1999). Further, there is a repeated emphasis on Rose's failures as a mother so that Cameron (1996: 29) suggests that it sometimes seems as though Rose was on trial as a mother and not as a murderer.

However, while Rose's monstrosity is inextricably linked to her mothering (or failure to mother), Fred's failures as a father generate little comment. If anything, it is Fred's failure to regulate his wives' sexuality and so 'father' the children in the first place that is at issue (both his wives had children to other men). *The Sun* (25 November, 1995), suggests that murdered Heather 'was the product of an incestuous union' between Rose and her father, repeating Rose's brother's claim that 'Fred never killed his own'. Fred, the mass murderer and serial abuser of women and girls, thus emerges as a protector of sorts: 'Despite all that happened to Anna [his daughter with his first wife] she was never murdered.' Not only is Fred's abuse of his daughters minimised (after all, he never murdered them) but also Rose's deviance is amplified – it is her children who could not be protected. Perhaps, as Cameron (1996: 26) suggests, it is simply more understandable that a father should behave like Fred than a mother should behave like Rose. Bronwyn Naylor (2001b: 173) observes a similar silence regarding 'the failures of the fathers' and argues, 'the law has tended to treat motherhood as obligation, as responsibility, while characterising fatherhood as choice and opportunity.'

In Chapter 3, I noted the press's reluctance to deal with stories of child sexual abuse within families. However, an Australian study of press reporting of all forms of child abuse (Wilczynski and Sinclair, 1998, cited by Naylor, 2001b) adds an important caveat to that finding – namely, that most media reports of sole female abusers deal with familial abuse, while most coverage of sole male abusers deal with non-familial abuse. Further, as we saw in Chapter 3, familial abuse was reframed in the late 1980s as abuse to the family as a result of inappropriate (and often implicitly feminist) intervention or therapy. Both of these findings point to women's position within the family as the focus of key concern and leave men's position relatively unexamined.

There is, then, a real ambivalence about women's capacity to mother in Western culture. On the one hand, becoming and being a mother is consistently represented as the most natural thing a woman can do and, indeed, as a result of pregnancy and childbearing, women are culturally identified with nature.[5] On the other hand, pregnancy and childbearing have long been seen as sites of female power, a power that men have attempted to erase or usurp via religious, medical and legal surveillance and management of women's menstruating, pregnant or lactating bodies.

So, women's capacity to bear and mother children is culturally inscribed as both natural (biological, instinctual) and pathological (an unfeminine usurption of power). This ambivalence has an important role in telling stories about women who kill or harm children. On the one hand, this is the most unnatural thing a woman can do; on the other, it brings to the surface men's fear of women's (powerful) bodies.

To illustrate this ambivalence, we need only return to Rose West and the representation of her 'monstrous' maternal body, both giving and destroying life. A number of press reports specifically locate Rose's deviance in her body – her lusts, her fertility, above all, her femaleness. For example, a report in *The Sun* on 23 November, 1995 claimed:

> as she grew into full womanhood Rose turned more and more to prostitution and sordid lesbian orgies ...
> Fred once confided: 'When Rose was pregnant her lesbian tendencies were at their strongest. I had to go out and get her a girl. She gets urges that have to be satisfied.'

In this and other, similar, accounts Rose represents the threat of the undiscplined female body. Not only are puberty, pregnancy and her pleasure in pregnancy linked with her growing appetite for sex and violence, but her excessive body is presented as a site of fascination, embarrassment and fear for those who encountered her. Rose's apparent pleasure in exhibitionism is repeatedly mentioned – the close-up photographs of her genitals displayed at 25 Cromwell Street, the flimsy clothing she wore for her clients, her repeated exposures of herself in public, her noisy sex sessions. Her body, like her sexual appetite, is excessive and excessively female. Rose West is not unique in this respect. In the context of a detailed discussion of a very different Australian maternal child killing, Naylor (2001b) similarly notes that the focus on the excesses of the mother's body and sexuality works to position her as a bad mother and, hence, criminal.

Indeed, women's bodies – particularly their reproductive capacities – have long figured in accounts of women's criminality and violence. For example, Susan Edwards (1984) notes that in the mid nineteenth century, crimes from shoplifting to murder were ascribed to problems of menstruation and women's attendant lack of psychic control.

In the late nineteenth century, menstruation, pregnancy, childbirth, and lactation were all linked to insanity and, hence, criminality. As Ann Jones (1991: 171) writes in relation to this period, 'Almost naturally insane, a woman might easily be a natural criminal.' This construction worked to pathologise women's bodies (their natural state was diseased) and, thus, legitimate patriarchal surveillance and control of those bodies.

That this is more than an historical curiosity is further illustrated by the crime of **infanticide**. Even today, the offence of infanticide (with which only women can be charged) assumes that women are ruled by biology, their/our minds unbalanced by childbirth and lactation. Allison Morris and Ania Wilczynski (1993: 206–7) note that puerperal psychosis – a relatively rare and severe mental disorder – is the legal basis for a plea of infanticide. Puerperal psychosis is, however, present in very few cases that are classified as infanticide (they estimate five cases per year in Britain) and evidence of mental disturbance is inconsistently presented in infanticide trials. Indeed, they note that about half of the mothers convicted of infanticide in England could not be classified as suffering from any mental disorder. It would seem that there is no need to prove that the maternal body/mind is diseased and in need of medical intervention and surveillance – this remains common sense. Further, as Morris and Wilczynski argue, the relative elasticity of the term 'infanticide' means that the social conditions and pressures that so often lead to maternal child killings are obscured by a focus on supposed disease. An acknowledgement of these conditions – which might include incessant crying, cramped living conditions, unemployment, lack of financial and emotional support, fathers deserting, depression and unsuccessful pleas for help with childcare – would raise crucial questions about mothering and society's evaluation of and (lack of) support for mothers (Naylor, 2001b). As Naylor (2001b: 163) notes, these narratives of 'ordinary mothering' are, therefore, meticulously suppressed and the maternal killer is, instead, 'constructed from a repetition of horrors' – the repetition emphasising the deviant mother's excess and working to repress the knowledge of what she shares with other mothers.

Sexual murder as gendered discourse

In what ways do the representations of Rose West discussed in this chapter differ from those of male sexual murderers discussed in Chapter 3?

Premenstrual tension (now more commonly termed premenstrual syndrome and known by its acronym, PMS) functions similarly, closing down consideration of the social circumstances in which women commit violent and criminal acts, negating women's conscious agency and anger and legitimating men's surveillance of, and control over, women's bodies (Benn, 1993). It is not, of course, incidental that it was in the 1970s – against the background of the women's liberation movements' demands for women's reproductive and sexual freedom – that PMS began to emerge in the defence of women accused of violence, legitimating once more the surveillance and medicalisation of women's bodies. A 1992 report from *The Independent*, quoted by Benn (1993: 153), illustrates these points perfectly:

> A computer expert who was sacked after she hit her head of department while suffering from Pre Menstrual Tension was unfairly dismissed, an industrial tribunal ruled yesterday.
>
> Yvonne Tibbles, 34, of Swindon, a software support assistant, was sacked from the electronics firm Fujitsu after hitting Mike Slaughter. When, during a row over a report she had been working on, Mr Slaughter told her to stop 'copping out' of her responsibilities, she screamed and swore at him, and told him never to say that again. The tribunal was told she then hit him around the head and threw a waste paper bin across the room. She said at the time of the incident she had been suffering from PMT *and the attack followed two and a half years of sexist abuse and being continually checked on by Mr Slaughter.* (Emphasis added)

Up until the final sentence of this report, Tibbles' anger is represented as hormonal, irrational, unprovoked and the two and a half years of sexist abuse is slipped in almost as an afterthought. While Tibbles' use of PMT may well be strategic, this medicalisation of women's experience – what we might call syndrome syndrome – focuses attention on the body of the individual. Whether violent, victimised or both (as in battered women's syndrome), this prevents us from seeing women's behaviour – and, specifically, women's anger – as a response, and perhaps even a reasonable response, to particular social and political contexts. It is easier to label women as 'mad', by virtue of their biology, than try to deal with the social causes of their anger.

The marginalisation of the social thus seems to be the common denominator in representations of male and female violence. However, while, as I have demonstrated, we are never allowed to lose sight of gender in representations of women's violence, representations of men's violence – as we saw in Chapter 3 – consistently ignore masculinity. More worryingly, perhaps, whether perpetrators or victims of violence, women's bodies and behaviour remain under surveillance. It is fitting, therefore, that the modes of looking at women's bodies will be a key concern in the next chapter.

Summary

- Women's anger, violence and rage pose a serious challenge to binary thinking about gender and, specifically, to ideas about women as passive and nurturing.
- Feminists have been understandably reluctant to engage with the issue of women's violence and much feminist work in this area has emerged from feminist work on male violence, examining the connections between women's violence and victimisation.
- It is not only feminists who have struggled with women's violent agency. Press reports demonstrate two major responses to the threat of women's violence: deny the woman's agency (she didn't do it, didn't mean to do it, isn't responsible for doing it) or her gender (she's 'unnatural', masculine, a lesbian, not really a woman at all). Both variations prevent us from looking at the social conditions in which women's violence is embedded.
- Women's sexual and violent agencies are linked because both demand a subjectivity that women have historically been denied.

Notes

1 For details of this and other cases referred to in this chapter, see the Appendix.
2 Such representations also depend on an assumption that victims have no agency. See the essays collected in Lamb (1999) for a variety of feminist perspectives on conceptualising victimisation in relation to women's experiences, agency and survival.
3 Hindley's reported deathbed plea for her own mother featured prominently in tabloid reports of her death, many of which also reprinted the transcripts of the harrowing Downey tape. Here, then, the juxtaposition was one of daughters – the innocent Downey and the monstrous Hindley.
4 Ann West died in 1999, but Winnie Johnson (mother of Keith Bennett, another of Hindley and Brady's victims) has been similarly used to maintain the Myra/mother opposition.
5 Feminists have long argued that the identification of women with nature provides the rationale for most, if not all, oppression of women. For a useful introduction to key feminist debates about women's reproduction and oppression see Brook (1999: Chapter 2).

Further reading

Birch, H. (ed.) (1993a) *Moving Targets: Women, Murder and Representation.* London: Virago.

Cameron, D. (1999) 'Rosemary West: motives and meanings', *The Journal of Sexual Aggression,* 4 (2): 68–80.

Hart, L. (1994) *Fatal Women: Lesbian Sexuality and the Mark of Aggression.* London: Routledge.

Kelly, L. (1996b) 'Feminist perspectives on violence by women', in M. Hester, L. Kelly and J. Radford, (eds), *Women, Violence and Male Power.* Buckingham: Open University Press.

Morrissey, B. (2003) *When Women Kill: Questions of Agency and Subjectivity.* London: Routledge.

PART THREE
Screening violence

Seeing (as) violence: film, feminism and the male gaze

Chapter outline

This chapter picks up on the challenge set at the end of Chapter 2 to think through our own conscious and unconscious investments in violence as entertainment. It does so through the lens of feminist film theory and focuses on some of the popular American genres that have generated concern and critical interest for their portrayal of violence, gender and sexuality.

- The violence of the **male gaze**   Laura Mulvey; **voyeurism**; **sadism**; **fetishism**.

- Killing and thrilling   **slasher** films; **masochism**; seriality; gendered investigation.

- **Rape** and revenge   rape revenge; mainstreaming feminism; male rape.

- The male body   disavowing objectification; the politics of action; new brutalism.

- Women, violence, sexuality   *film noir* and neo-*noir*; post-feminism.

The violence of the male gaze

As we saw in Chapter 1, films feature prominently in media effects stories surrounding specific crimes, but it is not just in the pages of the popular press that such stories are told. Feminist anti-violence activists have also sought to connect violence against women in film – and in **pornography** and '**gorenography**' in particular – to real-world violence. In a fairly typical, if polemical, piece, Chris Domingo (1992: 196) argues:

> The public and media reaction to **serial killings** is quite disturbing. Not only is **femicide** ignored by mainstream news and **discourse**, it is joked about and used as grist in the R-rated movie mill. Serial murder is actually enjoyed – not only by the woman-haters who commit the murders, as evidenced by the usual presence of semen at crime scenes – but by a large percentage of the male population, as evidenced by attendance at 'slasher' films and the popularity of photographs in which women are victims of violence.

Domingo raises valid and troubling questions about the entertainment function of serial murder. However, her argument is based on an assumption that the pleasures of these texts are entirely straightforward and their relationship to the sexual serial murder of women in reality is self-evident. She assumes that male viewers identify with the slasher killer and take pleasure in the sexualised spectacle of violence against women. Is this a safe assumption, though, and, if so, how do these films work to position male viewers in this way? Are these the only pleasures on offer? Where does this leave women in the audience? What happens when a man's body is mutilated on screen (as is frequently the case in the slasher film)? Can enjoying violence on screen really be equated with enjoying violence in real life? These are just some of the questions raised – but rarely answered – by criticisms such as Domingo's. Rather than assuming that the pleasures of violence in film are entirely straightforward, this chapter seeks to explore the nature of these pleasures, putting the viewer – you, me – back in the picture.

Violence has been central to feminist film theory and criticism since its inception. Early studies were primarily concerned with how images of women on screen related – or, rather, didn't relate – to the changing lives of women off screen.[1] So, for example, the focus on relationships between men in films from the late 1960s onwards was read as a symbolic annihilation of women in light of the contemporaneous rise of women's liberation movements. However, it was not just metaphorical violence against women that was of concern. These studies also noted the ways in which anxieties about changing gender roles were played out in spectacles of violence against women and, to a lesser extent, in films focusing on women's violence. However, like Domingo's much later criticisms, these early works focused on content at the expense of form. That is, there was little consideration of film as film.

The publication of Laura Mulvey's hugely influential article 'Visual pleasure and narrative cinema' in 1975 shifted the focus of feminist film studies away from images of women (or their absence) and towards a consideration of how films seek to position and gender their spectators.[2] Mulvey's argument is still useful for a discussion of film violence as, by using **psychoanalysis** to examine how the **patriarchal unconscious** has structured film form, she raises questions about the gendered violence of spectatorship. As Mulvey's argument is so central to the development of feminist film theory – and is specifically relevant for a discussion of film violence – it is useful to reiterate her main points here.

Mulvey argues that there are two aspects of pleasurable looking in the conventional cinematic situation: identification and objectification. Identification Mulvey explains with reference to Jacques Lacan's notion of the mirror stage – the moment when a child recognises their own image in the mirror. At this stage in children's development, their physical ambitions exceed their physical abilities and so this moment is a joyous (mis)recognition – the self in the mirror is imagined to be more complete, more ideal than the child's experiences of their own body. For the male spectator, cinematic identification involves a similar process in that the spectator (mis)recognises in the on-screen protagonist a more complete, more ideal version of himself and identifies with the image seen. The male spectator also takes voyeuristic pleasure in using another person (woman) as an object of sexual stimulation through sight – his gaze here is both controlling and curious. The peeping tom is the extreme expression of this instinct, his victim (and Mulvey uses this word) both unknowing and unwilling. Of course, feminists in other fields have identified this kind of voyeurism as a form of violence against women as it is a reminder of women's object status, sexualisation, lack of power, as well as (in a very real sense) a violation.

How, though, are we to understand the cinema spectator as voyeur, given that those on screen are (for the most part) neither unwilling nor unknowing? Mulvey points out that mainstream cinema works to produce a sense of separation between audience and screen that facilitates voyeuristic fantasy as the film unfolds with no reference to the audience watching it. This, then, is not to argue that those on screen are necessarily victims (in the way that we might understand those violated by the peeping tom), but that mainstream film creates for its male spectator a voyeuristic fantasy that gives the illusion of mastery and control.

However, Mulvey also makes use of Freudian psychoanalysis to investigate the meanings attached to the female figure. According to Freud, the female figure poses something of a problem for the male unconscious as – because she lacks a penis – she symbolises for the male the threat of castration. Thus, Mulvey (1975: 42) notes:

> the woman as icon, displayed for the gaze and enjoyment
> of men, the active controllers of the look, always threatens
> to evoke the anxiety it originally signified.

Mulvey goes on to outline the two possible 'avenues of escape' from this castration anxiety for the male unconscious.

The first response is to re-enact the moment the male child discovers sexual difference (his sight of the female genitals) and so develops a fear that he, too, might be castrated. Cinematically, she suggests, this is rendered by means of a narrative fascination with the female figure – the emphasis is on 'investigating the woman, demystifying her mystery' (Mulvey, 1975: 42). In other words, the female figure is made the object of the male character/spectator's investigation and his gaze. This process can, perhaps, be best illustrated in relation to *film noir* of the 1940s and 1950s – films such as *Double Indemnity* (Wilder, 1944) or *The Postman Always Rings Twice* (Garnett, 1946) – where the real mystery the male character/spectator must unravel is that surrounding the *femme fatale*. Is she what she seems to be? What are her motivations? Is she a (sexual) threat to the protagonist? It is not enough, however, to simply demystify this figure – she must also be contained or controlled. In *Double Indemnity*, for example, the *femme fatale* is shot dead and in *The Postman Always Rings Twice* she is killed in a car crash. There is, as Mulvey (1975: 42–3) notes, a sadistic aspect to this:

> pleasure lies in ascertaining guilt (immediately associated
> with castration), asserting control and subjugating the
> guilty person through punishment or forgiveness.

I will return to the *femme fatale* later, but for now I want to turn to the second 'avenue of escape' for the male unconscious discussed by Mulvey. Fetishistic **scopophilia** involves a complete disavowal of castration, substituting a fetish object for the woman's lack (of a penis) or, indeed, turning the female figure herself into a fetish, 'so that it becomes reassuring rather than dangerous' (Mulvey, 1975: 42). Here the containment and control is rendered visually (Mulvey, 1975: 43):

> The beauty of the woman as object and the screen space coalesce; she is no longer the bearer of guilt but a perfect product, whose body, stylised and fragmented by close-ups, is the content of the film and the direct recipient of the spectator's look.

Obvious examples of this can be found in striptease films of the mid 1990s – *Barb Wire* (Hogan, 1995), *Striptease* (Bergman, 1995) and *Showgirls* (Verhoeven, 1995). In these films, the actor/character's body is fragmented by close-ups of, for example, breasts, well-oiled legs and painted lips, while the clothing (PVC, lace, high heels) partially encases the body in a clearly fetishistic way. The body is indeed presented as a perfect product (it is no accident that Demi Moore's role in *Striptease* made her the highest-paid female actor of the time), inviting a direct gaze from the male spectator.

The crux of Mulvey's argument, then, is that Hollywood cinema is structured along the same lines as the patriarchal unconscious and so the act of looking is itself imbricated in gendered psychic and political structures characterised by power, control and submission. Indeed, in a 1981 article, Mary Ann Doane (1981: 86) suggests:

> Cinematic images of woman have been so consistently oppressive and repressive that the very idea of a feminist filmmaking practice seems an impossibility. The simple gesture of directing a camera toward a woman has become equivalent to a terrorist act.

For a discussion of film violence, this reminds us that it is not only what we see but how we are positioned to see it that is important.

Mulvey concludes her article by arguing that a central goal of feminist criticism must be to make these structures explicit and, in so doing, destroy the visual pleasure associated with narrative cinema.

Mulvey's theory and conclusions have been widely debated, contested and complicated in subsequent feminist work (including her own). In particular, Mulvey has been criticised for adopting a psychoanalytic framework that positions the spectator within a set of linked and fixed binary oppositions (male/female, masculine/feminine, active/passive) in which the sexual difference and those resulting from it are paramount. Later work complicates Mulvey's theory by addressing issues of female spectatorship, examining the masochistic possibilities of male spectatorship, investigating the objectification of men on screen and exploring the ways in which sexuality and race structure the 'right to look'.[3] The notion of the 'male gaze' is also complicated by audience studies that reveal the multiple and sometimes contradictory investments both men and women make in films (see Chapter 2). Nevertheless, Mulvey's article provides a still-provocative starting point for thinking about the ways in which the act of looking may be structured by power and violently enacted. As we will now see, these themes are taken up – and partially disputed – in feminist analyses of that most controversial of genres, the slasher film.

Killing and thrilling

In her influential account of male psychic investments in horror, Carol Clover (1992: 168) writes, 'The horror movie is somehow more than the sum of its monsters; it is itself monstrous.' This notion of the horror movie as monstrous is a recurring one, but Clover's concern here is with the self-reflexive aspects of horror or, more specifically, how looking is imagined as horrific. Indeed, Clover suggests that horror films repeatedly present a challenge to, if not a direct assault on, the viewer and the act of viewing. Eyes are attacked (sliced open, plucked out, splashed with acid) and widened in horror while the act of viewing makes characters vulnerable to violation as, for example, in *Videodrome* (Cronenberg, 1982) or *The Ring* (Nakata, 1998). So, instead of the viewer-as-sadist invoked by writers such as Domingo (and theorised by Mulvey), Clover suggests that there is a masochistic investment in horror, a pleasure in being subjected to pain, horror and fear.[4]

At this point, the sceptics among you might, rightly, point out that this does not change the fact that it is women's viewing and horror we are generally talking about here. In Brian de Palma's words, 'Women in peril work better in the suspense genre', or, in Hitchcock's, 'I always believe in following the advice of the playwright Sardou. He said, "Torture the women!" The trouble today is that we don't torture women enough' (in Clover 1992: 42). Certainly, as Clover (1992: 51) demonstrates in her discussion of the slasher films of the 1970s and 1980s, much screen time is taken up showing women in terror and pain. Abject terror, she notes, 'is gendered feminine'. Moreover, while, in the slasher, sex equals death for male and female teens alike, it is only women's deaths that are sexualised.

Feminists and other critics have also suggested that, in the sequences of terror, we are allied with the terrorist, the killer. It is not only at the moment of 'slashing' that such identification is solicited.

For much of the film we – along with the killer – stalk the teens who will become his victims (it is no accident that slashers are also referred to as 'stalker' movies (Dika, 1990)). We see through his (and it is usually his) eyes and hear his breathing, heartbeat and footsteps on the soundtrack. Our vision is compromised as his is – obscured by bushes, window blinds and so on – and as we literally see through his eyes, the killer himself remains unseen. Perhaps the classic example of this is the opening sequence of *Halloween* (Carpenter, 1978) where we are positioned with the killer, go with him into the kitchen, up the stairs and into the bedroom where we look through the Halloween mask he wears as he/we kill his post-coital teen sister. The killer himself is not revealed until he exits the house and his parents' unmasking reveals an emotionless six-year-old boy – a shocking revelation that arguably undercuts the spectator's sense of mastery in this film.

Clover points out that the slasher killer is rarely a figure with whom we would want to identify: he is typically juvenile or scarred, drooling, overweight, gender-confused or deformed.[5] Further, Clover notes that the sequences from his point of view, while striking, are few and far between and there is rarely a stable point of identification in the first stages of the film. Indeed, part of the way in which the slasher film creates suspense and tension is by playing around with the point of view to implicate other characters in the killings and/or to suggest a pervasive sense of threat. Early in *Friday the 13th* (Cunningham, 1980), for example, we adopt the perspective of the unseen killer lurking in the woods as she watches the camp counsellors at the river.[6] When two of the counsellors return to the river, we are again allied with an unseen voyeur as we watch them making out. In this instance, the voyeur is their friend and allying his point of view with that of the killer makes him (briefly) a subject of suspicion before he becomes the real killer's next victim. More significantly, by the end of the film, the point of view is most definitely that of the female survivor – the character Clover labels the 'Final Girl', whose flight, fight and fright are the focus of the final section of the film. The Final Girl is terrified, her screams and cries dominating the soundtrack, but she is also resourceful and determined, surviving where her friends do not.

What are we to make of the fact that this victim-hero is female despite the fact that the majority of the audience is male? A discussion of the Final Girl's function leads Clover to suggest that the psychic investment in slashers may not be as sadistically simple as some have assumed. Clover argues that the Final Girl is the only coherent point of identification in the typical slasher and suggests that identification with her provides the male spectator with the opportunity to live out masochistic fantasies in relative safety. It is not accidental, then, that the Final Girl is masculinised, in name (Laurie, Stretch,

Sidney, for example), appearance (distinctly less feminine and less sexual than her female friends) and at the level of the cinematic apparatus as Clover, (1992: 48) notes:

> her unfemininity is signaled clearly by her exercise of the 'active investigating gaze' normally reserved for males and punished in females when they assume it for themselves; tentatively at first and then aggressively, the Final Girl looks *for* the killer ... and then *at* him, therewith bringing him, often for the first time, into our vision.

The Final Girl is, Clover (1992: 51) suggests, 'a congenial double for the adolescent male':

> She is feminine enough to act out in a gratifying way, a way unapproved for adult males, the terrors and masochistic pleasures of the underlying fantasy, but not so feminine as to disturb the structures of male competence and sexuality.

While Clover is wary of making claims that this renders the slasher 'progressive' – not least because the surface image remains so manifestly problematic – she does suggest that, 'in its own perverse way', it constitutes 'a viable adjustment in the terms of gender representations' (1992: 64).

Horrifying audiences

Go back to the notes on your own horror film viewing from Chapter 2. Can Mulvey's and/or Clover's theories offer a way of understanding your pleasures or lack of them? Why or why not?

As a critique of the sadistic position assigned to the male spectator in Mulvey's 1975 article, Clover's account has been influential beyond the terms of the slasher movie. However, her conclusions have been contested in some subsequent work. As Tony Williams (1996) notes, Clover's analysis elevates the Final Girl as a rigid model and fails to take account of the contradictions and historical developments in the genre. Indeed, Williams' examples demonstrate that the Final Girl is not consistently 'final' (in a number of the early slashers, including *Halloween*, she must be saved by someone else), nor consistently a 'girl' (in the 1980s horror franchises there are male and female survivors). Moreover, her 'survival' looks very different when we consider films in series rather than as individual texts. So, for example, *Friday the 13th's* Alice (Adrienne King) is dispatched in the sequel (Miner, 1981) and Laurie (Jamie Lee Curtis) survives *Halloween* to be submissive and terrified in *Halloween II* (Rosenthal, 1981) and then become an alcoholic living in the shadow of Michael's violence (*H20*, Miner, 1998).

Most importantly, while the killer may be a marginal figure in individual films, Clover downplays the extent to which the slasher cycles present the killer as a celebrity. Certainly, Freddy Kreuger, Jason Voorhees and Michael Myers are the most enduring and memorable characters in the franchises in which they appear. Merchandising exploits this, rendering the killer safe and even fun by transforming him into a doll or other commodity at the same time as revelling in his splatter killings. He may be represented as a or the bogeyman, but it is worth remembering that the bogeymen of children's rhymes typically can be traced back to real-life cases of **sexual murder**. In this respect, as we saw in Chapter 3, the relationship of fact to fiction is never entirely straightforward and, indeed, Freddy, Jason and Michael become the hooks on which subsequent stories of real-life violence are hung:

PSYCHO 'FREDDY' IS JAILED

The Sun, 19 August, 1991

HALLOWEEN MONSTER HACKS GIRL TO DEATH
The Daily Mirror, 2 November, 1990

FREDDY PSYCHO FLEES GUARDS.
The Sun, 11 June, 1996

In linking real-life crime to the horror monsters, the effect is – as I argued in Chapter 3 – to dissociate the criminal from 'normal' men. In the films themselves, the horror monsters are mythical figures about whom we learn little beyond a cursory back story that provides a psycho-sexual motivation for their crimes. Their ability to survive for sequel after sequel, not to mention the increasingly bizarre means of their resurrection, render the narrative obviously and deliberately implausible and the films are typically both self-reflexive and self-deprecating in this regard. In the first *Halloween*, for example, Michael survives a stabbing and six bullet wounds to the chest to walk away at the film's end. In the sequels he survives much more. Indeed, the special effects are a key part of the films' appeal, with each film pushing the boundaries that bit further in terms of bloody spectacle and literally incredible methods of killing. In this respect, the criticisms of Domingo et al. seem particularly wide of the mark. At least part of the fascination with the most popular slasher killers (and killings) is that they themselves are so patently unreal, even if the fears they tap into are not.

Clover's psychoanalytic account also rather ignores the specific sociopolitical context in which the slasher film emerges and flourishes (see Wood, 1986; Ryan and Kellner, 1988). Particularly significant in the context of this book, Williams (1996: 171) suggests that the slashers of the later 1980s become increasingly focused on the dysfunctional family, linking this development to, among other factors, the increasing visibility of child **sexual abuse** as an issue during this period (see Chapter 3). At a time when more mainstream films – from *Fatal Attraction* (Lyne, 1987) onwards – dealt with abuse within the family by demonising career women and victimising men, the slashers offered one of the few fictional spaces where families and fathers were not being uncritically celebrated. Indeed, the return home of the male figure is frequently the source of terror as, most obviously, in the *Halloween* films where Michael's homecomings are deadly for family and community alike. However, as before, we should be wary of simply celebrating these developments as feminist. Indeed, to the extent that the slashers offer any explanation at all for the killing, they often return to the killer's relationship with his mother and/or his experience of child sexual abuse (often at her hands) – a discourse of women-blaming that should be familiar from our discussion of the press in Chapters 3 and 4.

At the conclusion of *Men, Women and Chain Saws*, Clover (1992: 235) claims that 'the slasher film proper has died down', but, since she sounded its death knell, the slasher has had something of a revival. Films such as the *Scream* trilogy (Craven, 1996, 1997, 2000) and *I Know What You Did Last Summer* (Gillespie, 1997) and its sequel, *I Still Know What You Did Last Summer* (Cannon, 1998), self-consciously use and transform aspects of the slasher genre. Yet, the sexualisation of violence against women is one thing that remains relatively consistent. It is no accident that Jennifer Love Hewitt and Sarah Michelle Gellar reputedly referred to the film in which they co-starred as 'I Know What Your Breasts Did Last Summer' (in Vint, 2002)! Also, while *Scream* may, in other respects, be extremely knowing and, indeed, ironic in its use of generic conventions, it is telling that the **diegetic** movie buffs do not comment on the differential fates of male and female characters. Rather, the film simply reproduces these conventions, so that the killings of female characters are significantly more protracted than those of the male characters, the women have time to register the danger they are in and their fear and (attempted) flight takes up considerable screen time. The 12-minute opening sequence in which Casey (Drew Barrymore) is tormented by a menacing movie buff clearly demonstrates this point. While her boyfriend is dispatched quickly and silently (he is gagged), Casey's dawning terror is the focus of the scene and her death, when it comes, is long and bloody, as she is repeatedly stabbed, then dragged across the ground and her body hung from a tree.

This discussion of the slasher genre suggests that these films in many ways have little in common with fact-based serial killer narratives (Chapter 3). Greater continuity can, however, be found in thrillers centred on serial killings and serial killers. The thriller, far more than the slasher, is interested in the individual character of the serial killer and the distinctive aspects of his crimes (Williams, 1983; Taubin, 1993). The process of detection focuses on the 'signature' of the killer (the killer is an artist, a unique and talented individual), on patterns in killing (when, where, how and who he kills) and on the bodies and lives of the victims. This gives a structure to the thriller narrative, pitting the investigator – with whom the spectator is most often aligned – against the killer in an intellectual battle conducted against the time pressures inherent in the serial nature of the killing and the running time of the film. As Richard Dyer (1997b: 16) writes:

> Seriality emphasises anticipation, suspense, what will happen next? It also emphasises repetition, pattern, structure. We may enjoy the excitement of the threat posed by a serial killer – when will he strike next and whom? when will they get him? – but we can also enjoy discerning the pattern in his acts. This may be the same basic pattern in each act – the same selection of victim, the same method of killing – or it may be that a pattern emerges out of all the killing seen as a sequence. The commonest form of the first kind of pattern is explanation – each act becomes an expression of the same underlying pattern of motivation. A classic example of the second kind of pattern – that virtually only exists in fiction – would be a series of killings based upon some numerical or alphabetical sequence.

Seriality, then, is a source of pleasure and reassurance, rendering the puzzle as solvable, the killer containable, the crimes explicable. While these serial killers are recognisably human in a way that serial slashers often are not, they are not 'normal' men either. Rather, as in fact-based accounts, they are typically evil geniuses and/or madmen, fascinating and somewhat romanticised figures. With the notable exception of Hannibal Lecter, it is unusual for serial killer characters to return outside the slasher. However, as so many serial killer films use the same real-life cases as their inspiration (or are reported to do so), there is a sense in which they, too, are involved in a process of demonic resurrection by replaying real killings, contributing to the celebrity of the killer.

Serial television

Do my observations about serial killer thrillers hold for an analysis of television serial killer dramas?

To illustrate some of these points, I want to briefly consider *From Hell* (Hughes Brothers, 2001) – the latest in a long line of films focusing on the killings attributed to Jack the Ripper (see Chapter 3). Here, the real women murdered in Whitechapel are given a fictional back story that provides a link between them and a pattern to the brutal killings (rendered in bloody detail in the film). What they share is knowledge, most of which is fictionalised, that the Duke of Clarence (Queen Victoria's grandson) had an affair with a prostitute who gave birth to his child. The killer, Sir William Gull (Queen Victoria's physician), is trying to cover up this indiscretion by killing the women. Establishing a pattern undoubtedly heightens the narrative tension – we know, and the women themselves know, that they are in specific danger – but the imposition of pattern also deflects the more disturbing randomness and **misogyny** of the original killings. In 1888, these women were killed because they were women, they were poor and they were available, not – as *From Hell* would have it – because they were linked by exceptional circumstances.

Moreover, by establishing a pattern, the film's investigator, Inspector Abberline (Johnny Depp), is able to solve the crimes that eluded his historical namesake and provide closure to the narrative. Although a stroke had left the real Gull with little strength and made him an extremely unlikely suspect, Gull's intelligence, professional standing and status make him an attractive suspect in Ripper fictions. Further, the conspiracy theory in which Gull becomes embedded allows the fictional police to solve the crime but not arrest the criminal, restoring the hero to a position of narrative authority and downplaying any understanding of the Ripper killings as gendered. Killer and investigator can thus be paired in a conventional manner as exceptional individuals. As Dyer (1997b: 17) notes of serial killer films more generally:

> Though women are central to the serial-killer phenomenon, the *raison d'être* for killer and investigator alike, much of the actual action in a serial-killing movie is between men, on-screen between killer and pursuer, and also to a considerable extent between screen and audience ... these films tend to posit men as the only possible saviours of women.

From Hell assigns the saviour position to Abberline, as he alerts Mary Jane Kelly (Heather Graham) – whose murder, in reality, was the final one attributed to the Ripper – to the danger she is in, causing her to flee to Ireland and escape her fate. Unlike the Final Girl, then, the investigator is rarely in mortal danger himself. Rather, the dangers he faces are moral (he must not get too close to his subject) and emotional (as he puts his loved ones in jeopardy). *From Hell* has Abberline fall in love with Kelly precisely so that he has something to lose and someone he must protect.

Female investigators are, unsurprisingly, very differently positioned. While, as Yvonne Tasker (1998) notes and we will see in Chapter 6, the female investigator has a more distinguished history on television than film, a number of films do, nevertheless, position women in this role and merit brief comment here. Notably, the female investigator rarely works alone and is usually positioned in relation to a male mentor in a world dominated by men. As Chris Holmlund (1993b) notes, the anxiety around women's assumption of active and violent roles means that the female investigator is frequently provided with multiple motivations for taking on these roles – motivations that her male counterparts rarely require. As with representations of real-life violent women (see Chapter 4), the investigator's assumption of the violent role is frequently allied to experiences of victimisation. For example, while Clarice Starling (Jodie Foster) has an active, investigating role in *The Silence of the Lambs* (Demme, 1991), her gendered identification and empathy with the victims is in contrast to the male investigator's typical identification with the killer (Tasker, 2002). Starling is thus able to read the bodies and lives of the victims in a way that eludes her male colleagues. Starling is the only woman, other than the victims, to inhabit the male-dominated world of serial murder and its investigation. Her gendered isolation is consistently underscored by positioning her in male groups where her small stature and clothing underline the fact that she is out of place (see Figure 5.1). The incarcerated killer's probing also reveals her motivations for following this career path (motivations male characters rarely require) and this flags up her vulnerability. The oscillation between positions of action and vulnerability is even more obvious in the rape revenge film, to which I now turn my attention.

Figure 5.1 *Out of place in the world of serial killer investigation – Clarice Starling (Jodie Foster) in* The Silence of the Lambs *(Demme, 1991).*

Rape and revenge

Rape itself, according to Sarah Projanksy (2001), has been both ubiquitous and elusive in Hollywood film. In other words, while rape is pervasive, it is not always recognised as rape. Rape appears on screen in many guises, including as seduction (most notoriously, perhaps, in *Gone with The Wind* (Fleming, 1939)), a justification for ethnic violence in the Western, an expression of evil to differentiate villain from hero in contemporary action films, the cost of women's independence and motivation for the hero's quest. While it is clearly outside the scope of this book to discuss how rape functions in all of these narratives, it is worth noting that in many of the examples listed, rape is something that, though enacted on a female body, is given meaning and significance by men. In her historical survey, Projanksy (2001: 35) further demonstrates how rape narratives engage, in often contradictory ways, with women's vulnerability and independence, yet, ultimately represent the family as a refuge and heterosexual romance as the raped woman's salvation.

In this section, however, I want to focus on rape as rape, beginning with a discussion of the rape revenge horror film. Rape revenge, like the slasher genre, has generated considerable controversy and concern for its portrayal of **sexual violence** against women. For example, in an infamous article that begins with his experience of viewing

I Spit on Your Grave (Zarchi, 1978), critic Roger Ebert condemns these 'women-in-danger' films for aligning their spectator with the point of view of the rapist. Ebert's article (1981: 54) – which is repeatedly cited in discussions of the rape revenge film – provides disturbing examples of male audience members' enthusiasm for and approval of the rape scenes, recalling the concerns expressed by Domingo about the slasher:

> the audience seemed to be taking all this as a comedy, and there were shouts and loud laughs at the climaxes of violence. And then, beneath these noises, as a subtle counterpoint, I could hear my neighbour saying, 'That's a good one ... Ooh-eee! She's got that coming! That'll teach her. That's right! Give it to her! She's learned her lesson ...'

While, as we later learn, the men in Ebert's audience were silenced by the heroine's subsequent revenge, their apparent appreciations of the rape scenes cannot be easily dismissed. The film may work to de-legitimate these pleasures, as we will see, but there are questions to be asked about men's public and communal enactment of the gendered pleasures of spectatorship and how this impacts on the enjoyment and safety of women in the audience (see Chapter 2). However, it soon becomes clear that it is not simply men's responses that trouble Ebert. As the revenge section of the film progresses, he notes that women's voices begin to dominate. Differentiating the 'women-in-danger' films from horror films he admires (including *Halloween* and *Dressed to Kill*), Ebert argues that the former are problematic because they do *not* allow the (male) spectator the luxury of voyeurism, but implicate him in the unfolding violence. He (Ebert, 1981: 56) concludes:

> Horror movies, even the really bloody ones, used to be fair game for everyone – diversions for everybody. Pop psychologists could speculate that they were a way for us to exorcise our demons. Terrible things were happening all right – but to the victims who were safely up there on the screen. Now that's not the case in some of these new women-in-danger films. Now the terrible things are happening *to women*, and the movie point of view is *a non-specific male killing force*. These movies may still be exorcising demons, but the identity of the demons has changed. Now the 'victim' is the poor, put-upon traumatised male in the audience. And the demons are the women on screen. (emphasis added)

Of course, the victims 'up there on the screen' are also likely to have been women. The difference is that the rape revenge film makes the gendered nature of horror violence explicit and this is profoundly discomfiting for the male spectator/critic (Read, 2000). Herein lies one of the central contradictions of rape revenge horror – although presenting graphic scenes of sexual violence as 'entertainment', it is also one of the few spaces where feminist analyses of violence as a gendered and structural phenomenon are literalised. As Clover notes (1992: 138), in its portrayal of a rape-supportive culture in which *all* men 'are directly or indirectly complicit', rape revenge horror owes a debt to feminism. Yet, while *all* men on screen may be implicated, the pool of men is often small. Many of the films unfold in an isolated, rural location where locals (poor, white, uneducated men) rape and abuse relatively wealthy outsiders. In this respect, the rural rape revenge films draw on a long tradition of positioning rape – and rapists – outside of, or other to, so-called civilised American society (Projanksy, 2001).

Both Clover and Peter Lehman (1993) note that, in the rape revenge film, the rape scenes are typically brutal and unerotic and we are positioned with the rape victim rather than with the rapist. In *I Spit on Your Grave*, for example, the rape scenes are, in Lehman's (1993: 104) words, 'free of the conventional ways of eroticising such scenes'. Much of the outdoor scene is in long shot (see Figure 5.2) and there is considerable emphasis on the rapists' faces and reactions (Figure 5.3), frustrating the voyeuristic look at the female body to align us with the point of view of the raped woman. There is absolutely no suggestion here that Jennifer (Camille Keaton) enjoys the rape – her violation and degradation are horrifying to watch (and listen to – her cries dominate the soundtrack), but then, shouldn't rape be horrifying? Challenging Ebert's reading of *Spit*, Lehman (1993: 104) argues:

> The protracted nature of the scenes, far from extending pleasurable eroticism, work to make the rapes painfully difficult to watch, though not for the reprehensible reasons Ebert suggests. The reverse is closer to the truth. Watching these despicable men engage in this atavistic brutality allows the audience to feel that what follows is justified.

What follows is Jennifer's protracted and bloody revenge. If sex is used as a weapon to victimise Jennifer, in her transformation to hero/avenger, sex becomes her weapon. She lures two of the rapists with the promise of sex before hanging one and castrating the other (the remaining two men are dispatched with an axe and boat propeller respectively). Like other avenging women, Jennifer plays on men's willingness to believe in rape myths (she asked for it, she

Figures 5.2 and 5.3 *Rape is violent, not erotic. The use of long shots and the focus on the rapist in* I Spit on Your Grave *(Zarchi, 1978) frustrate the voyeurism of the spectator.*

enjoyed it) in order to seduce/kill her rapist(s), manipulating both her appearance and demeanour in the process.

While such self-conscious performances of rape myths arguably draw attention to their absurdity, Barbara Creed's assessment of this tradition is more critical. Creed (in Emerman 1995: 73) suggests that the effect of sexualised revenge is to present women's sexuality as dangerous and, therefore, justify male violence. Indeed, the pleasures on offer for the male spectator are not only those of cross-sex identification, as the representation of the often naked avenger also offers relatively conventional fetishistic pleasures (Lehman, 1993; Read, 2000). As the rapist is rarely presented as a point of identification for the male spectator, Lehman suggests that he can take pleasure in this display without having to confront the ways in which his own gaze might mirror that of the rapists'. Yet, he continues, 'it is not just the women who are watched – it is also the men in their horror and pain' (Lehman, 1993: 107). The pleasure in other men's pain comes not only from the trans-sex identification but also, Lehman argues, from a homosexual sadism that resolves the heterosexual male spectator's anxiety about his gaze at (and desire for) other men (an issue that I will confront more directly later in this chapter).

Virgins and vamps?

Recall Benedict's (1992) argument, outlined in Chapter 3, that raped women tend to be portrayed as virgins or vamps. Does the rape revenge tradition support or challenge this view?

As Clover and others demonstrate, *I Spit on Your Grave* depends on feminist anti-rape discourse for its presentation of rape as both horrific and actionable, and for its portrayal of a rape culture. The portrayal of the victim avenger as active and self-sufficient also owes something to feminism, but the individualist and violent nature of her revenge arguably undercuts a feminist analysis. Clover (1992: 143) writes, 'if women are as capable as men of acts of humiliating violence, men are off the guilt hook that modern feminism has put them on'. Despite this, some of the publicity for the film sought to position it in relation to broader debates about rape, women who kill and justice:

> THIS WOMAN HAS JUST … CUT, CHOPPED, BROKEN AND BURNED FOUR MEN BEYOND RECOGNITION … BUT NO JURY IN AMERICA WOULD EVER CONVICT HER!

This publicity perhaps refers to the contemporaneous case of Francine Hughes – an abused woman who, in a widely publicised case that I return to in Chapter 6, was acquitted on charges of murdering her abusive ex-husband (by setting fire to his bed while he slept) not long before *Spit*'s release.[7] However, while the Hughes trial's jury accepted the 'temporary insanity' defence and did not convict her (Jones, 1991: 306–9), to suggest that 'no jury in America' would ever convict Jennifer – whose actions are clearly coded as revenge – is ridiculous. Legal arguments aside, the publicity claim seems to suggest – as Projansky (2001) claims is common in more mainstream rape narratives of the 1980s – that feminist anti-rape discourse has entered the mainstream and so become redundant. It goes something like this: now that we know and accept that rape is a bad thing and individual women like Jennifer or Francine Hughes are able to act without censure, there is no need for feminism.

More than a decade after *Spit*, two mainstream films – *The Accused* (Kaplan, 1988) and *Thelma & Louise* (Scott, 1991) – brought the heroine of rape revenge to a much wider audience. On one level, these films arguably owe a more explicit debt to feminism, drawing on feminist anti-rape discourse to make sense of and contextualise the women's experiences and draw attention to the legal difficulties in prosecuting rape and defending women who kill. However, Clover (1992: 147) suggests that something was nevertheless lost in the transition to mainstream films. While *The Accused* is, in many ways, a powerful critique of the legal processing of rape (and rape victims), the happy ending shows the law to be victim-friendly after all. Importantly, the case at the film's centre hinges on the testimony not of the raped woman herself (Sarah Tobias, played by Jodie Foster), but Kenneth Joyce (Bernie Coulson) – a male witness. Although the film is loosely based on the Big Dan's case (see Chapter 3), Joyce is a fictional construct who provides a safe point of identification for the male spectator, notably absent in the low-budget films. Indeed, when the rape is finally shown, it is anchored by Joyce's courtroom testimony and shown from his point of view. It is the good man's willingness to help that makes the rape speakable and actionable. Tobias' dependence on others (her lawyer, Joyce, the jury) to act on her behalf is in stark contrast to Jennifer's violent agency.

In this respect at least, Thelma (Geena Davis) and Louise (Susan Sarandon) are more like Jennifer, operating outside the law, which, the film makes clear, is inadequate for dealing with their experiences. Nevertheless, here, too, the male spectator is offered a sympathetic screen surrogate in Hal (Harvey Keitel) – the cop who consistently gives voice to feminist arguments about rape and justice.

Despite this, much of the controversy surrounding the film related to its lack of sympathetic male characters. Of course, individual films without sympathetic female characters rarely merit such public opprobrium and the controversy surrounding *Thelma & Louise* perhaps points out the extent to which – as Mulvey (1975) suggests – Hollywood films characteristically construct a male viewing position. Moreover, while there remains a reluctance to address the gendered and sexist nature of men's violence against women, reviewers and commentators were only too willing to see Thelma and Louise's violence as both: they were women killing/assaulting men because they were men.

In popular and academic debate, the feminism of the characters/film was also a central and recurring issue. Indeed, discussions of the *Thelma & Louise* controversy demonstrate that such representations 'participate in the discursive production of what feminism is and can be' (Projansky, 2001: 52).[8] For our purposes here, it is sufficient to note that, whether a film like *Thelma & Louise* can be understood as feminist or not, it creates a public forum whereby feminism, rape and justice can be discussed (an issue I return to in Chapter 6).

Finally, a brief word on male rape revenge. In an article written almost a decade on from Clover's influential work, Joe Wlodarz (2001) discusses a range of films from the 1990s that present a male rape revenge narrative including *Pulp Fiction* (Tarantino, 1994), *The Shawshank Redemption* (Darabont, 1994) and *Sleepers* (Levinson, 1996). However, he highlights important differences between the female and male rape revenge traditions.

First, he argues that the male rape revenge films – due to their incessant scapegoating of gay men – go 'out of their way' to recuperate patriarchy and heterosexual masculinity. In other words, there is no critique of normative constructions of masculinity here. Second, for this recuperation to be effective, the male rape revenge films reverse two of the commonplaces of the female rape revenge film, by characterising the rapist as a deviant rather than a 'normal' man and by presenting the rape victim's revenge as unerotic. This latter point is particularly important and recalls arguments about the cycle of violence presented in Chapter 4 – the male victim can only move into the hero position if he moves out of a position of sexual objectification. The relationship between men's victimisation, violence and erotic objectification is my concern in the next section.

The male body

While female bodies – abused, violated and sometimes surviving – are at the centre of slasher, serial killer thriller and rape revenge films, in the action genre, male bodies are typically the focus.

Steve Neale's 1983 article 'Masculinity as spectacle' returns to the propositions set out in Mulvey's 'Visual pleasure and narrative cinema' to explore – and problematise – the relationship between the male spectator and his on-screen surrogate. For Mulvey, the implicitly heterosexual male spectator's investment in the screen male is based on identification, not desire. However, Neale argues that the process of identifying with the 'ego ideal' on screen can be profoundly contradictory for the male spectator, arousing anxieties about his own inadequacies. According to Neale, the male spectator thus oscillates between identification with and contemplation of the screen male. As such, the screen male is not only the subject of the action (and identification), but also the object of a contemplative gaze.

However, in a patriarchal society, the male body cannot be explicitly marked as the erotic object of another man (or woman's) gaze the eroticism of the gaze has to be disavowed. Thus, Neale argues, the pleasures on offer oscillate between sadistic voyeurism (pleasure in seeing the male body mutilated, hurt) and fetishistic looking. However, in psychoanalytic terms, the male body cannot signify castration and so cannot be fetishised. Instead, Neale suggests, the pleasure of display is displaced from the male body as such and located more generally in the overall components of a highly ritualised (and generally violent) scene. Neale (1983: 18) notes:

> We are offered the spectacle of male bodies, *but bodies unmarked as objects of erotic display*. There is no trace of an acknowledgement or recognition of those bodies as displayed solely for the gaze of the spectator. ... We see male bodies stylised and fragmented by close-ups, but our look is not direct, it is heavily mediated by the looks of the characters involved. And those looks are marked not by desire, but rather by fear, or hatred, or aggression. (emphasis added)

The spectacle of male bodies is one of action and movement. The characters act (fight, attack and defend) and their actions have clear narrative purpose (defeating or escaping an enemy, gaining information or status). These bodies are not, therefore, simply passive objects of the gaze, but drive the narrative forward.

While Neale's psychoanalytic reading is not genre-specific, it is in relation to the Western and the action movie that his arguments have arguably proved most productive. To illustrate this, I want to turn now to *Terminator 2: Judgement day* (Cameron, 1991) and, specifically, to the scene introducing Arnold Schwarzenegger's character – the Terminator himself. Brought back from the future, the Terminator is reborn (naked) in the film's present and immediately heads for a biker bar, where he acquires clothes and a vehicle from a patron. As the naked Terminator walks through the bar, male and female patrons alike look him up and down with both bemusement and admiration. However,

Figure 5.4 *Seeing through the Terminator's eyes in* Terminator 2: Judgement Day *(Cameron, 1991).*

it is his desire (for clothes and a vehicle) that drives this scene and, as Neale suggests, the looks of the bar patrons are heavily mediated – we see him, seeing them, looking at him (see Figure 5.4). The Terminator's body is fragmented by close-ups of his muscular torso, legs and arms, but it is a body in action, a body in motion, a body that is both the subject and object of violence (see Figures 5.5 and 5.6). The display here is not superfluous (as it is, for example, in female striptease films that I mentioned earlier), but drives the narrative forward.

So far, this sequence would seem to offer a fairly clear-cut example of the processes Neale describes. However, this reading is complicated when we factor in the star image of Schwarzenegger himself. After all, our look in this sequence is not just at the (non-human) Terminator, it is also a look at a human, champion body. Yet, where once muscles and a tan signified manual labour and man's productive role, Schwarzenegger's built body carries none of these connotations. His bulk is not the by-product of labour, but an end in itself, the result of wealth and leisure, of hours in the gym, on the sunbed and so on (Faludi, 2000). Moreover, as the built body is a body built-to-be-posed (recalling Mulvey's phrase 'to-be-looked-at-ness'), It carries feminine connotations and some critics have suggested that such built bodies symbolise the instability of masculinity (Holmlund, 1993a; Tasker, 1993). This tension is perhaps even more explicit in the birthing sequence in the latest instalment of the *Terminator* saga. More than a decade on, *Terminator 3: The Rise of the Machines* (Mostow, 2003) sees Schwarzenegger's Terminator seeking clothing and a vehicle not in a

Figures 5.5 and 5.6 *A body, fragmented but muscular, strong and in action. Arnold Schwarzenegger in* Terminator 2.

biker bar, but in a club where a male stripper performs for a female audience. The Terminator's aggressive appropriation of the male stripper's outfit can, in some ways, be seen as consistent with Neale's arguments about the disavowal of male objectification. However, the presence of the stripper and the female audience also point to the increasing ornamentalisation of masculinity in contemporary culture and to an anxiety about the status of the muscular male body.

Partly because of these tensions, the display of the naked body carries – or can carry – connotations of vulnerability, reducing the body to object. In his book *White* (1997a), Richard Dyer notes that while, prior to the 1980s, it was rare to see a white man naked, or semi-naked, in media representations, non-white male bodies were regularly on display in Westerns, plantation dramas, jungle adventure films and dance numbers with body-baring chorus boys. In contrast, the white male body was generally only displayed in two genres – the boxing film and the action/adventure film in a colonial setting. In both cases, the look at the white male body was legitimated by context (sport, historical epoch or geographical location) and the body on display was, typically, a champion or built body (for example, Johnny Weissmuller as Tarzan). These images were, therefore, amenable to being understood in terms of white superiority, drawing on both classical and fascist ideology and iconography.

In this respect, it should not be surprising that the hard bodies of the 1980s – bodies like Schwarzenegger's, Stallone's, Willis', Van Damme's – have been read in relation to Reaganite political ideology: an association reinforced by the political affiliations of many of the hard body stars themselves. The late 1970s and 1980s were periods when masculinity – white, American masculinity in particular – was popularly represented as being in crisis (not for the first or the last time). This specific crisis was the result of at least four overlapping factors: the American defeat in Vietnam, what were perceived to be the failures of the 'soft' presidency of Jimmy Carter, the social movements for civil rights, women's liberation and gay liberation and the decline of heavy industry (Tasker, 1993; Jeffords, 1994; Faludi, 2000). As a counterpoint to this crisis, in the early years of his Presidency, Reagan was consistently portrayed in ways that emphasised his masculinity, strength and toughness, often drawing explicitly on the iconography of the Western (he was pictured chopping wood, riding horses and so on). Similarly, Hollywood action films of the period offered a space where the crisis of masculinity could be articulated and resolved in and through male violence, reinforcing the ideological project of the Reagan era. Not surprisingly, then, these films were generally derided by feminists and those on the left, and a number of critics have examined the relationship between nationalism, masculinity and Reaganite ideology in 1980s action films (Wood, 1986; Traube, 1992; Tasker, 1993; Jeffords, 1994) – a relationship that is nicely parodied in a widely reproduced image of the time, collapsing the figures of the President and Rambo (see Figure 5.7).

My own concern, however, is with the male hero's oscillation between victim and hero positions. It is significant to note here that the body of the Terminator can be damaged as well as do damage and in this the Terminator is not alone among action heroes. The vio-

Figure 5.7 *The male body and the Reaganite right in the composite figure of 'Ronbo'.*

lence done to the heroic body is one of the means whereby the eroticism of the gaze at that body is disavowed (Willemen, 1981; Neale,
1983), but there is something more at stake here. Whether man or
machine, these bodies withstand the abuse and heal themselves.

So, for example, John Rambo (Sylvester Stallone) stitches his own wounded arm in *First Blood* (Kotcheff, 1982) and spectacularly cauterises a shrapnel wound in his side using gunpowder in *Rambo III* (MacDonald, 1988). These scenes, as Jeffords (1994: 50) notes, typically provoke discomfort from audiences. They are visceral scenes, the camera lingering on the wound, demonstrating both the vulnerability and exceptional strength of the hero. While the heroes are not victims in any straightforward sense, the focus on the violence done to their bodies – of which their scars, torn and bloodied clothing serve as continual reminders – arguably legitimates the violence done by these bodies.

Moreover, the hard body is made vulnerable not only by physical injury but, more importantly perhaps, by relative isolation and marginalisation. The hero is typically an outsider, a straight, white male whose traditionally masculine values of individualism, aggression and stoicism are no longer valued post-Vietnam, post-civil rights, post-feminism. In films of the 1980s, the hero's placelessness is often linked (implicitly or explicitly) to his service in Vietnam – he is a soldier without an army, a veteran uncelebrated by the country for which he fought. This, certainly, is the story of Rambo in *First Blood*. For all the muscles, he is a victimised figure, 'wrongly, harshly mistreated by enemies foreign and domestic who would like to redefine and reshape that body and its presentations' (Jeffords, 1994: 31). He is a survivor of torture (his body still bears the scars and he has vivid flashbacks) and indeed the only surviving member of his Special Forces Unit from Vietnam. Back in the US, he is discriminated against because of his appearance and difference and – as he emotionally acknowledges towards the end of the film – ostracised from a society ashamed by the Vietnam war. So, white American men are positioned as the heroes and victims of Vietnam, displacing the reality of American atrocities against the Vietnamese. The villains of the piece are also white American men – the soft-bodied police and National Guard who push Rambo to the edge, but have none of his discipline, stamina or strength. As Jeffords, (1994: 32) notes:

> *First Blood* clarifies the consequences of the 'weakened' years of the Carter presidency, when strength and preparedness were, according to the Reagan historians, abandoned in favor of negotiation and capitulation. ... Consequently, *First Blood* shows audiences that inadequate, unprepared, and weakened masculine bodies cannot compete with the forces of a strengthened and prepared body.

The hard body and the qualities associated with it were, therefore, not only a masculine ideal, but a national ideal, too, in the Reagan era – and the Rambo trilogy, though attracting more criticism than most films of the period, was hardly unique in this respect. Indeed, masculine regeneration through violence is a generic action staple and depends on precisely this oscillation between victim and hero positions. Although *First Blood* is more ambiguous than most (the film ends with Rambo giving himself up to the police), by the sequel, Rambo's body is accorded something of the proper recognition – his is the only body for the job. In other films, those who would ostracise, suspend from duty or otherwise doubt the methods and morals of the hard body end up dependent on him for their very survival (King, 1999). The body is bruised, yes, but ultimately it is a body triumphant and, moreover, only this body can triumph. Indeed, some commentators predict that we are likely to see lot more of this regeneration of masculine and national identity through action in the post-9/11 period as social and political anxieties are again imagined on screen.

There are, perhaps, certain parallels here between the action hero and the serial killer. For both, it is their capacity for violence that affirms their identity and differentiates them from ordinary mankind. As Neale (1983: 12) notes of the Western and action/adventure films, 'the hero's powers are rendered almost godlike, hardly qualified at all.'

Further, and at the risk of stating the obvious, action in *First Blood* – as in the vast majority of action movies of the 1980s, 1990s and beyond – is an exclusively male preserve. Indeed, Yvonne Tasker (1993: 3) writes that, while researching her book on action cinema, she 'became convinced that that the figure of "woman" was in the process of being eclipsed from the Hollywood cinema altogether'. Although Tasker's conviction was subsequently shaken, it remains true that action women are still in the minority, both within the genre as a whole and, typically, within the narratives in which they function. Action heroes may be diegetically isolated, but it is not the fact of their violence (or capacity for violence) that isolates them from other men.

Twenty-first century heroes

Do twenty-first century action heroes have much in common with their counterparts from the 1980s and 1990s?

Consider how contemporary social events and anxieties – such as those aroused by the terrorist attacks on New York and Washington in 2001 and the subsequent 'war on terror' – might have shaped the representation of these heroes.

The action genre is not the only space where men's violence and victimisation typically co-exist – Westerns, gangster movies and war films are other obvious examples. In addition, since the early 1990s, a group of films variously labelled as 'new brutalism' (Hill, 1997) and 'neo violence' (Rich, 1992) have been of interest to critics in relation to their treatment of masculinity and violence.[9] However, we might well ask, what is new about the brutalism of films like *Reservoir Dogs* (Tarantino, 1991), films that, as noted in the introduction, have become virtually synonymous with screen violence? In defining the term, Hill (1997: 9–11) suggests that the films associated with this label are uncompromisingly and explicitly violent and focus on interpersonal, physical violence by men against men. As well as the perceived extremity – symbolised by *Reservoir Dogs'* infamous torture sequence – Hill (1997: 11) argues that new brutalism is distinguished by 'the use of *realism* when representing violence'. However, the 'real' has an often contradictory status within debates about screen violence and what appears realistic on screen is certainly generically and historically contingent (Hallam, with Marshment, 2000). Tarantino (in Dargis, 1994: 19), for example, argues that the violence in *Reservoir Dogs* and *Pulp Fiction* is both realistic and self-consciously cinematic:

> Every time you try to show gore realistically, it looks absurd, operatic. People go on about Tim Roth bleeding to death in *Reservoir Dogs*, but that's the reality. If someone is hit in the stomach, that's how they die. Put them in one spot in a room and they're going to have a pool growing around them. That might look crazy, but it's the truth and it's because you're not used to seeing the truth that it looks pushed. ... To me, even though it's got a foot in real life, it also has a foot in Monty Python.

Tim Roth's bloody demise is realistic in terms of cause and effect – 'If someone is hit in the stomach, that's how they die'. Yet Tarantino also foregrounds the aestheticism and potential humour of the bloody scene. Certainly, both *Reservoir Dogs* and *Pulp Fiction* consistently draw attention to their own artifice or unreality, to remind us that we are watching a movie, and watching violence within a movie. This self-reflexivity has become increasingly commonplace in genre films, such as slasher and action movies, as mentioned earlier. However, while such reflexivity can open up possibilities for subversive pleasures, it can also function to reinforce hegemonic power relationships by, for example, replicating misogynist patterns of looking, speaking or killing, at the same time using irony to stay any attempt to critique these representations. In her discussion of Tarantino's early work, bell hooks (1995: 64) sums this up brilliantly:

> Tarantino ... represents the ultimate 'white cool': a hard-core cynical vision that would have everyone see racism, sexism, homophobia, but behave as though none of that shit really matters, or if it does it means nothing cause none of it's gonna change, cause the real deal is that domination is here to stay – going nowhere and everybody is in on the act. Mind you, domination is always and only patriarchal – a dick thing.
>
> ... The fun thing about Tarantino's films is that he makes that shit look so ridiculous you think everybody's gonna get it and see how absurd it all is. Well, that's when we enter the danger zone. Folks be laughing at the absurdity and clinging to it nevertheless.

Although by no means an exclusive characteristic of new brutalism, it seems to me that this 'dick thing' is what links the films lumped together under the 'new brutalist' label. They are films that speak to a certain cultural (re-)construction of white, straight masculinity in 1990s culture. The explicitness with which brutalism and its effects are staged may be new, but the characters and the relationships between them are not. Tarantino may make white, macho violence look absurd, but he also effectively reinvents and legitimates its politics of domination (racism, misogyny and, especially, homophobia) in much the same way as we might argue that late 1990s horror repackages classic slashers (see also, Tudor, 2002). 'New brutalism', Tarantino-style, would seem to be defined by old politics, albeit in a new wrapping.

Women, violence, sexuality

Staying with 'new brutalism', I want to begin my discussion of women's violence with Oliver Stone's *Natural Born Killers* (1994) – a film that, with its very different constructions of the male and female mass murderer, usefully highlights some of the difficulties and tensions in representing women's violence. Reflecting on the motivations of his anti-heroes, Mickey and Mallory Knox, Stone (quoted in Williams, 1994: 16) suggests:

> Mickey is a total predator. He understands the universe only from a predatory standpoint and he justifies what he does that way. Mallory is a different question because

she comes from a whole different space, and we clarify their different motives.

This 'whole different space' – like the spaces accorded some of the women discussed in Chapter 4 – is one that is defined by victimisation (Mallory's sexual abuse at the hands of her father) and sexual objectification (throughout the film, there are moments where she embodies Mulvey's idea of 'to-be-looked-at-ness'). Of the child sexual abuse story, actor Juliette Lewis (quoted in Kaye, 1995: 29) notes:

> ... I mentioned that [Stone] might wanna show that something happened to this girl in her background. *It's hard to see a girl be that cruel.* I didn't want to disgust the audience; I want them to understand the character a little. (emphasis added)

Notably, Lewis suggests that it is specifically because Mallory is female that such a strategy is deemed necessary, as cruelty on the part of a woman would otherwise invite audience disgust and preclude identification. This oscillation between victim and perpetrator positions is, therefore, rather different than that undertaken by the action hero – she is victimised on the basis of her sex in a way male heroes very rarely are. Further, while Mickey, too, comes from an abusive home, his back story functions quite differently, establishing a continuity between him and his abusive father. As Mickey comments, 'I come from violence. It's in my blood. My dad had it, his dad had it. It's my fate.' Mickey is positioned as the latest in a long line of violent men: in his own family, in the diegetic world of *NBK* (the prison inmates, abusive guards and cops are all male) and in a broader, sociocultural context (references to Charles Manson, Ted Bundy, John Wayne Gacy and the Menedez brothers, among others, provide a recognisable context for Mickey's behaviour and the public consumption of it). Clearly, it is not hard to imagine a man being that cruel, as we have seen throughout this book.

In a survey article exploring the representation of violent women on screen from the mid 1980s to early 1990s, Christine Holmlund (1993b: 129) describes 'Hollywood's queasiness' about women who kill in comparison with the popularity of male killers such as the Terminator, Rambo or even Freddy Krueger. However, while feminists have replicated this 'queasiness' in their reluctance to tackle real women's violence, Hollywood's violent women have been the focus of considerable feminist interest. For many feminists, these women offer rare glimpses of female agency and sexuality, particularly lesbian sexuality, on screen – but what is the price for such visibility?

Mulvey's reference to the *femme fatale* of *film noir* offers one response to this question. Mulvey, you will remember, found in *film noir* the paradigmatic example of the sadistic aspects of the male gaze, with its narrative emphasis on demystifying the *femme fatale* and punishing or controlling her sexuality. Yet, other critics have pointed out that, for this punishment to be meaningful, the *femme fatale*'s sexual strength and threat must first be convincingly established. Precisely because such representations are relatively rare, it is, Janey Place (1978) suggests, the *femme fatale*'s strength and sassiness that we remember rather than her inevitable demise. Moreover, the *femme fatale*'s machinations clearly expose both men's fallibility and the fragility of the nuclear family, providing possibilities for feminist rereadings that complicate Mulvey's monolithic, ahistorical formulation of the gaze (see, for example, Gledhill, 1978; Harvey, 1978; Place, 1978).

Film noir emerged in a pre-feminist period of gender-role flux in the aftermath of the Second World War. As such, the *femme fatale* has been read not only (following Mulvey) as a manifestation of men's unconscious fears of female sexuality, but also as a historically specific response to men's anxieties about shifting gender roles (see, for example, Harvey, 1978). In this respect, it is significant that the themes, characters and visual style of *noir* experienced something of a resurgence from the 1970s against a backdrop of feminist activism and the almost simultaneous **backlash** against the movement. However, like classic *noir*, the *fatale* figure of neo-*noir* has been both celebrated and condemned by feminist critics, who have variously delighted in her assertiveness and rallied against the equation of women's sexual subjectivity with criminal violence.

Neo-*noir* clearly owes something to the feminist movement, but typically positions itself **'post'-feminism**, in the sense that it depends on and repudiates feminism. In planning her violent schemes, the more contemporary figure frequently employs a feminist discourse concerning sexual pleasure, men's violence and women's work. However – in a move that recalls the press construction of **'date' rape** and false memory stories in the 1990s (see Chapter 3) – these arguments are transformed so that feminism's threat to male privilege becomes a threat to individual men's lives and livelihood. Moreover, the feminist discourse on women's sexual autonomy here legitimates a sexualised display of women's bodies and sexual pleasure. While the very self-consciousness of the display and the explicit threat to male subjectivity that it poses presents the possibility of an active and ironic construction of 'to-be-looked-at-ness', nevertheless, this depends on a conventional equation of woman with sexual objectification and sexual objectification with women's power over men. This is explicit in *Disclosure* (Levinson, 1994), advertised with the slogan 'sex is power' and an accompanying image of the sexually harassing *fatale* figure (Demi Moore) pinning down Michael Douglas' beleaguered male (see Figure 5.8). In the context of a film dealing with workplace **sexual harassment**, this equation of sexual objectification by men with women's power over men is particularly troubling and works to negate men's responsibility for their actions and reactions. This argument found a particularly bizarre expression in the Automobile Association's complaint that Moore's 'power' to draw the gaze of male motorists from the road and onto the billboard could have catastrophic results (in *The Sunday Times, Cinema* section, 12 March, 1995)!

Julianne Pidduck (1995: 65) has coined the term 'fatal femme' to describe the 1990s incarnation of the *femme fatale*, noting that, while the fatal femme shares her predecessor's smart mouth and sexual savvy, she 'ups the ante of earlier, more muted cinematic codes of sexuality and graphic violence'. The shift in emphasis in Pidduck's term – the fatal femme is fatal because she is femme (feminine and/or lesbian femme), rather than a femme (woman/wife) who is fatal – reflects the importance of gender and sexual performance in these more recent films. The authenticity of the sexual performance and the nature of the fatal femme's sexual identity become the central questions to be investigated, an investigation that takes us from one sexual 'number' to another in a manner that, Kate Stables (1998: 174) suggests, mimics pornographic films. More generally, the linking of women's sexual subjectivity with violence has obvious implications for representations of lesbian-and bisexuality, as we saw in Chapter 4. In this respect, it is hardly accidental that the two genres in which lesbians have most commonly appeared are heterosexual pornography (where the performance of lesbianism can be recouped for the male gaze) and horror (where the lesbian is made monstrous).[10]

To illustrate some of these points, I want to briefly consider *Basic Instinct* (Verhoeven, 1992) – a film that, as noted in Chapter 2, generated considerable controversy for its equation of lesbianism, bisexuality and murderousness. The film begins with an unindentified naked blonde woman killing her sexual partner at the moment of his climax. As the film progresses, we are offered a series of explicit sex scenes and sexual displays in place of criminal investigation, as the cop investigating the murder (Michael Douglas again) becomes sexually involved with both of the main suspects. The investigation of their guilt is thus inextricably tied to the investigation of their sexuality. Both women have had sexual relationships with men and women, their bisexuality evidence of a refusal of binaries and boundaries that makes them threatening to the hero and potential criminal suspects. The authenticity of their heterosexual acts is the key to the case

Figure 5.8 *Sex is women's power. The sexually harassing* femme fatale *of* Disclosure
(Levinson, 1994).

both for the cop (for whom misreading the signs might mean death) and for the viewer (legitimating the 'investigative' gaze at the female body).

Interestingly, J. Hoberman (1995: 32) describes Michael Douglas' men-in-peril films – *Fatal Attraction* (Lyne, 1987) and *Falling Down* (Schumacher, 1992) as well as *Basic Instinct* and *Disclosure* – as role-reversing slasher movies. The comparison is a striking one, underlining the extent to which challenges to white male privilege are explicitly envisaged as a form of violence against white men. Indeed, Douglas himself frequently recasts interviewers' questions about his films' treatment of women and minorities in order to focus on political correctness as a censoring discourse, victimising and restricting white men.[11] In this context, women's violence is a sexy issue, both aesthetically and politically, while men's violence against women is once more rendered unspeakable.

Moreover, by condensing the threat to the nuclear family and heterosexual couple into the figure of the fatal femme, these contemporary films, 'ominously skew actual patterns of gendered violence' (Pidduck, 1995: 67). **Domestic violence** thus takes on quite a different meaning in the contemporary fatal femme film, as the threat posed to family and heterosexual harmony is both externalised and feminised. Men's domestic violence is rarely confronted in Hollywood films (Holmlund, 1993b: 128–9) and this makes the fatal femme's transformation and manipulation of feminist anti-violence discourses all the more troubling. In *The Last Seduction* (Dahl, 1993), for example, the fatal femme draws both on a pre-feminist stereotype of fragile, white womanhood and on feminist anti-violence discourse to manipulate men for her own advantage. Bridget's (Linda Fiorentino) self-presentations as a victimised woman may be patently unconvincing to the film's spectator (Bruzzi, 1997: 171), but, within the diegesis, men are only too willing to accept these stories at face value. The film's relationship to feminism is, therefore, complex. On the one hand, Bridget's performance exposes femininity as a fiction and begins to unpick the investments men have in it. On the other, the unquestioning acceptance, by a variety of male characters, of Bridget's false or exaggerated accusations plays into contemporaneous debates about 'victim feminism' and falsely accused men. In this respect, we might think of *The Last Seduction* – as well as its contemporaries *Disclosure* and *To Die For* (Van Sant, 1995) – as backlash variations on the rape revenge narrative, where the sexualised revenge proceeds from a false claim of rape (or other male violence) that is only believable because of the popular acceptance of feminist anti-rape discourses (Boyle, 1998). Here, it is men who are failed by the implicit assumption that women are incapable of desire or aggression and that men are guilty until proven innocent – a cinematic variant of the news media's fascination with false accusations and memories (see Chapter 3).

As we saw earlier in this chapter, Mulvey argued that the sexual woman's threat is typically contained by the end of the classic *noir*. Neo-*noirs* are less uniform in this respect and the fatal femme's ability to outwit the male characters and survive on her own terms in films such as *Basic Instinct* has been celebrated by some feminists. Indeed, Carr (1992) and Taubin (1992) ask if the outraged responses of some male critics to *Basic Instinct* may be a reflection of the anxieties aroused by the bisexual killer rather than a concern about the film's misogyny. In this spirit, Paula Graham's review of *Basic Instinct* poses the question, 'What could be wrong with a film in which women sleep with each other and kill men?', while Ruth Picardie comments, 'a dyke with two Ferraris who kills men? Now there's a positive image!' (quoted in Keesey, 2001: 50). Nevertheless, it is striking how often the sexual and aggressive woman is still contained or punished in protracted and excessive scenes of violence, of which *Fatal Attraction*'s stabbing, drowning and shooting of the fatal femme is still perhaps the most obvious example.

Significantly, not only is the threat to family harmony posed by a woman in *noir* and neo-*noir*, but, frequently, the violent restoration of the family unit is also accomplished by a woman. In this context, women's violence is justified, even celebrated, as an extension of her familial role. This, for example, is the case in *Fatal Attraction* when the final shot is fired by the wife/mother whose place Glenn Close's character has tried to usurp. The juxtaposition of fatal femme and the good woman (who is defined by her familial relationships, whether wife, mother or daughter) further emphasises the former's sexual deviance and justifies the good woman's deployment of violence in defence of family, home and self. Notably, the final showdown frequently takes place within the family home – a space invaded and polluted by the fatal femme's sexuality and from which, in death, she is violently expelled.

This takes us to relatively familiar ground: women's violence requiring explanation in relation to their gender role and/or their deviance from it. In conclusion, I want to turn to screenwriter Hilary Henkin's account (quoted in Francke, 1994: 120–1) of trying to put an alternative version of the violent woman in a mainstream movie. From script to screen, the heroine of Henkin's *Fatal Beauty*, Rita Rizzoli, went through an interesting transformation. Rizzoli, started out as a female version of Dirty Harry – obsessive, violent, lacking in back story – a concept apparently too frightening for the studio:

'It seems that similar sorts of male characters within the genre are allowed to indulge their obsession, with almost no reason, and when they indulge their obsession they are applauded by the film-making establishment and the audience. But the notion of the female character who does things for the sake of doing them seems to be frighteningly out of control for the system and its perception of how the audience would react to that idea … the studio didn't think that an audience wanted to see such a violent woman. Hence they built in a back story. The movie went through many incarnations on the way to production. It was turned into a comedy, and from being a comedic tragi-comedy, it became a broad comedy. Rita was given the quintessential abused female back story – which gives her a motive, but it is a far less profound motive than she might have had.'

Henkin's account provides a clear example of how women's on-screen violence – like that committed by the real women discussed in Chapter 4 – requires explanation and personal, gendered motivation that is rarely an issue for their male counterparts. While I make no claims that Henkin's heroine in her original form is necessarily more feminist, it is the job of feminist criticism to identify the ways in which gender determines what can and cannot be said and shown about violence.

Summary

- Feminist explorations of gendered violence in film consider both the surface image (what is shown) and the ways in which we are positioned in relation to that image. The tensions between surface image and patterns of identification and objectification produce a variety of feminist perspectives on genres such as the slasher, action, rape revenge film and neo-*noir*.
- The sexual objectification of violent women on screen typically works to contain their agency, while the agency of violent men typically guards against their sexual objectification.
- Film representations of rape and other forms of violence against women both initiate and respond to broader sociocultural debates about feminism, violence and justice.
- The self-reflexivity that has become increasingly commonplace in violent movies since the late 1980s opens up possibilities for subversive (and possibly feminist) pleasures, but also functions to reinforce hegemonic power relations, replicating misogynist patterns of looking, speaking or killing while using irony to hold critique at a distance.

Notes

1 The most influential of these studies are Marjorie Rosen's *Popcorn Venus* (1973) and Molly Haskell's *From Reverence to Rape* (1974), both of which focus primarily on images of white, heterosexual women in Hollywood. Subsequent work has addressed the pervasive stereotyping of other marginalised groups, including black men and women (Bogle, 1994), lesbians and gay men (Dyer, 1977; Russo, 1981) and disabled men and women (Norden, 1994).

2 For an accessible introduction to feminist film theory and an overview of its development see Stacey (1994: Chapter 2) or Smelik (1995). Although I am positioning

Mulvey here in relation to developments within feminist film theory, it should be noted that her article was equally an intervention in debates about psychoanalysis and cinema being conducted in the pages of the British film journal *Screen*. Mulvey's article is easily the most reprinted article in feminist film theory and has made feminist analyses central to film studies as a discipline.

3 On the female spectator, key texts include Mulvey (1981), Doane (1982; 1988–9), de Lauretis (1984) and Stacey (1994). The special issue of *Camera Obscura* (1989, 20/21) devoted to the question of female spectatorship is also useful. On male masochism, see Silverman (1980), Studlar (1985) and Clover (1992). Neale's 'Masculinity as spectacle' (1983) opened up the debate on male objectification. Stacey's work (1987, 1994) challenges the heterosexual assumption of Mulvey's approach and work by Jane Gaines (1988) and bell hooks (1992) explores how race has also structured the 'right to look' in historical and political terms.

4 Audience studies suggest that this claim has a certain empirical basis (Chapter 2).

5 The apparent gender confusion or transgression of horror monsters and fictional serial killers alike has long been a source of concern for feminists, lesbian and gay critics. Benshoff (1997) and Creed (1993) provide very different starting points for exploring these issues. The linking of physical difference with monstrosity is problematised by disabled writers and activists who highlight the ways in which the disabled or deformed monster functions as the repository of the fears non-disabled people have of disabled people (see, for example, Longmore, 1985; Norden, 1994). Writing from a feminist perspective, Morris (1991) demonstrates how these stereotypes are gendered.

6 Unusually, *Friday the 13th*'s first killer is a woman. However, the film works to make us think that the killer is male up until the final moments. For example, we catch glimpses of the killer's clothing (sturdy black shoes, a plain shirt), we know the killer is physically strong and she appears considerably taller than her victims.

7 The poster is reproduced in Read's *The New Avengers* (2000). On the Millennium Edition Region 1 DVD, the slogan becomes: 'THIS WOMAN HAS JUST CHOPPED, CRIPPLED AND MUTILATED FOUR MEN BEYOND RECOGNITION ... BUT NO JURY IN AMERICA WOULD EVER CONVICT HER!' This is more accurate in relation to Jennifer's actions (she does not burn men in the film) and suggests that the burning in the original may well be a direct reference to the Hughes case, with which contemporaneous audiences would be familiar.

8 See also Rapping (1991), Grundmann (1991), Sturken (2000) and Read (2000).

9 The films to which this label has been most consistently applied are *Reservoir Dogs* (Tarantino, 1991), *True Romance* (Scott, 1993), *Pulp Fiction* (Tarantino, 1994), *Natural Born Killers* (Stone, 1994), *Killing Zoe* (Avary, 1994), *Bad Lieutenant* (Ferrara, 1992), *Man Bites Dog* (Belvaux, Bonzel and Poelvoorde, 1992) and *Henry: Portrait of a Serial Killer* (McNaughton, 1986). Although linked because of their extreme portrayals of violence, these films are otherwise very different.

10 On lesbian representations in film more generally, see Weiss (1992), Whatling (1997) and the essays collected in Wilton (1995). All of these texts engage with the question of violence.

11 For a more detailed discussion of Douglas' roles and persona, see Davies and Smith (1997), Boyle (1998: Chapter 7) and Watts (1995).

Further reading

Clover, C. (1992) *Men, Women and Chain Saws: Gender in the Modern Horror Film*. London: BFI.

Hart, L. (1994) *Fatal Women: Lesbian Sexuality and the Mark of Aggression*. London: Routledge.

Jeffords, S. (1994) *Hard Bodies: Hollywood Masculinity in the Reagan Era*. New Brunswick, NJ: Rutgers University Press.

Kaplan, E.A. (ed.) (1998) *Women in Film Noir,* rev. edn. London: BFI.

Tasker, Y. (1993) *Spectacular Bodies: Gender, Genre and the Action Cinema*. London: Routledge.

6

The days of whose lives? Violence, (post-) feminism and television

Chapter outline

In Chapter 1, I argued that we cannot separate acts of violence on screen from the contexts in which they take place, nor can we equate violence with physical acts. Despite its recurrent use in policy debates, therefore, 'television violence' is an indefinable object and studying violence on television cannot be divorced from studying television. This chapter explores how interpersonal violence is made meaningful in specific televisual contexts. The concerns of feminist television critics frame this chapter, but are also interrogated and challenged within it as I discuss representations of violence in genres – including the talk show, soap opera and contemporary action television – which have in various ways tackled questions about women's agency, feminism and violence.

- Letting men off the hook
- Soap operas and male violence
- The personal and the political
- Crime-time
- Putting men (back) in the picture

feminist and **post-feminist** television criticism and the problem of women.
narrative structure and everyday violence.
talk shows, consciousness-raising and women's speech; made-for-TV movies.
heroine television; law and order; **rape**.
the problem of post-feminism; sitcoms; action heroines; male violence.

Letting men off the hook?

Writing in 1995, Charlotte Brunsdon identified four main categories of feminist television scholarship: the real world of women working in television, content analyses of the presence of women on the screen, textual studies of programmes for and about women and studies focusing on female audiences.

What unites feminist research in each of these categories is a concern with women, whether behind the scenes, on screen or in front of their television sets. This, of course, is in sharp contrast to feminist film criticism, where male viewing pleasures have also been a central concern (see Chapter 5). More specifically, in the introduction to *Feminist Television Criticism*, Brunsdon et al. (1997: 1) suggest that feminist television criticism is defined by an engagement 'with the problems of feminism and femininity – what these terms mean, how they relate to each other, what they constitute and exclude.'

With the focus on women and femininity, it is perhaps not surprising that violence on television – which, as we saw in Chapter 1, is an overwhelmingly male preserve – has been of somewhat tangential interest. Yet, as has been repeatedly demonstrated in this book, male violence has been a central feminist concern and this makes the relative silence of feminist television critics on the issue rather troubling. Indeed, the first feminist books focusing specifically on violence on television – all of which deal with **sexual violence** on US prime-time programmes (Cuklanz, 2000; Projansky, 2001; Moorti, 2002) – were not published until relatively recently. This chapter, therefore, begins with a consideration of feminist television criticism more generally before moving on to consider how we might extend this work in order to analyse televisual representations of violence in those genres and shows which have been of most interest to feminists.

Of Brunsdon's four categories, it is the latter two – textual and audience studies – that have dominated feminist television criticism, with interest focused on a relatively small range of texts and their audiences. Daytime and early evening television – largely neglected in debates about violence on television – have been central to feminist television criticism. In the early days of the women's liberation movements, these genres were heavily criticised by activists for not reflecting the diverse realities of women's lives and instead focusing on a narrow range of roles for women centred on home and family.

By the late 1970s, feminists within the academy began to reject this realist paradigm and take soaps – and women's pleasure in them – more seriously. The concern with these texts and their audiences was part of a broader feminist project of re-evaluating critically derided 'women's genres' and investigating how women constructed meaning from these texts in the contexts of their lives (Hobson, 1982; Modleski, 1984). The interest in soaps, however, was not restricted to the daytime and some of the most influential feminist studies of the 1980s and 1990s focused on prime-time US soaps, such as *Dallas* (1978–90) and *Dynasty* (1981–89). Research examining how these programmes were received in specific communities within the US (Press, 1990) and in different national contexts (Ang, 1985; Liebes and Katz, 1990; Gripsrud, 1995) brought questions of class, race, nationality and cultural imperialism to the fore and began to complicate the relatively homogenous 'women's audience' imagined in early feminist work.

There have been few published studies focusing specifically on representations of violence in soaps,[1] but, the nature and frequency of violence against and by women is a recurring if peripheral concern in more general studies of both UK and US soaps (see, for example, Geraghty, 1991, Williams, 1992). Moreover, the textual attributes that some have argued create the space for feminist readings within the soaps – multiple points of view and overlapping stories, narratively central women, the privileging of talk over action – have particular implications for representations of male violence, as I demonstrate in this chapter.

Of course, it's not just soaps that have been of interest to feminist television critics. Other genres for and/or about women – most notably, talk shows and made-for-TV movies – have also attracted attention. With their focus on interpersonal relationships, these genres also engage with men's physical and emotional violence against women (in the home, on the streets and at work) and women's responses to that violence. In addition, there has been great interest in what Brunsdon (1995: 34) dubs 'heroine television' – primarily, but not exclusively, situation comedies and crime shows that focus on female characters trying to cope with the multiple and often contradictory demands placed on them in a **patriarchal** society. As Brunsdon (1995: 34) notes, 'These shows are all, in some fundamental way, addressing feminism, or addressing the agenda that feminism has made public about the contradictory demands on women.' 'Addressing feminism' in the context of crime inevitably raises questions about gendered violence and justice.

Since Brunsdon's article was written, critical responses to shows such as *Ally McBeal* (1997–2002), *Sex and the City* (1998–2004) and *Buffy the Vampire Slayer* (1997–2003) have focused less on the agenda that feminism has made public than a post-feminist agenda in which violence (or men's violence at least) has an even more marginal position. As post-feminism emerges repeatedly in debates about television, it is useful to clarify how the term has come to be used and how I am using it here.

Post-feminism was itself initially a media term, implying, variously, a periodisation, a development and a rejection of **second-wave** feminism. In popular representations of post-feminism, the second wave is represented as a historically specific (1970s) movement, the **liberal** (equality) wing of which has been successful, while the **radical** wing (concerned with challenging male power and violence and changing society) is dismissed as extremist and essentialising. As befits its popular origins, post-feminism has never been a concrete political, activist movement. The American writers most associated with the term – Naomi Wolf (1994) and Camille Paglia (1993), as well as Katie Roiphe (1994) and Christina Hoff Sommers (1994), who we encountered in Chapter 3 – in many ways have little in common, except, perhaps, a general concern with rejecting what is seen as the victimising tendency of radical feminism and exploring issues of women's autonomy and sexual desire.

With the popularisation of these media-friendly women's views, post-feminism has come to be associated with a focus on the individual (generally white, middle-class, female) subject. This is a subject divorced from any understanding of oppression as actively constructed not only in terms of gender but also, for example, along the lines of race, ethnicity, class and sexuality. Against this background, a feminist analysis of violence is deemed both unnecessary and victimising (Roiphe, 1994; Sommers, 1994) and it is hardly surprising, then, that there has been very little attention devoted to men's violence in those television shows most consistently dubbed post-feminist. It is in this respect that post-feminism is perhaps most effectively aligned with what Susan Faludi (1992) dubs the **backlash** against feminism. With feminism redefined in individualist terms, the radical demands of women's liberation – demands that men change – are allowed to disappear from the media landscape.

I do not want to suggest that this is the only or indeed the definitive meaning of post-feminism – it is a term that carries a range of often ill-defined meanings in both popular **discourse** and academic scholarship (Gamble, 2001; Lotz, 2001). However, as this individualist definition is associated with the term both in popular culture and critiques of popular television, it is the one I want to retain here. Arguably, with its primary focus on women (in the audience and on screen), feminist television criticism has facilitated the 'post-ing' of feminism in these debates by allowing representations of men to remain relatively underexplored. This chapter examines the implications of this emphasis for an understanding of gendered violence on the small screen.

Soap operas and male violence

Interpersonal violence – murder, **domestic violence**, rape, **sexual harassment**, incest – has been a staple feature of the soap opera landscape since at least the 1970s. In her 1992 study of US soaps, Carol

Traynor Williams notes that women are almost always the victims of violence in soap stories and links soap opera representations of rape to a longer **misogynist** tradition of rape as entertainment. In the 1970s and 1980s in particular, US soaps were accused of perpetuating extremely anti-feminist myths about men's violence against women, not least by means of the figure of the rapist turned romantic hero (Williams, 1992; Dutta, 1999).

The realist tradition in British prime-time soaps has resulted in a rather different treatment of men's violence against women, although the incentives soap producers have for developing violence against women storylines are unlikely to be entirely shared by feminist activists. For example, drawing on interviews with industry personnel in Britain, Henderson (2002) describes how the Jordache family were introduced to *Brookside* (Channel 4, 1984–2003) in 1992 specifically to develop a story on domestic violence, child **sexual abuse** and the defence of provocation in murder trials.[2] This fitted the social issue ethos of *Brookside* and provided a long-running sensationalist story to boost flagging ratings. It proved a phenomenally successful strategy, with Channel 4 achieving their highest audience share to date when mother and daughter went on trial for the murder of their abuser in May 1995. Similarly, *Emmerdale*'s (ITV, 1972–) first child sexual abuse story was developed in 1992 in order to boost ratings and bring younger viewers to the programme. Even *Coronation Street* (ITV, 1960–) – a soap not known for its social issue storylines – nevertheless achieved its highest viewing figures to date when Alan Bradley beat up his partner, Rita, in 1989.

Although the ratings-grabbing nature of violence storylines might be a source of concern, studies with female audiences have demonstrated that, by making visible what is still too often hidden behind closed doors, soaps can help to end abused women's sense of isolation, provide a language with which they can name their experiences (sometimes for the first time) and provide an impetus to begin the support-seeking process (Schlesinger et al., 1992; Kitzinger, 2001; Henderson, 2002). Indeed, British soaps have frequently been praised for their sensitive, critical and pro-feminist treatment of violence against women. A textual analysis of soap opera can help us to understand some of the contradictions in telling stories of gendered violence in this format by focusing our attention on how soap opera as a form both facilitates and contains feminist discourse.

With their multiple, overlapping storylines, soaps are structured on patterns of repetition and interruption that mirror the daily experiences of women watching in the home – a space of simultaneous work and leisure for women. Tania Modleski (1979) – whose article 'The search for tomorrow in today's soap operas' was one of the first to explore the feminine form from a feminist perspective – argues that this narrative structure denies the viewer the opportunity to identify with a single protagonist, forcing the viewer into multiple identifications. Instead of the **sadistic**, controlling **voyeurism** of narrative cinema's **male gaze** (Chapter 5), Modleski argues that soap's spectator is akin to the 'ideal mother', identifying with everyone and attempting to balance contradictory demands. Further, soaps, again unlike narrative cinema, are characterised by a lack of closure – they do not have a beginning, a middle and an end that wraps everything up and restores order. The mini-climaxes of soaps (weddings, shootings, births, shocking revelations and so on) do not simplify characters' lives but introduce new difficulties, complications and pleasures. Indeed, action is of secondary importance – it is not what happens but how it happens, and how the characters make sense of it when it does, that matters most.

A further characteristic of the soap is the centrality of (predominately white) women and their experiences. While women's roles in soaps have arguably changed in the period since the first feminist studies were written, soaps still consistently present (predominately white) women's experiences of work, family, love and relationships. For feminist critics this is something of a double-edged sword. On the one hand, they privilege the experiences of some women, but, on the other, they arguably make those women responsible for the maintenance of the family and community and, thus, for the crises that beset both on a regular basis. Further, feminists have been critical of the ways in which white women – in all media forms – are used to represent a universal female experience, ignoring the ways in which women's experiences are inflected by racial, national and class positions (Projanksy, 2001; Moorti, 2002).

In Modleski's (1979: 43) words, then, 'soap operas are not altogether at odds with a possible feminist aesthetics'. They privilege a non-controlling female gaze, focus on process, resist closure and centralise the experiences and emotions of (some) women. The difference between this and Mulvey's characterisation of narrative cinema could not be more stark. That soaps are not at odds with a feminist aesthetics, does not, of course, mean that the form and content necessarily privileges feminist understandings of male violence in any straightforward way. However, the soap opera form does arguably create spaces for such discourse.

To illustrate this, I want to turn now to the prime-time British soap, *EastEnders* (1985–) and, more specifically, to the Slater family, around whom overlapping stories concerning domestic violence, child sexual abuse and prostitution developed in 2001–2.[3] I make no claims that the Slater family's stories are representative of the treatment of violence against women in soaps (or even in British soaps). Rather, I hope that my analysis will highlight some of the issues at stake in examining soap opera violence and open up ideas for further study.

First, a brief introduction to the Slaters is necessary. The core family group comprises father Charlie, his mother-in-law Mo, and four of his daughters, Lynne, Little Mo, Kat and Zoe. Not long after their arrival in Albert Square, we learned that Little Mo (Kacey Ainsworth) had been abused by her estranged husband, Trevor (Alex Fearns). Against her family's wishes she returned to Trevor and the physical, sexual and emotional abuse began again, culminating in a particularly vicious attack on Christmas Day 2001. While Trevor's abuse of Little Mo escalated in secret, the family was shocked when Kat (Jessie Wallace) revealed that her Uncle Harry (Michael Elphick) had sexually abused her in her adolescence. Further, it emerged that Zoe (Michelle Ryan) – who had been brought up as Kat's sister – was in fact Kat and Harry's daughter, the product of the rape (1–5 October 2001). Shocked and distressed by this disclosure, Zoe ran away from home and – with no money or shelter – was in the process of being recruited into prostitution before she was returned to her family. While Zoe was on the run, her attempts to contact Little Mo were frustrated by Trevor. This was the final straw for Little Mo, who left Trevor, only for him to track her down and threaten her again. This time, however, Little Mo struck back, hitting Trevor over the head with an iron and leaving him for dead on New Year's Eve, 2001. She was later tried and convicted of attempted murder (14–19 April 2002), but subsequently freed after Trevor violently assaulted Kat (July–August 2002). After Little Mo's release, Trevor stalked her and, finally, attempted to kill both Little Mo and himself in a Halloween-night fire. Just over a year later, in the run up to Christmas 2003, Little Mo was raped by a punter in the bar where she worked.

As is apparent from this brief account, *EastEnders* developed these stories over a considerable time period. Although there were moments of sensational climax (Kat's disclosure, Little Mo's trial, the fire), the soap was particularly effective in rendering the everyday nature of domestic violence. Whereas, in other media forms, domestic violence only tends to become a story after it results in severe physical injury or murder (as we saw in Chapter 3), *EastEnders* showed the cumulative effects of Trevor's repeated physical, sexual and psychological abuse of Little Mo over a number of years. Moreover, the overlapping of the domestic violence, child sexual abuse and prostitution stories – both in terms of the time period in which they developed and the characters involved – arguably served to highlight the links between different forms of male violence against women.

However, it has also been suggested that the victimised woman has replaced the strong woman as the central character in the soap opera world. This is a legitimate concern, particularly as so many of the *EastEnders'* women are or have been victims of male violence or **commercial sexual exploitation**. Yet, the very nature of soap means that these characters are not always and only victims, in contrast to women in other entertainment genres (Moorti, 2002). Not only are soap women usually allowed to survive – so taking on roles in future storylines not focused on their victimisation – but, even during the period of their abuse, they never exist solely in that storyline. Rather, they continually interact with others (neighbours, family, lovers, colleagues) and are shown from the perspective of these other characters, meaning that the abuser's perspective of the victim is never allowed to dominate. As women in Henderson's (2002: 179) study noted, the overlapping narrative structure thus allows for violence to appear as a part of everyday life.

Similarly, the abusive man is not only an abuser and this makes it more difficult to see him as a monster, as completely 'other' in the way rapists, for example, are so often portrayed in fact-based media (Chapter 3). Also, the relatively closed world of the soap opera means that abusers are likely to be known to their victims. So, in *EastEnders*, we knew Harry as Charlie's brother and Peggy's fiancé before we learned that he had abused Kat. While, as both Cuklanz (2000) and Moorti (2002) note, the majority of rapists on US prime-time television are known to their victim, they are rarely recurring characters and so are not known to the audience in the way soap characters are.

However, in British soaps at least, the soap opera abuser is unlikely to be completely integrated into the soap community. Both Trevor and Harry, for example, were marked as outsiders, joining the show after the Slater family had been established and never having a permanent home on the Square. Reflecting on this, former Executive Producer John Yorke notes that when the possibility of running a child sexual abuse story in *EastEnders* was first discussed, the preferred option was to develop this story around long-established characters, gradually revealing a hidden history of abuse. The idea was abandoned as there was concern that the audience would feel betrayed by such a revelation about a long-established and well-liked character.[4] Of course, such a betrayal would, in a small way, mirror the real-world experience of discovering that a friend, lover, neighbour or family member – a 'normal' man – is an abuser. However, as Yorke acknowledges, *EastEnders* is an entertainment programme and the dramatic potential of such a story has to be weighed against the potential impact on viewer pleasure and ratings. Clearly this places certain limitations on the realism of the representation.

That the abuser is a relative outsider also means that he can be easily expelled from that community (Trevor died in a fire, Harry was banished to Spain where he died of a heart attack). While it is clearly preferable to see the abusers punished rather than rehabilitated as romantic heroes (see Dutta, 1999), there is a whiff of divine justice about Trevor and Harry's deaths that negates the necessity of social change. The bad guys get what's coming to them without anyone else (neighbours, family, police, courts) having to take decisive action.

Of course, Little Mo did attempt to take decisive action earlier in the development of this story (hitting Trevor over the head with an iron), but Trevor – like the horror movie monster he increasingly came to resemble – could not be easily killed. Little Mo's attempt to fight back landed her (like *Brookside*'s Mandy and Beth before her) in the dock and her trial, conviction and subsequent appeal went some way towards highlighting the inequities of the legal system. However, while the exceptional cases of women who fight back might make for gripping drama, this arguably undermines the more mundane, persistent realities of domestic violence that the soap – patterned on repetition and the deferral of closure – is otherwise well positioned to deal with.

The centrality of talk to the genre is also important here. As we have seen in previous chapters, making previously hidden and unspeakable acts of male violence visible was and is a key feminist concern. In the 1970s, it was through consciousness-raising groups and 'speak outs' that women first began to collectively name and develop an analysis of their experiences of male violence. With its focus on talk as action, the soap arguably draws on these modes. The episodes following Kat's disclosure of child sexual abuse, for example, focus almost exclusively on talk as Kat tries to explain both her experience and her prior silence. Indeed, one episode is almost entirely taken up by a dialogue between Kat and Zoe and – as is common in soaps – the viewer/listener is given few distractions from the words. Kat's disclosure takes place in a setting that is confined, familiar and (importantly) domestic and extreme close-ups are used to heighten the emotional impact of the scene (see Figures 6.1 and 6.2). Unusually, in this instance the characters talk with no interruptions from other characters and with few cuts away to other stories, thus marking the importance of this speech act. At other points in the development of the Slater stories, the characters note the connections between these different forms of male violence. So, for example, during Little Mo's trial, Kat and Billy (Little Mo's friend and, later, husband) share their childhood experiences of being abused by male adults and make connections with Trevor's treatment of Little Mo. When Little Mo is raped again, she explicitly links the rape to Trevor's abuse and voices her determination not to be victimised by the experiences.

This talk extends beyond the primary text. While neither Little Mo nor Kat seek support from external organisations, viewers are explicitly encouraged to do so. At the end of each relevant episode, a voiceover

Figures 6.1 and 6.2 *The disclosure of child sexual abuse in a familiar setting, Jessie Wallace as Kat in* EastEnders *(BBC1, 2 October, 2001).*

invites viewers who have been affected by the issues to call the BBC's Action Line or go to the *EastEnders'* website where feminist organisations Rape Crisis and Women's Aid are prominently listed. Further, in numerous interviews, the actors outline the continuities between their characters' experiences and those of the real women they have encountered while preparing for the role or, later, in letters and responses to the story. Underlining the relationship between fiction and reality, Little Mo's story was the subject of a documentary during the BBC's 'Hitting Home' season on domestic violence (BBC1, 16 February, 2002) and actor Kacey Ainsworth fronted appeals for domestic violence charities during the Comic Relief telethon (BBC1, 14 March, 2003).

These secondary texts can work to create a collective, potentially feminist, identity for abused women and enlarge the show's more limited discussion of domestic violence and incest. Indeed, survivors and feminist support agencies alike have generally been extremely positive about soap's role in making hidden violence visible in everyday contexts, thus allowing viewers to name their own similar experiences and seek support (Schlesinger et al., 1992; Kitzinger, 2001; Henderson, 2002). After Kat's disclosure of child sexual abuse, for example, calls to the NSPCC's child protection helpline soared by 60% (*The Observer*, 7 October, 2001). To give an earlier example, as the Jordache storyline unfolded on *Brookside*, women's refuges and support agencies saw a marked increase in calls and specialist telephone helplines advertised after key episodes had an unusually high response from young people (Henderson, 2002: 9). However, specialist helplines are now rarely advertised on screen – the BBC's Action Line is a generic information and referral service that does not offer specialist counselling – and there is justified concern that soaps may thus increase victims'/survivors' isolation by raising the issue without providing appropriate follow-up.[5] Further, it could still be argued that the onus here is on women to seek help, not on men to change. Non-abused viewers are encouraged to view victims as vulnerable women in need of their support and charity, but are not confronted with the ways in which their own behaviour can challenge or condone male violence.

Stories about domestic violence

How does the treatment of domestic violence and child sexual abuse in *EastEnders* compare to representations in fact-based media (see Chapter 3)?

Finally in this section, I want to comment briefly on *EastEnders'* treatment of prostitution and link this to more general questions about the portrayal of prostitution and other forms of commercial sexual exploitation on television. I have already suggested that the multiple overlapping storyline structure of the soap allowed for connections to be made between prostitution and other forms of violence in the Slater story, creating possibilities for a radical feminist understanding of prostitution as a form of commercial sexual exploitation rather than simply 'work' (Jeffreys, 1997). However, the gendered nature of this commercial exploitation was only partially revealed in Zoe's story. While Zoe was clearly targeted because of her age and sex, her pimp was an older woman and men's involvement in creating the demand for prostitution was not visible. In another roughly contemporary prostitution story, Janine (a classic soap opera villainess who would later add murder to her list of crimes) prostituted herself in order to support a drug habit and give her additional leverage to exploit vulnerable and rather pathetic men. While Zoe and Janine's experiences were otherwise very different, they shared an implicit understanding of prostitution as a system in which women exploit women (themselves or others) and tempt or take advantage of men. The men do not create the demand (as radical feminist analyses of prostitution insist) but are peripheral to the prostitution story, simply responding (sometimes stupidly) to what is on offer. It is on offer everywhere in *EastEnders*. At the beginning of 2004, no fewer than four of *EastEnders'* central female characters – Zoe, Kelly, Janine and Pat – had at some time been involved in prostitution.

It is not only in *EastEnders* that it is on offer. Prostitutes and other women involved in the sex industry are arguably more visible now than ever – in soaps, crime dramas, documentary series, reality TV shows and talk shows. While there has been little critical work focusing specifically on representations of prostitution and commercial sexual exploitation, a cursory glance at the schedules would suggest that it is women – whether prostitutes, porn stars, or lapdancers – who are the focus of voyeuristic interest, while punters and pimps escape scrutiny.

Feminists' analyses of **pornography** (see Chapter 2) may provide useful frameworks for an analysis of shows such as Sky One's *Porno Valley* (2004) or ITV's *Personal Services* (2003), but there is also scope for a consideration of these shows as television. For example, how do these shows use the conventions of the documentary or reality TV show to position their viewers and what are the pleasures on offer here? Indeed, are we – as viewers – encouraged to participate in this commercial sexual exploitation?

In a rather different context, Lisa McLaughlin (1993) focuses on representations of prostitution in another 'women's genre' – the daytime talk show. She argues that talk show debates about prostitution continually return to the prostituted woman's body, her sexual technique, earnings and morality. Such discussion places prostitution as a job or lifestyle choice made by women, ignoring the social conditions that make prostitution seem like a viable choice and rendering invisible the demand and sense of sexual entitlement that creates the conditions for prostitution. For the women in the talk show audience challenging the prostitute guests, controlling (or ending) prostitution is the responsibility of the prostitute women rather than the men who buy them – an argument that, as McLaughlin notes, recalls Victorian debates about chastity, sexual morality and prostitution.

The personal and the political

McLaughlin's work suggests some of the potential contradictions of the talk show format. On the one hand, the talk show creates a public space for women's speech and experiences, recalling the feminist maxim that the personal is political. Even more obviously than soaps, talk shows – and in particular those US shows that established the popularity of the genre, *Oprah*, *Geraldo* and *Donahue* – are modelled on the format of consciousness-raising groups.[6] Indeed, the *Oprah Winfrey Show*, to take the most famous example, was, from the outset, explicit in its goal to empower the women who make up 80% of the talk show audience (Squire, 1994: 99; Shattuc, 1997: 8). On screen, women's talk is privileged – the majority of guests, experts and featured audience members are women and black women achieve a rare visibility here (Shattuc, 1997). The orchestration of their talk can also function similarly to the consciousness-raising group as an individual, personal experience is recounted in emotive detail, commented on, questioned and added to by audience members, experts and the host. As the individual's experience of abuse – a regular topic on the talk show circuit – becomes a collective story, there is the potential for understanding violence as a social rather than individual problem (Squire, 1994; Shattuc, 1997; Moorti, 2002). Moreover, the emphasis on personal experience establishes victims/survivors as the experts, while the featured experts – speaking impersonally and on behalf of others – are routinely challenged (Livingstone and Lunt, 1994).

However, while talk shows in some ways dramatise the slogan 'the personal is political', as McLaughlin's discussion of prostitution suggests, feminists have not been universally optimistic about the potential of the genre.[7] Indeed, a number of critics note that talk shows work to resist explicitly political (feminist) analysis in favour of personalising the political. So, as we have seen, McLaughlin (1993: 50) criticises the way in which talk shows relentlessly focus on the prostituted woman herself, ignoring both the punters and the broader social and political questions raised by the practice and regulation of prostitution. In telling stories about interpersonal violence, there is a similar emphasis on women's experiences, as victims/survivors are questioned in detail about incidents of abuse and about their feelings and actions. While such testimony was indeed an important aspect of early feminist speak-outs on male violence, critics argue that talk shows consistently marginalise or reject any attempts to connect this personal experience to an analysis of society (Alcoff and Gray, 1993; Armstrong, 1994). The experts most frequently invited on to the shows are not sociologists, criminologists or feminist advocates, but psychologists who focus on the individual storyteller and suggest ways in which she can overcome her problem.[8] Almost by definition, the talk show cannot do other than seek individual solutions as it presents a daily success story only to return the next day with more harrowing stories (Squire, 1994: 102). Thus, men's violence becomes reframed as an issue of women's mental health and the perpetrators remain virtually invisible.

In a British context, critical responses to the audience discussion programme *Kilroy* suggest that, here too, personal stories are privileged over 'expert' analysis yet carefully managed by the host to construct a relatively coherent, but usually conservative, social message (Haarman, 2001; Wood, 2001). Andrew Tolson (2001: 18), for example, notes that, 'in this type of show, people are not free to speak their experiences or tell their stories unless these closely conform to the dominant agenda.'

To further explore some of these tensions, I want to look in some detail at an edition of *Kilroy* broadcast on 26 September, 2003 and entitled 'My partner beats me'. While the programme certainly displays an awareness of feminist discourse on male violence – in terms of the language adopted by lay speakers and the host, for example – the tension between the personal and political/social can never be satisfactorily resolved and, as a result, the show's agenda or message is far from clear.

The programme is introduced, as usual, with Kilroy-Silk's direct-to-camera address which – in the instance – positions abused women as the object of his somewhat bemused interrogation: 'Your husband constantly beat you. And yet, you stayed with him for 21 years?'. However, following the title music, Kilroy-Silk's second to-camera address poses a different set of questions:

> Yesterday morning the Metropolitan Police carried out a dawn raid on 100 suspected wifebeaters. What's going on?

How did the police suddenly discover 100 wifebeaters? Did they have new information? Or were they, as one report implied, merely following up the calls that they had over the weekend and recent complaints of men breaking their injunctions but left until yesterday to deal with in one big swoop. Is this a publicity stunt or a real crackdown on domestic violence?

Here it is the police rather than the women who stay whose behaviour is interrogated, but, again, male perpetrators escape scrutiny. It is also striking that Kilroy-Silk does not attempt to link the two sets of questions – that is, women's failure to leave is not related to the lack, or inappropriate nature, of institutional support. The personal and political aspects of the question are clearly separated and as the discussion progresses, Kilroy-Silk is swift to redirect the discussion if women themselves attempt to explore these connections.

Extract

Key: W1 = first woman speaker; W2 = second woman speaker; W3 = third woman speaker; K = Robert Kilroy-Silk, Square brackets indicate overlap between speakers.

W1:	Well there's a lot more to it. Domestic abuse isn't just about being hit.
[*Audience*:	murmurs of agreement]
	That's the smallest part of it as far as I am concerned.
[*Unidentifed*:	Yes]
[*K:*	Right.]
	It's the psychological thing. A lot of it is about being in control of you and if the police then come and take control you're still not in control. The point is giving the woman back control.
[*K:*	So you don't ...]
	And she won't stay away until she's ready to stay away.
K:	So you, so you, what you're saying, you wouldn't have wanted, you don't approve of the the dawn swoop and the the 100 men being lifted by the police, like, as if ...
W1:	I don't see that it will do an awful lot of good, really, because

[K: Why?]
      the woman has to feel in herself, the woman has to be ready
      to leave. I've been there, I've done it.
K: Why are you puffing up there?
W2:   I disagree with you. If the police had come and helped me and
      lifted my ex-husband I would have been absolutely grateful.
[W1: Well I, but I]
[K: Why?]
W2:   Because you're not allowed to smack children and yet how
      come a husband can smack his wife or his partner?
[W1: Well, he isn't allowed.]
[K: What was he doing to you?] What was he doing to you?
W2:   A good hiding if there wasn't pop in the house. Good hiding if
      the house wasn't tidy, yet it was always immaculate. Em ...
K: Good hiding?
W2:   Right.
K: What's a good hiding?
W2:   Smack. Punch in the face.
K: Punch in the face? A punch or slap?
W2:   Punch. Slap. Kick. Pulled hair. You name it.
K: How long was it going on for?
W2:   Seven years.
K: How many times a week?
W2:   As many as he wanted.
K: What would it be? [What would be the number?]
W2:   [Em. Worse on a week]end.
(Kilroy-Silk's questioning continues in this vein, until Woman 3 inter-
rupts, off screen.)
W3:   Did you call the police when he hit you?
W2:   There was once I had an injunction but not power of arrest and
      he come at midnight and he wanted to speak to the children.
      I phoned the police. The police came and all they said was,
      well you haven't got power of arrest but we'll take him away
      so you can get some sleep.
K: Did he cause bruises and damage to your body?

In the extract, we can see some of these tensions at work. The first speaker attempts to connect the two framing narratives by suggesting that police intervention without the woman's consent mirrors the abusive situation. She also introduces questions of women's agency – taking back control, deciding to leave – in contrast to the way Kilroy-Silk

Figure 6.3 *The close-up isolates the speaker and the title of the programme in the bottom left of the screen reinforces the individualised nature of the story (Kilroy, BBC1, 26 September, 2003).*

has framed domestic violence, as a story about women's helplessness. The second speaker is clearly selected to introduce conflict and Kilroy-Silk prevents any dialogue between the women, focusing his attention on this speaker and ignoring the other women who attempt to contribute. The use of close-ups during most of this sequence also works to isolate individual speakers from the audience (see Figure 6.3), while Kilroy-Silk's movement within the studio – he sits some distance from the first speaker but moves to sit beside the second speaker – privileges the second speaker's account. More importantly, Kilroy-Silk's management of the second speaker's story seems designed to emphasise the woman's powerlessness. He interrupts and redirects, focuses on assault and injury in almost voyeuristic detail (despite the first speaker's insistence that physical violence is the 'smallest part of it') and ignores anything she says that does not fit this narrative (note the redirect in the final line, for example).

There are parallels here with press treatment of **sexual murder** and rape (see Chapter 3), but perhaps more obviously, Kilroy-Silk's interrogation – his short, sharp questioning, the demand for detail – is reminiscent of the treatment of victimised women in the courtroom – a process many women describe as being like a 'second rape'.[9]

Importantly, then, domestic violence is framed as a woman's story – a story told by women and addressed to women, but also a story about women, about their bodies, violence done to those bodies and their inability/failure/responsibility to end that violence. In his closing address to camera, Kilroy-Silk makes this explicit:

> If it's happening to you now it's wrong. A man beating a woman – whatever woman – is wrong. It's not right. It's not acceptable. It should not happen. And you must not put up with it. If it's happening to you, or if you're children and it's happening to your mother, then it's wrong and you must do something about it and ring the helpline number we've given you, or ring the police. Now.
>   And take care of yourselves.

Although Kilroy-Silk names men as perpetrators, this is immediately (if unconsciously) qualified so that man's agency is rendered invisible – it's not the man who's wrong, it's the beating ('it's not right', not 'he's not right') – and the responsibility for ending the violence is placed on women and children. As with *The Sun*'s domestic violence campaign to which this programme explicitly refers (see Chapter 3), the idea that viewers could be perpetrators is not entertained. Indeed, it is significant that in framing topics for discussion, Kilroy-Silk refers not only to personal narratives but also news stories and, in other instances, high-profile soap plots (a programme on rape aired the week of Little Mo's rape, for example).

In all of these sites – soaps, talk shows, news – there is a real tension between personal narratives of violence and an analysis of gendered violence as an experience of structured and systematic inequalities. This intertextuality again points to the difficulty of separating out an object labelled 'television violence'.

A similar tension between the personal and the political exists in the made-for-TV movie, another America-originated 'women's genre' that, in the 1980s and early 1990s in particular, repeatedly dramatised stories about gendered violence. Television movies frequently take news stories as their subject matter and virtually all of the high-profile US stories discussed in Chapters 3 and 4 have had the television movie treatment. Unsurprisingly, it is exceptional stories of gendered violence – those that have brought about legal reform (Cuklanz, 1996) or feature women killers (Rapping, 1992; Savage, 1996) – that have attracted most interest. Nevertheless, both Lisa Cuklanz (1996) and Sujata Moorti (2002) suggest that the made-for-TV movie offers more scope for presenting women's stories and feminist demands for legal reform than television news, which 'hails the white male subject as the normative citizen of the public sphere' (Moorti, 2002: 72). Where the news story typically has a short lifespan focused on criminal investigation and/or court proceedings (see Chapter 3), the television movie is more interested in making sense of criminal violence in the context of the lives of those (primarily women) affected by it. As Elayne Rapping (2000) suggests, the focus on women's lives allows the movie to place gendered violence within its social context. It is precisely this context that is typically lost in those other genres, such as news, court room TV or law and order dramas, which centre on legal processes and procedures – the gathering of evidence, questioning suspects, the adversarial criminal trial and so on.

In her earlier work, Rapping (1992: xxxi–xlii) also notes the centrality of the family (and women's role within it) to the television movie. She argues that the genre provides a space where the 'conflicts and contradictions inherent in the existence of the family as an institution' are publicly played out, creating space for the 'oppositional voices of feminists and other women'. In television movies of the 1980s, these oppositional voices reached a mass audience: for example, *The Burning Bed* (Greenwald, 1984), a television film focusing on an abused woman's trial – and acquittal – for the murder of her abusive ex-husband, aired to an audience of 75 million in 1984 (Rapping, 2000).

However, the family focus of the genre means that the narratives have little space for a consideration of women's collective experiences or responses to male violence. This is particularly stark in *The Burning Bed*. The Francine Hughes' case on which the film is based was initially brought to national prominence by feminist campaigners, but, in the film, the feminists are absent and Hughes' struggle is recast as that of an exceptional individual overcoming the odds. Further, the aesthetics (an emphasis on close-ups that mark the story as personal) and narrative structure tend to work to contain such oppositional voices, as Moorti (2002: 187–8) notes:

> Blending fact and fiction, the storylines in this hybrid genre tend to follow a formulaic trajectory: they begin with a problem that threatens or at least has an impact on the functioning of the nuclear family; at midpoint, the crisis escalates, but by the end of the movie, the family [though not necessarily in its original form] is rehabilitated. With their focus on the family, the made-for-TV narrative domesticates social issues, personalizes them and allows the viewer to respond emotionally.

Further, as Rapping (1992) notes, all families are not treated equally in narratives of abuse. Domestic violence, for example, is portrayed as a primarily white, working-class problem and working-class men who abuse are not given the same opportunity for redemption as their middle-class counterparts.[10] Here too, as elsewhere on television, black families are rarely the narrative focus.

A comparison of two of the most successful television movies of the 1980s – *The Burning Bed* and *Something About Amelia* (Haines, 1984) – illustrates Rapping's point. While the working-class wife-batterer of *The Burning Bed* 'is seen as the ultimate slob and beast', the middle-class incestuous father of *Something About Amelia* 'is never seen at his worst moments. He is never out of control, drunk or brutally abusive, at least to the camera's eye' (Rapping, 1992: 76). Moreover, the middle-class incestuous father – played by Ted Danson of *Cheers* fame – is given the opportunity for redemption in the form of counselling once he confesses his sins (see also Chapter 3).

Whether the focus is soap opera, talk shows or made-for-TV movies, feminists have argued that 'women's genres' have feminist potential. All consistently offer women's experiences of male violence – drawing, in different ways, on the feminist tradition of speak-outs and consciousness-raising groups. Also, they do so without using a male hero/narrator to interpret that experience, as is commonly the case in other dramatic forms (Projanksy, 2001; Moorti, 2002). Although we are offered women's experiences – experiences that are often articulated and dramatised in a language that owes a clear debt to feminism – these genres are, however, ideologically contradictory. There is a resistance to making the personal truly political and there is a focus (on screen at least) on individual solutions to the problem of men's violence. However, the critical work reviewed and expanded on here only tells half the story as the focus on women's genres, women characters and women viewers in feminist television criticism has largely been at the expense of a critical consideration of men and masculinity.

Crime-time

Crime on television, as in life, is an overwhelmingly male preserve (see Chapter 1), although, in other respects, television crime largely adheres to the 'law of opposites' (see Chapter 3). Ray Surette (1998: 47) explains the law of opposites in the following terms: 'whatever the truth about crime and violence and the criminal justice system in America, the entertainment media seem determined to project the opposite'. So, violent crime is overemphasised, individual personality traits are presented as the cause of crime, violence is presented as the solution and crimes are tidily solved by the conclusion of the show.

As in press reporting, there is an emphasis on the early stages of the justice process – law enforcement, investigation and arrest – and women are over-represented as victims of violent crime relative to criminal statistics (Surette, 1998: Chapter 2). However, while such broad brushstrokes can be useful in establishing a general sense of the televisual landscape, as I argued in Chapter 1, the content analyses that allow us to arrive at these conclusions are, in themselves, rather limited. Can feminist television criticism help to shed any more light on these gendered patterns?

In the 1980s and early 1990s, feminist work on law and order shows tended to concentrate on what Brunsdon dubs 'heroine television' – shows that placed women at their narrative centre. Perhaps more than any other series of the period, *Cagney and Lacey* (1982–88) attracted popular and academic attention for its negotiation of feminist concerns.[11]

With two female cops at its centre, much of the show's drama comes from the difficulties Christine Cagney (Meg Foster/Sharon Gless) and Mary-Beth Lacey (Tyne Daly) daily encounter as women working in a man's world, trying to balance work and personal relationships. In the first episode ('Bang, Bang You're Dead', 1.01), for example, the crime narrative (focused on drug-dealing and the murders of prostitute women) is intertwined with Chris and Mary-Beth's interactions with sexist colleagues and their struggle to be taken seriously by their boss. The boss patronisingly refers to them as 'girls' and 'broads', gives them sexualised assignments (posing as prostitutes) and passes them over for 'real' police work until he sends them to a investigate a grusome **femicide** with the explicit intention of reminding them of their gendered position. Moreover, his sexist attitudes are made plain in dialogue with male colleagues – 'You tell me why guys with families are getting laid off and broads are getting promoted?', for example. Meanwhile, Mary-Beth herself struggles with the contradictory demands of being, in her words, 'a mother-wife-cop', with 'the emphasis on mother-wife'. This brings her into conflict with Chris, a single, career-orientated woman who is prepared to work extra hours and put herself in danger in order to secure promotion. Throughout the series, the tension between Chris and Mary-Beth – as well as the strong bond between them – gives rise to **diegetic** debates about women's choices (and lack of choices) that owe an obvious debt to feminism, even if the characters themselves are not straightforwardly feminist.

However, it is not only in terms of plot lines and character that *Cagney and Lacey* has been of interest to feminists. Generically, the show's combination of the public, action-orientated world of the cop show and the private, talk-centric world of the soap also creates spaces for feminist discourse. Significantly for our purposes here, gendered violence is a recurring concern throughout the series – from the murders of prostitutes in episode one to later episodes dealing with domestic violence, rape (including, as early as 1983, an episode on **'date' rape**) and sexual harassment. Unlike soaps, *Cagney and Lacey*, by definition, brings these instances of men's violence against women into the public sphere as criminal actions, even when the women victims are themselves reluctant to label their experiences as such. Like the soap, however, the show also provides space for women's experiences of male violence and other crime to be articulated and for female characters to support one another and challenge systems of inequality.

Nevertheless, as a commercial venture, the show's feminism was subject to containment to appease network, advertisers and anti-feminist critics – as Julie D'Acci's (1994) discussion reveals. In particular, the transformation of Christine Cagney during the show's early years – the role was re-cast (with Sharon Gless replacing Meg Foster), the character physically feminised and her difference from Lacey emphasised – was an explicit attempt (much criticised by female viewers) to make the show's feminism less overt and threatening.

Focusing on relatively exceptional shows such as *Cagney and Lacey* can illustrate some of the pleasures and contradictions inherent in attempting to place feminist concerns in a popular television format. However, such a focus can also divert attention from the everyday nature of men's violence against women in other, more conventional, programmes. Three more recent studies (Cuklanz, 2000; Projanksy, 2001; Moorti, 2002) go some way towards rectifying this in providing an overview of rape representations on US prime-time television between the mid-1970s and the mid-1990s and I want to briefly summarise the major points emerging from these studies.

Interestingly, all three studies found that representations of rape on prime-time television incorporate feminist anti-rape discourses, by, for example, acknowledging the victim's experience, challenging rape myths (that she provoked it, rape is the cost of female independence, men 'can't help it' when they rape) and condemning the rapist. The 'soapification' of prime-time television – the frequent use of ensemble casts and multiple, overlapping storylines in prime-time dramas – means that the rape story unfolds from the perspectives of several characters who debate not only the facts of a case (which most frequently hinge on consent), but also their meaning. As Judith Mayne (1988: 90) argues in an interesting reading of *L.A. Law* (1986–94),

> The centrality of multiple and overlapping narration in the series suggests the possibility of a more complex engagement with rape, defined as a problem of representation as well as a problem of sexual violence, than is usually the case on prime-time television.

The narrative structure thus allows women's experiences to emerge, at the same time as the focus on legal debate and argument demonstrates the ways in which the story-telling and image-making with which the law is primarily concerned can distort those experiences or render them unintelligible. *L.A. Law* thus acknowledges some of the failures of the legal system in handling rape cases (Cuklanz, 2000). However, it is male characters – such as the sympathetic Kuzak – who are given narrative authority here, making the women's experience intelligible and commenting on the inequities of the system (Mayne, 1988).

More generally, Cuklanz, Projanksy and Moorti all argue that prime-time television's rape narratives are essentially male stories. It is a recurring male character (a lawyer, cop, private eye, sometimes even a medic) who most often forwards the narrative (by seeking justice within or outside of the law), gives voice to feminist arguments and helps the victim – who is often resistant to these arguments – to make sense of her experience. More accurately, they are white, male stories without ever being stories about masculinity. The authoritative recurring characters are predominately white as, indeed, are the rapists they chase, capture or condemn, and the raped women they protect. Even in those rare cases where black men or women feature as perpetrators or victims, there is no acknowledgement that the experience of rape is inflected by race (and racism) as well as gender (and sexism) (Moorti, 2002). Further, these white men condemn the rapist and define the woman's experience from within the very institutions (the police, the criminal justice system, the medical profession) long criticised by feminists for their inadequate treatment of abused women. There is, therefore, a contradiction at the very heart of these representations. On the one hand, they demonstrate a popular acceptance of some feminist anti-rape discourses as common sense and challenge misogynist myths. However, on the other, that the feminist understanding is provided by a male authority figure undermines the need for any structural feminist analysis or collective action. By incorporating some aspects of feminist anti-rape discourse and having male characters 'do' feminism, the shows contribute to a cultural representation of (liberal) feminism as already successful and, so, no longer necessary. Thus, Projansky (2001) argues, contemporary prime-time television rape narratives are essentially post-feminist.

Male gazing on television

To what extent is Mulvey's (1975) concept of the male gaze (as discussed in Chapter 5) relevant to a study of television?

Putting men (back) in the picture

Projanksy's labelling of prime-time television's rape narratives as 'post-feminist' is critical, intended to draw attention to the limitations of these narratives in understanding men's violence against women. However, Projanksy is one of the few writers to have interrogated post-feminist television in relation to violence. More generally, the post-feminist frame has allowed men to slip from the picture, as we will now see.

In the late 1990s, shows such as *Ally McBeal* and *Sex and the City* became focal points for discussions about the meaning(s) of feminism and post-feminism in the press as well as in academic texts. What seems to define these shows as post-feminist for critics (popular and academic) – regardless of whether they celebrate or condemn the shows on these grounds – is the way in which their heroines both enjoy the gains of feminism and celebrate femininity (Moseley and Read, 2002: 236–7). There are two things to note about this. First, feminism (without the 'post') and femininity are constructed as exclusive categories. Much of the popular debate and even some of the academic debate about these shows therefore tends to label as feminist the heroines' usurpation of 'male' roles in their pursuit of career, sexual satisfaction and (post-Mulvey) sexual looking. In contrast, these heroines are not feminist (but, are, perhaps, post-feminist) when they express vulnerability and worry about appearance and romance. Second, the critical debate surrounding these shows' ideological positioning is often more narrowly focused on whether the character is feminist/post-feminist or not and, therefore, whether or not she is an appropriate role model for women.

So, we have women (critics) judging women (characters and, frequently, the actors who play them) as more or less suitable role models for other women (viewers). More seriously, these judgements are often based on precisely those factors that serve as markers of women's worth within patriarchy – physical appearance, weight, clothing, sexual assertiveness. The terms of the debate thus render feminism safe for men by focusing on conflict or consensus between women. So, where Tania Modleski (1991) suggests that post-feminism is a 'feminism without women', it seems to me that television criticism (both popular and academic) frequently imagines a feminism without men. Televisual representations of men, masculinity and violence remain largely unscrutinised, while representations of female agency are continually troubled and debated. Meanwhile, on screen, as Projanksy's (2001) discussion of rape narratives suggests, it seems that only male characters can unapologetically adopt the label and language of feminism.

Of the post-feminist shows, *Ally McBeal* merits particular consideration here for the way in which it transforms feminist discourses concerning sexual violence and justice into post-feminist comedy. Many of the cases dealt with by the legal firm for which Ally (Calista Flockhart) works have a clear feminist origin (Kim, 2001; Moseley and Read, 2002). In the first episode ('Pilot', 1.00), for example, Ally leaves one job for another because of her own experience of sexual harassment. However, for Ally work is a sexualised space and she is happy and willing to use her sexuality. Indeed, when the harasser reappears in a later episode, he (like the male motorists captivated by Demi Moore – see Chapter 5) is rendered relatively powerless by his attraction to Ally ('The Kiss', 1.03) and the show routinely presents harassment as an issue of representation rather than power.

Moreover, the courtrooms of *Ally McBeal* are crammed full of men and women who no longer know how to communicate with one another. In her courtroom speeches and performances, Ally connects these cases to her own relationships and the boundary between public and private is further blurred by the use of voiceovers and fantasy to render Ally's private thoughts and emotions in the public sphere. This, Moseley and Read (2002: 245) suggest, involves a reconfiguring of 'the personal is political' in 'a distinctly post-feminist manner'. Although they do not expand on this, I would suggest that this 'distinctly post-femininst' reconfiguring imagines that the feminist project to make the personal political has been successful, but the consequences have been absurd. So, although Ally and her colleagues do make connections between their own lives and the experiences of their clients, it is frequently to reject the distorting 'orthodoxy' of feminist discourse on equal opportunities, sexual harassment, commercial sexual exploitation and so on. Ally and her colleagues also find their own lives under legal scrutiny on a number of occasions, as, for example, when Ally has Internet sex with a boy she later discovers is 16 and is charged with statutory rape ('Do You Wanna Dance', 3.19).

The absurdity of many of these cases (the romantic, hopeless Ally is a rapist?) seems designed to render the legal system equally absurd, at least to the extent that it attempts to regulate interpersonal relationships. In this respect, *Ally* reflects the politics of the backlash – and the writings of Roiphe (1994) and Sommers (1994) in particular – in rejecting as illegitimate, extremist and downright absurd feminist attempts to make violence and abuse in private relationships public and to hold abusers legally accountable.

Thus, while – as we saw in the previous section – Mayne suggests that *L.A. Law* defines women's experiences of rape as a problem of representation as well as a problem of sexual violence, the sexual violence in *Ally McBeal* is only a problem of representation. Issues of violence, power and control are routinely evaded and, as representations are open to different, personal and frequently idiosyncratic interpretations within the text itself, the structural politics of representation are disavowed. Women use feminist arguments in the courtroom only when it is strategically beneficial to represent themselves in this way. For example, in the show's second season, Ling Woo (Lucy Lui) sues a misogynist radio personality for contributing to sexual harassment at her steel plant in one episode ('They Eat Horses Don't They?', 2.02) and in another episode is herself the defendant in a nuisance claim brought by Mothers Against Pornographic Entertainment relating to the operation of her female mud wrestling club ('Just Looking', 2.08). Further, the generalising claims about women made in court are repeatedly undercut by the distinct lack of solidarity between the women in the law firm. In 'They Eat Horses', to give just one example, Ally – appalled by what she sees as her colleague, Nelle Porter's (Portia DiRossi) dishonest treatment of the radio host – agrees to go on his show. Undercutting Nelle's prior courtroom arguments about the relationship between the radio show and the oppression and discrimination of women, Ally explicitly enjoys his construction of her as a sexual object. That she is – as another colleague comments – distinctly not herself in the broadcast (she is more confident, sexual) simply underlines Ally's point that the show is only representation (not oppression, not violence, not discrimination). Moreover, Ally's personal interactions with the radio host render him sympathetic, suggesting that his radio persona is an exaggeration, that it, too, is unreal and cannot have effects in the real world.

The use of humour is, of course, key here. Making sexual harassment and sexual exploitation the joke means that those who don't get it (both inside and outside the text) are cast as humourless (it is no accident that the anti-porn group is known by the acronym MOPE). In this sense, *Ally* arguably dramatises the backlash against feminism, but the programme is by no means unique in this respect. In a British context, Imelda Whelehan notes that magazines and television programmes aimed at 'new lads' employ a retro-sexism where the very knowingness of the representation seems to undercut critical analysis. She comments (2000: 69), 'as long as the message is intended as a "joke" no one can touch you for it', recalling bell hooks' critique of Tarantino's work (see Chapter 5). Similarly, both *Ally McBeal* and the diegetic radio show mentioned above are knowing about the ways in which they perform sexism and so attempt to undercut any feminist critique. Admittedly, the men in *Ally* are portrayed as rather absurd and pathetic figures, ruled, as Ling memorably puts it, by their 'dumbstick'. However, while the show holds men up to ridicule, it also – as Whelehan (2000: 26) argues in relation to the British show *Men*

Behaving Badly – sanctions their behaviour, asking women to indulge masculine 'weaknesses', 'not necessarily because they are inevitable or right, but purely because they are so absurd'. That these 'weaknesses' may include various forms of sexual harassment and discrimination in the workplace or plain sexism in interpersonal relationships does, however, suggest why some feminists might not get this particular joke.

Alongside Ally and her post-feminist sitcom sisters, a rather different kind of post-feminist heroine emerged in shows such as *Buffy the Vampire Slayer* (1997–2003), *The X-Files* (1993–2001), *Xena: Warrior Princess* (1995–2001) and, later, *Alias* (2001–). The physically strong, agile, resourceful and quick-witted heroines of these shows are, indeed, striking figures in a television landscape in which violence is largely a male preserve (see Chapter 1). However, by focusing on the agency and feminism of these heroines, the everyday nature of male violence on screen is again left unscrutinised. Pender (2002), for example, notes that much of the debate surrounding *Buffy* concerns opposing value judgements about the central character and the show – a good (feminist)/bad (not feminist) Buffy binary. However, even the term 'feminism' is contentious here, with critics variously labelling Buffy (the character) as feminist, post-feminist, third-wave feminist or discussing her 'girl power' credentials.[12] As Amanda Lotz (2001: 105) writes in her more general discussion of post-feminist television criticism:

> Confusion and contradiction mark understandings of feminism in US popular culture at the turn of the 21st century. Surveying the terrain of both feminist theory and popular discussions of feminism, we seem to have entered an alternate language universe where words can simultaneously connote a meaning and its opposite.

However, it seems to me that the questions we should be asking are not whether or not a character (or show) is feminist – as though 'being feminist' is something we can measure – but, more generally, how these texts engage with and negotiate feminist questions. Feminist questions are not only questions about individual choice. Rather, I want to get back to a conceptualisation of feminism as an active and relational process. This pre-post-feminism (or feminism as it used to be known!) is a way of thinking about the world and our position within it, rather than – as much of the writing on these television shows would seem to suggest – a way of thinking only about oneself.

It is in this respect that I think a show like *Buffy* merits particular consideration, and, indeed, a number of articles have explored the show's engagement with structural feminist concerns (Early, 2001; Miller, 2003). However, here, too, the treatment of men, masculinity and violence has remained critically underexplored, although it seems to me to offer a particularly productive way in to thinking about the show's relationship to feminist discourse and, moreover, of bringing together many of the themes of this book.

If we use the prefixes simply to imply a periodisation, Buffy is a 'post'-feminist heroine who does battle with 'pre'-feminist males on a nightly basis. The heroine may be strong, confident and sexually assertive, but this means little if the broader context in which she and her friends live, desire, go to school and work has not changed. This is explicitly acknowledged in the show's finale ('Chosen', 7.22) when Buffy (Sarah Michelle Gellar) and her lesbian Wicca friend, Willow (Alyson Hannigan), not only save the world (again), but, more importantly, change it by sharing Buffy's power with other young women:

> *Buffy:* In every generation one Slayer is born, because a bunch of men who died thousands of years ago made up that rule. They were powerful men. This woman [*pointing to Willow*] is more powerful than all of them combined.
>
> So I say we change the rule.
> I say my power shall be our power.
> Tomorrow Willow will use the essence of this scythe to change our destiny. From now on every girl in the world who might be a Slayer, will be a Slayer. Every girl who could have the power, will have the power. Can stand up, will stand up. Slayers. Every one of us.

It is not only the (literally pre-feminist) 'men who died thousands of years ago' who pose problems in the Buffyverse. That the majority of *Buffy's* monsters – vampires, demons, power-hungry frat boys – are white males is not in itself exceptional (as my brief discussion of quantitative content studies in Chapter 1 demonstrates).[13] However, what strikes me as more unusual is the extent to which the male investment in violence is critically highlighted within the show, though, rarely, in the responses to it. The ways in which male characters use violence to establish their own position in homosocial hierarchies and exert power over others is, for example, the subject of recurring commentary. The all-male group – human, demon or vampire – is consistently shown to be misogynist, competitive and violent and the naming of monsters and the symbolic forms that they take often further highlight the connections between violence and masculinity. It is not incidental, then, that the sympathetic male characters are feminised. Buffy's 'Watcher', Giles (Anthony Stewart Head), is fastidious in manner and dress, associated with books and learning rather than physical activity and one of the show's recurring jokes is the frequency with which he is knocked unconscious and requires rescuing by a girl. Her friend, Xander (Nicholas Brendon), is perhaps the character who most often gives voice to fear and he is, sometimes painfully, aware of his physical limitations and gendered reversal of roles with Buffy: 'It's time for me to act like a man. And hide' ('Bewitched, Bothered and Bewildered', 2.16) The sheer frequency of such remarks means that the difference between the masculine ideal and reality is consistently kept in view.

Nevertheless, Buffy's (and the show's) erotic investments are in male characters who are, in many ways, more conventionally masculine – strong, well-built, resilient, relatively fearless – although they, too, are defined primarily by their relationships with women. The fact that these characters – Angel (David Boreanaz), Riley (Mark Blucas) and Spike (James Marsters) – are, however, regularly the objects of an explicitly erotic, female gaze complicates their agency in a way more typical of the female figure in film. In contrast, Buffy herself is not routinely represented as the object of another character's gaze (Daughtery, 2002) and, in both fight and love scenes, the camera avoids the kind of **fetishisation** of the female form discussed in Chapter 5 to linger on the male body. This is particularly stark during Buffy's sexual relationship with Spike when his naked body is repeatedly lingered upon while Buffy remains clothed, is off screen or even (literally in one episode) invisible.

However, the relationship between Buffy and Spike is of interest here primarily for the attempted rape that follows their break-up (in 'Seeing Red', 6.19). As we have seen in a number of different contexts in this book, even in dealing with rape – such an obviously gendered expression of violence – there is a marked reluctance to represent rapists as men in popular accounts. In contrast, when Spike (who is a vampire) attempts to rape Buffy, he is quite clearly marked as man rather than monster. Buffy's relationship with Spike is complex and merits more discussion than there is room for here. However, it is sufficient for my purposes to note that, up until this point, Buffy has always called the shots. For Buffy it is a relationship based on sexual desire, violence and a self-loathing that she frequently projects on to the lovestruck, morally complex vampire. The attempted rape thus takes place in the context of a pre-existing relationship and Buffy and Spike do not easily fit the stereotypes of rape victim (virgin or vamp) and rapist (one-dimensional monster) identified elsewhere in this book. Further, as already noted, while acquaintance rape has become increasingly visible on US prime-time television, it is rare for both characters to appear as regulars (before and after) as Buffy and Spike do here. For the would-be rapist and his intended victim to be characters viewers have invested in over a number of years makes for extremely uncomfortable viewing – the implications of which cannot be easily dismissed (and, indeed, are repeatedly returned to, both in the show's final season and in online fan discussion).

In the attempted rape scene, Spike's actions are firmly anchored in the real rather than the fantastic and, thus, become part of the show's critique of (normative, human) masculinity. As a vampire, Spike is associated with darkness – his home is a candle-lit crypt, most of his scenes take place at night and, in daytime scenes, he must remain out of direct sunlight, inhabiting the shadows or hiding under a blanket. In the attempted rape, however, Spike moves out of the vampire's shadow world – both literally, as the scene takes place in the bathroom in Buffy's house, and aesthetically, as the bathroom is decorated in light, bright colours and starkly lit (see Figure 6.4). Stylistically, this scene is differentiated both from Buffy's fantastical battles and Spike and Buffy's passion. It lacks a musical soundtrack, takes place in a very confined space that restricts the characters' movement and employs an unusual (for *Buffy*) shot structure. The almost claustrophobic alternating close-ups of Buffy and Spike during the attack, interspersed with high-angle long shots, make for a disorientating viewing experience that manages to convey both the sense of personal violation and the emotional distance between the characters (see Figures 6.4, 6.5 and 6.6).

While this scene clearly references the horror genre, these references are reworked to underline *Buffy*'s difference from exploitation fare. The most obvious allusion here is to *Psycho*. The attack takes place in the bathroom, as Buffy falls, she brings down the shower curtain and the shot, reverse shot structure (see Figures 6.5 and 6.6) conventionally heightens the tension by giving both perpetrator's and victim's points of view. However, the differences are equally obvious and underline the way in which the series rewrites the gendered conventions of horror. There is no attempt to sexualise the victim or eroticise the attack. Buffy is dressed in a grey robe and sneakers throughout, her hair pulled back from her face, wearing little make-up. There are no fetishising close-ups of Buffy's body and her attacker is not shadowy, nor anonymous. After the attack begins, Spike is in every frame. Spike's actions may be evil, but his emotions are all too human and he makes a clear decision to act in the face of Buffy's verbal and physical attempts to push him away. It is clear that he doesn't attempt rape because he is inherently bad – he does so because he is angry and hurt by her rejection of him and wants to feel powerful and in control again. Most significantly, perhaps, Spike looks human throughout, never morphing into the vampire's 'game face' that the show typically uses to mark the vampire as evil and/or supernaturally strong (see Figure 6.7).

Figures 6.4, 6.5 and 6.6   *The alternating use of close-ups and high-angle long shots in the rape scene is disorientating and reminiscent of the rape revenge film. As he attempts to rape Buffy, Spike remains in human face (*Buffy the Vampire Slayer*, 'Seeing Red', 6.19).*

Figure 6.7 *The vampire's 'game face' in an earlier episode (*Buffy the Vampire Slayer, *'Smashed', 6.09).*

The show might not let Spike off the hook, but a post-feminist criticism that focuses primarily on Buffy's actions and agency does. Yet, the continuity between man and monster facilitates a reading of the show that puts men (and feminism) back in the picture. If man and monster cannot be so easily separated (and, indeed, a number of the monsters in the show's seven seasons turn out to be simply men), then rape and other forms of gendered violence must be understood in relation to normative constructions of masculinity. Indeed, if online activity is anything to go by, fan debate continually (and often critically) returns to the question of Spike's (and Angel's) moral accountability as well as Buffy's (and fans') erotic investments in dangerous men. As Vint (2002) suggests in the context of a discussion of representations of Buffy/Gellar, contradictions both within the show itself and between the show and its secondary texts (interviews, merchandising, DVD commentaries and so on) require a certain activity on the part of viewers to construct meaning. The intertextual nexus in which the programme and its characters are situated reminds us of the difficulty of studying television in isolation and, further, of the absurdity of focusing on violent acts in isolation. The activity of the viewers – as consumers and often as producers of their own texts – also challenges the conceptualisation of the viewer as being passively exposed to violence. Instead, the show may well create a space where young women (and other viewers) can begin to develop (and see reflected) a critical consciousness about gender, violence and sexuality.

My rather tentative language in the last sentence is not accidental. Part of the difficulty in reaching any conclusions about the efficacy of popular representations in disseminating, undermining or negating feminist discourses around violence is the relative lack of empirical work with audiences of all kinds. Clearly, in calling for more of this research, I am not suggesting that we return to the cause and effect paradigm critiqued in Chapter 1. Rather, this is a call for more research investigating how media audiences make sense of representations of violence in the context of our own experiences of violence, gender, popular culture. I do not see this as a replacement for the kind of textual analyses undertaken in much of this book (as we saw in Chapter 1, work that focuses on only the audience side of the equation can be equally limited), but as a valuable companion to this work.

As I have argued throughout this book – in relation to film and print media as well as television – media representations have an important role to play in shaping our understandings of violence, gender and feminism. There is a rich variety of work in this area, but, as I have also demonstrated, there are also significant gaps in our knowledge. Despite, or sometimes because of, all the brouhaha about media violence, there are lots of things we don't yet know, lots of questions that haven't yet been asked and too much that has been taken for granted or rendered unspeakable. Hopefully, this book will encourage you to seek out some of the existing work and, through your own research and study, broaden the debate in ways that I haven't yet thought of.

Summary

- Feminist and post-feminist television criticism has been primarily concerned with women's genres, women viewers and women characters, meaning that men, masculinity and violence on television are rather under-researched from a feminist perspective.
- Popular forms can be more amenable to feminist understandings of men's violence against women than news programmes, which rarely explicitly acknowledge feminist expertise or analysis.
- Feminist interest in women's genres, such as the soap opera and talk show, demonstrate both the possibilities and limitations of these genres for representing male violence against women.
- There is still a considerable gap in our knowledge about how women (and men) understand and respond to violence in those television genres and shows that have generated the most feminist critical work.

Notes

1 See Hargreaves (1996) on *Brookside*'s domestic violence/murder storyline (1993–95) and Dutta (1999) on representations of rape victims in US daytime soaps. Audience studies by Jenny Kitzinger (2001) and Philip Schlesinger et al. (1992) discuss responses to child sexual abuse and domestic violence storylines respectively. Finally, in her unpublished PhD thesis, Lesley Henderson (2002) provides a detailed discussion of the production context in which child sexual abuse stories were developed in both *Brookside* and *Emmerdale* and considers audience responses to the *Brookside* storyline.

2 In British courts, provocation is one of the conditions in which a charge of murder can be reduced to manslaughter. Murder carries a mandatory life sentence, while manslaughter may result in variable terms. In the early 1990s, a number of high-profile cases of abused women who killed their abusers demonstrated that the emphasis on a momentary loss of control in provocation made it very difficult to account for the cumulative provocation of years of domestic violence. This is the context in which the *Brookside* story developed (see Kennedy (1992) or Radford (1993) for contemporaneous discussions of the law). Since the early 1990s, the position has improved and the cumulative effects of domestic violence can be admitted as evidence of provocation (as was the case in the trial of Jan Charlton, discussed in Chapter 4). However, feminist campaign groups, such as Justice for Women, point to the ways in which provocation remains a gendered defence in practice (see www.jfw.org.uk).

3 Clips from climactic episodes in the domestic violence and child sexual abuse stories discussed here can be found on the *EastEnders* website at www.bbc.co.uk/eastenders, just click on 'Episodes' and then click on 'classic' to choose which classic episodes you want to view (accessed April, 2004).

4 John Yorke, Head of Drama at the BBC and former Executive Producer of *EastEnders*, speaking at the Glasgow Film Theatre in September 2002. Yorke's comments are supported by Henderson's (2002) audience study in which she found a marked reluctance among viewers with no prior experiences of violence to accept that soap's 'man next door' could also be an abuser.

5 In an article in *The Guardian* following *Coronation Street*'s highly publicised rape story in 2001, the director of the Rape Crisis Federation suggests that the failure to publicise specialist, feminist services reflects the broadcasters' fear of 'saying the "R" word' despite building sensational stories around abuse. However, the article also points to the difficulty of dealing with the intense interest generated by such stories within the underfunded feminist voluntary sector ('Crisis? What crisis', *The Guardian*, 7 May, 2001). See also Henderson's (2002) PhD study.

6 The newer talk shows – *Rikki Lake*, *Jerry Springer* and others – are more orientated towards conflict (and the performance of conflict) than the consensus-building approach I describe here. See Shattuc (1997) for a fuller discussion.

7 See Tolson (2001) for a useful and succinct review of the literature.

8 Both Nancy Berns (1999) and Imelda Whelehan (2000) make a similar point about the treatment of feminist issues in women's magazines.

9 Notably, when two men who abused their female partners are called on later in the programme, Kilroy-Silk interrupts their storytelling infrequently and then not to ask for detail, but explanation.

10 Holmlund (1993b) makes a similar point about the representation of domestic violence in Hollywood film.

11 Julie D'Acci (1994) provides a useful critical consideration of responses to the show in the mainstream and feminist press (see also Clark, 1990). Although the series ended in 1988, Cagney and Lacey returned in a number of television movies between 1994 and 1996.

12 See, for example, articles by Fudge (1999), Owen (1999), Early (2001), Daughtery (2002), Helford (2002), Karras (2002), Playden (2002), Vint (2002), Wilcox (2002) and Miller (2003).

13 Clearly, this is not to suggest that *Buffy*'s female characters never act violently with evil or morally questionable intent. However, it is notable that morally reprehensible violence does not bring female characters together in the show in the way that it routinely unites male gangs (vampire, demon, human).

Further reading

Cuklanz, L.M. (2000) *Rape on Prime Time: Television, Masculinity and Sexual Violence*. Philadelphia, PA: University of Pennsylvania Press.

Moorti, S. (2002) *Color of Rape: Gender and Race in Television's Public Spheres*. Albany, NY: State University of New York Press.

Rapping, E. (2000) 'The politics of representation: genre, gender violence and justice', *Genders,* 32, and at www.genders.org/g32/g32_rapping.html (accessed April, 2004).

Whelehan, I. (2000) *Overloaded: Popular Culture and the Future of Feminism*. London: Women's Press.

Appendix

This appendix provides brief details of the cases of **sexual murder** and other violent crime referred to most frequently in this book. Their inclusion in this list should not be taken as an indication of an equivalence between the actions and their perpetrators. Dates in brackets refer to the period during which the crimes occurred and the crimes are listed by the names of the perpetrators, unless there is another name by which the case is more commonly known. See the Introduction at the beginning of this book for a brief discussion of some of the difficulties in representing the realities of sexual murder.

Bernardo, Paul (1987–92)

Between May 1987 and May 1990, Bernardo stalked and **raped** eight women in Scarborough, Toronto. In December 1990, Bernardo and his girlfriend, Karla Homolka, drugged and raped Homolka's younger sister, Tammy. She died the next day, but no foul play was suspected. In 1991 and 1992, the couple abducted, raped, tortured and murdered two teenage girls. They videoed all three girls' ordeals. In January 1993, Homolka left Bernardo because of his violence towards her and, shortly afterwards, his other crimes came to light. In 1995, with Homolka giving evidence against him, Bernardo was convicted of murder, kidnapping, forcible confinement, aggravated sexual assault and committing an indignity to one victim's body. It is highly unlikely that he will ever be released.

See also Homolka, Karla.

'Big Dan's' Rape (1983)

The case – on which *The Accused* (Kaplan, 1988) is loosely based – involved the gang rape of a woman in Big Dan's bar, New Bedford. While the woman was raped, other men in the bar stood by and watched, some cheered, no one came to her aid. The victim was a Portuguese-American, the perpetrators were Portuguese immigrants. The case received sustained national media coverage and was the first criminal trial to be nationally televised. Two of the perpetrators were found guilty, two were found not guilty, but the victim and her family were effectively exiled from their community. Less than three years after the trial, the victim died in a car accident in her Florida exile.

Brady, Ian (1963–65)

With his lover, Myra Hindley, Brady abducted, tortured and murdered five children (aged 10–17), burying the bodies of the first four victims on Saddleworth Moor – hence, they were known as the Moors Murders/ Murderers. Brady took **pornographic** photographs of Hindley and their victims and audio-recorded the torture of ten-year-old Lesley Ann Downey (in which Hindley can also be heard to participate). In 1966, Brady was found guilty of three murders and he has since confessed to two more. At the time of writing (February 2004), he remains in Ashworth Hospital from where, in 2001, he published *The Gates of Janus: Serial Killing and its Analysis*.

See also Hindley, Myra.

Bulger, James (murder of)

See Thompson, Robert, and Jon Venables.

Bundy, Ted (1974–79)

In 1977, Bundy was found guilty of kidnapping and was awaiting trial for murder in Colorado when he escaped from custody. The first time, he was recaptured within eight days; the second time, he escaped to Florida where his killing spree continued. His murderous career spanned at least five years (1974–79), during which time, Bundy later confessed, he murdered, raped and mutilated at least 38 women in 6 states. Some commentators argue that this is a conservative estimate and suggest that he killed over 100 women. Bundy was executed in January 1989.

Carr, Maxine

See Huntley, Ian.

Central Park Jogger rape (1989)

The Central Park Jogger was a professional, wealthy, white woman who was beaten unconscious with a lead pipe and a rock, raped and left for dead in New York's Central Park. She had no memory of the attack. Five black and Hispanic teenagers were convicted of assaulting her: all have now served their time. In September 2002, Matias Reyes, a convicted murderer and rapist who had never been charged in relation to the case, confessed to the rape, claiming that he acted alone. There is DNA evidence linking Reyes to the crime and questions have been raised about the safety of the original convictions.

Chambers, Robert (1986)

Chambers was 19 when he confessed to the killing of his friend, 18-year-old Jennifer Levin, claiming that her death followed 'rough', but consensual, sex that had 'got out of hand'. Both in the press and the courtroom, Levin's life was subjected to intense scrutiny, resulting in feminist protest and outrage. Chambers was allowed to plead guilty to manslaughter and received a 5–15-year sentence. Violations of prison rules added time to his sentence and affected his eligibility for parole. He was released in 2003.

Chapman, Jessica (murder of)

See Huntley Ian.

Charlton, Jan (2002)

Charlton killed her lover, Daniel O'Brien, with an axe. At her trial in Leeds, the jury found her guilty of manslaughter on the grounds of provocation, accepting her claims that she had been abused by O'Brien and feared that he would abuse her daughter. She was jailed for five years, but released in December 2003.

Columbine High School massacre (1999)

On 20 April 1999, two teenage boys – Eric Harris and Dylan Klebod – walked into their school – Columbine High in Littleton, Colorado – with a range of weaponry. After killing 13 people and injuring many more, they fatally turned their guns on themselves.

Dahmer, Jeffrey (1978–91)

The 'Milwaukee Cannibal' drugged, killed, dismembered and cannibalised his young male victims. Dahmer was found guilty of the murder of 15 young men, the majority of whom were black or from minority ethnic communities (Dahmer was white). His crimes came to light when one of the men he assaulted escaped and went to the police. An earlier victim – a 14-year-old Laotian boy – had also managed to escape and alert the police, but the police believed Dahmer's story (that they were lovers) and returned the drugged boy to Dahmer, who strangled, violated and dismembered him. Dahmer was killed by a fellow inmate in prison in 1994.

Hindley, Myra (1963–65)

Hindley, one of the 'Moors Murderers', was convicted, with her lover, Ian Brady, on two counts of murder and of being an accessory in a third murder. Jailed in 1966, Hindley finally confessed to her crimes – including her involvement (with Brady) in two additional murders – in 1986. Unlike Brady, Hindley fought for her release, generating intense revulsion in the British tabloid press. She died in jail in November, 2002.

Homolka, Karla (1990–92)

Along with her boyfriend (and later husband) Paul Bernardo, Homolka was involved in drugging, raping and killing three teenage girls, including her sister, Tammy. Each of the young women was videotaped during their ordeal, though the tapes – which showed Homolka taking an active role – did not come to light until after Homolka had made a highly controversial plea-bargain. She received a 12-year sentence for her role in each of the murders (to run concurrently) in exchange for her full cooperation in the prosecution of Bernardo. Homolka claimed, in her defence, that she was abused by Barnardo over a period of years. She was denied parole in 2001 and is due for release at the end of her sentence in 2005.

Hughes, Francine (1977)

The night Francine Hughes killed her abusive (ex-)husband James she had called the police following another attack, but they declined to arrest him. When he fell asleep, she set fire to his bed. Feminists and other interested people formed the Francine Hughes Defence Fund to raise money for her defence and raise public awareness of **domestic violence** and the gendered inequalities of the law. Hughes was acquitted on the grounds of temporary insanity.

Huntley, Ian (2002)

In December 2003, school caretaker Ian Huntley was found guilty of the murders of 10-year-olds Jessica Chapman and Holly Wells in Soham, Cambridgeshire, and given two life sentences. After his trial, it emerged that Huntley had a history of grooming young girls for sex, **sexual abuse** of young girls and women and a prior charge of rape (which had been dropped due to lack of evidence). His fiancée, Maxine Carr, a teaching assistant at the girls' school, was found guilty of perverting the course of justice for giving Huntley a false alibi for the night of the murders. She was sentenced to three and a half years in prison, with the recommendation that she serve half that sentence. There is some evidence to suggest that Carr was herself abused by Huntley.

Jack the Ripper (1888)

The name given to the man who murdered and mutilated prostitute women in Whitechapel, London. He was never caught and the fascination with Jack the Ripper continues to this day. The number of killings attributed to the killer remains a point of dispute. There were 11 unsolved **femicides** in Whitechapel between April 1888 and February 1891. The murders of five of these women are commonly recognised as being the work of one killer. However, some 'Ripperologists' argue that the killer's total number of victims during this period may be nearer to 13 or even more.

Levin, Jennifer (murder of)

See Chambers, Robert.

Lucas, Henry Lee (1975–82)

North American 'wandering' **serial killer** who courted celebrity with his confession to around 360 murders. The confessions followed his

1982 arrest on suspicion of the murder of the 80-year-old widow who had employed him as an odd job man. Prior to these killings, Lucas had already served time in prison for killing his mother and, in addition, he strangled the first girl he ever had sex with when he was 14 years old. He later recanted many confessions and police were able to disprove others. Although it is certain that he killed his former employer and his teenage wife, his involvement in many other murders remains unclear. In 1999, his death sentence was commuted to one of life imprisonment.

Moors Murderers

See Brady, Ian, and Hindley, Myra.

Sutcliffe, Peter – The Yorkshire Ripper (1975–81)

Sutcliffe murdered 13 women and attempted to kill another 7. Many of his victims were prostitutes and feminists have argued that it was not until he claimed his first non-prostitute victim that the police began looking for the killer in earnest. His modus operandi was to hit his victims on the head with a hammer and stab them repeatedly in the breasts and abdomen with a sharpened screwdriver. Sutcliffe claimed that he had a divine mission to cleanse the streets of prostitutes, but, at his 1981 trial, his defence of diminished responsibility owing to delusions was rejected and he was found guilty of murder. He was sentenced to 30 years imprisonment and has since been transferred to a special hospital.

Thompson, Robert, and Jon Venables (1993)

Thompson and Venables were 10-year-olds when they abducted 2-year-old James Bulger from a Merseyside shopping centre and killed him. Their crime and trial generated sustained media coverage and the judge in the case caused considerable controversy when he suggested (with little evidence) that the killers' consumption of violent videos may provide a partial explanation of the crime. Amid much media furore, the boys were released with new identities in 2001.

Wells, Holly (murder of)

See Huntley, Ian.

West, Fred, and Rosemary (1967–87)

In February 1994, police investigating the 1987 disappearance of the Wests' 16-year-old daughter, Heather, began searching for her remains at the couple's 25 Cromwell Street home. In total, the dismembered remains of nine young women – including Heather – were uncovered at Cromwell Street and three other bodies were found in nearby locations. The women had been sexually tortured before death. Fred was charged with 12 counts of murder, two of which (the murder of his first wife and his pregnant lover) predated his relationship with Rose. Fred hung himself on New Year's day 1995 before he could face trial. In November 1995, Rose – who insisted that Fred had acted alone and without her knowledge – was found guilty on ten counts of murder. She has been told she will never be released from prison.

Whitechapel murderer

See Jack the Ripper.

Wuornos, Aileen (1989–91)

Wuornos shot and killed seven white, middle-aged, heterosexual men in the space of 18 months. Wuornos, a lesbian who worked as a prostitute, initially claimed that on each occasion she acted in self-defence as the men, who had picked her up on Florida's Interstate 75, raped or attempted to rape her. Wuornos has been labelled the first female serial killer, although there was no evidence of the lust to kill or any suggestion that she derived sexual pleasure from the killings. Wuornos was executed by lethal injection in October 2002.

The Yorkshire Ripper

See Sutcliffe, Peter.

Glossary

backlash (against feminism) The conscious and unconscious efforts to reverse or contain gains made by feminism. Although most commonly used to refer to the backlash against **second-wave feminism**, backlashes have followed feminist gains in other historical periods (see Faludi, 1992).

commercial sexual exploitation Any commercial activity the profits of which come from the sexual exploitation of women and children. This includes prostitution, **pornography**, stripping and lapdancing.

'date' rape A contentious term that has no legal status and has been rejected by feminists, who argue that it undermines the seriousness of the **rape**. As popularly used, the term refers to rapes by acquaintances of all kinds and is not restricted to situations where the man and woman have made a date to go out together. This usage not only trivialises rape but also distorts the relationship between victim and perpetrator.

diegesis/diegetic The diegesis is the fictional world of a text. In terms of film, everything we see and hear that belongs to the on-screen fictional world is diegetic. So, music from an on-screen jukebox is diegetic, while soundtrack music is non-diegetic – that is, it does not have an on-screen source.

discourse: A group of statements that together produce a particular type of knowledge within specific social contexts. Discourses are 'practices that systematically form the objects of which they speak' (Foucault, 1972: 49). Discourses are both determined by their social context and contribute to the way that social context continues its existence. See Mills (1997) for an accessible introduction to the various uses of discourse.

domestic violence Physical, sexual and emotional abuse within intimate relationships, most commonly, men's abuse of women and children. The use of this term has been much debated in feminist research and activism as it is argued that it disguises gendered realities and, by labelling violence 'domestic', downplays the severity and criminality of abuse. In Britain, the term 'domestic violence' is still used by agencies supporting women (such as Women's Aid or Refuge), government and the public at large and so it is used throughout this book. In the US, 'battery' is the more commonly used term, although this, too, is gender-neutral.

femicide The murder of women because they are women. Also referred to as woman killing and gynocide.

fetish/ism In psychoanalytic terms, a strategy to disavow sexual difference by substituting a fetish object for the woman's lack (of a penis) or turning woman herself into a reassuring fetish object – for example, by a fragmentation and over investment in parts of the female body.

film noir A term coined by French film critics to refer to a group of American thrillers of the 1940s and 1950s (often adaptations of hard-boiled crime fiction) that typically dealt with dark or violent passions in a downbeat way. The themes and visual style of *film noir* witnessed something of a revival from the 1970s onwards. The *femme fatale* – the enigmatic, dangerous, sexual woman – is central both to *film noir* and its more contemporary variants and has been of particular interest to feminist film critics (see, for example, Kaplan, 1998).

gorenography Used by some feminists to refer to **slasher** movies and other representations of sexualised violence against women in mainstream entertainment genres. The term quite obviously seeks to establish a link between such representations and **pornography**.

infanticide A woman's killing of her child of less than one year in age because she is suffering from the effects of childbirth or lactation. This is an offence men cannot commit (although they can and do kill their infant children) and the penalty tends to be light as these women are seen as being victims of their biology.

liberal feminism Focuses on achieving equality for women within existing social structures.

male gaze from Laura Mulvey's hugely influential work on visual pleasure and narrative cinema (published in 1975). Now more generally used to refer to the male point of view or way of looking that is privileged in patriarchal culture and assigns to women the position of (sexualised) object.

masochism Pleasure or sexual gratification in receiving pain or suffering from another person.

misogyny Hatred of women. This should be differentiated from sexism, which is not gender-specific.

modality The relationship between a statement (or media text) and reality.

moral panic The theory that agents and institutions of control – which include the media – exaggerate forms of deviance and danger in order to justify the control of those persons or things portrayed as deviant/dangerous.

obscenity A subjective and a moral concept. In Britain, for example, obscenity is defined in law as material that is likely to 'deprave and corrupt', but who is likely to be 'depraved and corrupted' and how they are likely to be so affected is not specified.

patriarchy A form of social organisation in which men are dominant and the central institutions of society (family, church, government, media and so on) are controlled by men and/or organised in their interests.

pornography Three main definitions of pornography are adopted in academic writing on the topic. The first, associated with anti-pornography feminists, defines pornography as material that is both sexually explicit and sexist, violent, degrading, dehumanising and/or sexually objectifying. The second definition, often used by anti-censorship writers, sees pornography as sexually explicit material designed for arousal and/or for fantasy. Violence is not an inherent component of this definition. Third, a number of writers define pornography as that material identified by producers, distributors and consumers as pornography – that is, material sold in sex shops, magazines located on the top shelf or videos found in the adult section.

post-feminism The 'post' in post-feminism can and does variously imply a periodisation, a development and a rejection of **second-wave feminism**. Post-feminism has never been a concrete political, activist movement and the writers most associated with the term have little in common, except, perhaps, a rejection of what is seen as the victimising tendency of **radical feminism** and an interest in exploring issues of women's autonomy, subjectivity and desire. The emphasis of much post-feminist writing is on the agency of the individual, female subject. However, critics note that this is often at the expense of an understanding or analysis of oppression as actively constructed along the lines of gender, race, ethnicity, class and sexuality.

psychoanalysis A methodology for the study of the human psyche and for treating mental and emotional disorders based on revealing and investigating **the unconscious.**

radical feminism Sees **patriarchy** (and the institutions that support and perpetuate it) as the source of women's oppression and works to challenge and dismantle the patriarchal system. Radical feminists are particularly concerned with issues of sexuality, violence against women, **pornography** and **commercial sexual exploitation,** leading critics to rebrand radical feminism as 'victim feminism'. By suggesting that radical feminism focuses only on women as victims, the challenge radical feminists pose to men and male privilege is negated in this critique.

rape Historically, the spoiling of the chastity and value of a woman by a man who had no legal claim to have sex with her. The fact that a husband could not be charged with raping his wife (up until 1991 in England and Wales) was a reflection of this. In Britain, legally defined as the penetration (or attempted penetration) of the vagina or anus with the penis without consent. The focus on penetration distorts the ways in which many women experience rape.

sadism Pleasure or sexual gratification in inflicting pain or suffering on another person.

scopophilia The desire to see, the drive to pleasurable viewing.

second-wave feminism The women's liberation movements (note the plural) that emerged in the UK and US in the late 1960s/early 1970s. The term reminds us that feminist ideas and organising have a history – a 'first wave'. *See also* **liberal feminism, radical feminism.**

serial killing/serial murder A term coined by an FBI profiler in the 1970s to refer to a series of murders, often with a sexual component, committed by one person or group of people with significant periods of time between murders. It has been suggested that the term disguises the sexualised nature of the majority of these crimes and, thus, their meaning to (predominately male) perpetrators (see Cameron and Frazer, 1987).

sexual abuse Abuse in which victims are targeted on the basis of their sex and where sex is an explicit component of the abuse.

sexual harassment Deliberate or repeated sexual behaviour that is out of place and makes the recipient feel that they are being inappropriately sexualised. Behaviour in this category can range from belittling comments to demands for sex.

sexual murder Murder that has a sexual component. The sexual component may be the **rape** or sexualised mutilation of the victim or the sexual charge the killer derives from the murder.

sexual violence *See* **sexual abuse.**

slasher films Also known as 'stalkers' and 'splatter' films. A subgenre of horror in which a group of young people (male and female) are stalked and their bodies 'slashed' by a (usually male) killer.

snuff A **pornographic** movie culminating with the actual **sexual murder** (the 'snuffing out') of a person. The existence of commercial snuff has long been disputed, but the existence of non-commercial snuff – the filming of sexual murder and **rape** by perpetrators for their own viewing – is undisputed.

the unconscious That which is forbidden or repressed from consciousness. **Psychoanalysis** explores how and why thoughts and desires are repressed (particularly in childhood, as the young child becomes aware of sexual difference) and how this impacts on our subjectivity.

video nasties A term mainly (but not exclusively) used to describe low-budget horror films featuring explicit violence, gore, sex and/or nudity and aimed at a youth audience. It is a notoriously imprecise term, emerging in Britain in the 1980s and inextricably linked to fears about children and young people's 'unregulated' use of the then new video technology.

voyeurism Watching people without their permission or knowledge. Feminists have suggested that voyeurism is not only sexual but inherently violent in the attempt to control the (usually female) object of the **(male) gaze.**

References

Alcoff, L. and Gray, L. (1993) 'Survivor discourse: transgression or recuperation?', *Signs: A Journal of Women in Culture and Society*, 18 (2): 260–90.

Allen, M., D'Alessio, D. and Brezgel, K. (1995) 'A meta-analysis summarizing the effects of pornography II', *Human Communication Research*, 22: 258–83.

Andison, F.S. (1977) 'TV violence and viewer aggression: a cumulation of study results', *Public Opinion Quarterly*, 41: 314–31.

Ang, I. (1985) *Watching Dallas: Soap Opera and the Melodramatic Imagination*. London: Methuen.

Armstrong, L. (1978) *Kiss Daddy Goodnight*. New York: Profile Books.

Armstrong, L. (1994) *Rocking the Cradle of Sexual Politics: What Happened When Women Said Incest*. Reading, MA: Addison-Wesley.

Asselle, G. and Gandhy, B. (1982) '*Dressed to Kill*: a discussion', *Screen*, 23 (3–4): 137–43.

Assiter, A. and Carol, A. (eds) (1993) *Bad Girls and Dirty Pictures: The Challenge to Reclaim Feminism*. London: Pluto.

Atmore, C. (1998) 'Towards 2000: child sexual abuse and the media', in A. Howe (ed.) *Sexed Crime in the News*. Sydney: Federation Press.

Austin, T. (2002) *Hollywood Hype and Audiences: Selling and Watching Popular Film in the 1990s*. Manchester: Manchester University Press.

Barker, M. (ed.) (1984a) *The Video Nasties: Freedom and Censorship in the Media*. London: Pluto.

Barker, M. (1984b) *A Haunt of Fears: The Strange History of the British Horror Comics Campaign*. London: Pluto.

Barker, M., Arthurs, J. and Harindranath, R. (2001) *The* Crash *Controversy: Censorship Campaigns and Film Reception*. London: Wallflower Press.

Barker, M. and Brooks, K. (1998) *Knowing Audiences*: Judge Dredd, *its Friends, Fans and Foes*. Luton: University of Luton Press.

Barker, M. and Petley, J. (eds) (2001) *Ill Effects: The Media/Violence Debate*, 2nd edn. London: Routledge.

Baxter, T. and Craft, N. (1993) 'There are better ways of taking care of Bret Easton Ellis than just censoring him', in D.E.H. Russell (ed.), *Making Violence Sexy: Feminist Views on Pornography*. Buckingham: Open University Press.

Benedict, H. (1992) *Virgin or Vamp: How the Press Covers Sex Crimes*. Oxford: Oxford University Press.

Benedict, H. (1993) 'The language of rape', in E. Buchwald, P.R. Fletcher and M. Roth (eds), *Transforming a Rape Culture*. Minneapolis, MN: Milkweed.

Benedict, H. (1997) 'Blindfolded: rape and the press's fear of feminism', in M. Fineman and M. McCluskey (eds), *Feminism, Media and the Law*. Oxford: Oxford University Press.

Benn, M. (1993) 'Body talk: the sexual politics of PMT', in H. Birch (ed.), *Moving Targets: Women, Murder and Representation*. London: Virago.

Benshoff, H.M. (1997) *Monsters in the Closet: Homosexuality and the Horror Film*. Manchester: Manchester University Press.

Berg, L. (1999) 'Turned on by pornography: still a good girl?'. Paper presented to 'Women's Worlds: the 7th International Interdisciplinary Congress on Women', University of Tromsø, June, 1999.

Berns, N. (1999) ' "My problem and how I solved it": domestic violence in women's magazines', *The Sociological Quarterly* 40 (1): 85–108.

Bindel, J., Cook, K. and Kelly, L. (1995) 'Trials and tribulations – justice for women: a campaign for the 90s', in G. Griffin (ed.), *Feminist Activism in the 90s*. London: Taylor & Francis.

Birch, H. (ed.) (1993a) *Moving Targets: Women, Murder and Representation*. London: Virago.

Birch, H. (1993b) 'If looks could kill: Myra Hindley and the iconography of evil', in H. Birch, (ed.), *Moving Targets: Women, Murder and Representation*. London: Virago.

Bland, L. (1992) 'The case of the Yorkshire Ripper: mad, bad, beast or male?', in J. Radford and D.E.H. Russell (eds), *Femicide: The Politics of Woman Killing*. Buckingham: Open University Press.

Bogle, D. (1994) *Toms, Coons, Mulattoes, Mammies, and Bucks: An Interpretive History of Blacks in American Films*, 3rd edn. Oxford: Roundhouse.

Boyle, K. (1998) 'Violence and gender in contemporary cinema'. Unpublished PhD thesis, University of Bradford.

Boyle, K. (1999) 'Screening violence: a feminist critique of the screen violence debate'. Paper presented to 'Women's Worlds: the 7th International Interdisciplinary Congress on Women', University of Tromsø, June, 1999.

Boyle, K. (2000) 'The pornography debates: beyond cause and effect', *Women's Studies International Forum*, 23 (2): 187–95.

Boyle, K. (2001a) 'What's natural about killing? Gender, copycat violence and *Natural Born Killers*', *Journal of Gender Studies*, 10 (3): 311–21.

Boyle, K. (2001b) 'Domestic violence voluntary perpetrators' programmes: report for Wolverhampton Domestic Violence Forum', Centre for Applied Social Research, Wolverhampton.

Brady, I. (2001) *The Gates of Janus: Serial Killing and its Analysis*. Los Angeles, CA: Feral House.

Brady, K. (1984) 'Testimony on Pornography and Incest', in D.E.H. Russell (ed.) (1993) *Making Violence Sexy: Feminist Views on Pornography*. Buckingham: Open University Press.

Bragg, S. (2001) 'Just what the doctors ordered? Media regulation, education and the "problem" of media violence', in M. Barker and J. Petley (eds), *Ill Effects: The Media/ Violence Debate*, 2nd edn. London: Routledge.

Broadcasting Standards Commission, British Broadcasting Corporation & the Independent Television Commission (2002) 'Briefing update No. 10: the depiction of violence on terrestrial television', at www.ofcom.org.uk/static/archive/bsc/plain/pubs. htm (accessed April, 2004).

Broadcasting Standards Council (1993) 'Monitoring Report 2: 1993'. London: BSC.

Brook, B. (1999) *Feminist Perspectives on the Body*. London: Longman.

Browne, A. (1987) *When Battered Women Kill*. New York: Free Press.

Brunsdon, C. (1995) 'The role of soap opera in the development of feminist television criticism', in C. Brunsdon (ed.) (1997) *Screen Tastes: Soap Opera to Satellite Dishes*. London: Routledge.

Brunsdon, C., D'Acci, J. and Spigel, L. (1997) 'Introduction', in C. Brunsdon, J. D'Acci and L. Spigel (eds), *Feminist Television Criticism: A Reader*. Oxford: Oxford University Press.

Bruzzi, S. (1997) *Undressing Cinema: Clothing and Identity in the Movies*. London: Routledge.

Buckingham, D. (1996) *Moving Images: Understanding Children's Emotional Responses to Television*. Manchester: Manchester University Press.

Burn, G. (1998) *Happy Like Murderers: The True Story of Fred and Rosemary West*. London: Faber & Faber.

Busby, K. (1994) 'LEAF and pornography: litigating on equality and sexual representations', *Canadian Journal of Law and Society*, 9 (1): 165–92.

Cameron, D. (1992) ' "That's entertainment"?: Jack the Ripper and the selling of sexual violence', in J. Radford and D.E.H. Russell (eds), *Femicide: The Politics of Woman Killing*. Buckingham: Open University Press.

Cameron, D. (1996) 'Wanted: the female serial killer', *Trouble & Strife*, 33: 21–8.

Cameron, D. (1999) 'Rosemary West: motives and meanings', *The Journal of Sexual Aggression*, 4 (2): 68–80.

Cameron, D. and Frazer, E. (1987) *The Lust to Kill: A Feminist Investigation of Sexual Murder*. Cambridge: Polity.

Cameron, D. and Frazer, E. (1992) 'On the question of pornography and sexual violence: moving beyond cause and effect', in C. Itzin (ed.), *Pornography, Women, Violence and Civil Liberties: A Radical New View*. Oxford: Oxford University Press.

Caputi, J. (1988) *The Age of Sex Crime*. London: Women's Press.

Caputi, J. and Russell, D.E.H. (1992) 'Femicide: sexist terrorism against women', in J. Radford and D.E.H. Russell (eds), *Femicide: The Politics of Woman Killing*. Buckingham: Open University Press.

Carr, C. (1992) 'Reclaiming our *basic* rights', *Village Voice*, 28 April: 35.

Carter, C. (1998) 'When the "extraordinary" becomes "ordinary": everyday news of sexual violence', in C. Carter, G. Branston and S. Allan (eds), *News, Gender and Power*. London: Routledge.

Cavender, G., Bond-Maupin, L. and Jurik, N.C. (1999) 'The construction of gender in reality crime TV', *Gender and Society*, 13 (5): 643–63.

Chancer, L. (1987) 'New Bedford, Massachusetts, March 6, 1983–March 22, 1984: the "before and after" of a group rape', *Gender and Society*, 1 (3): 239–60.

Chandler, D. (n.d.) 'Cultivation theory', at www.aber.ac.uk/media/Documents/short/cultiv.html (accessed April, 2004).

Cherry, B. (1999) 'Refusing to refuse to look: female viewers of the horror film', in M. Stokes and R. Maltby (eds), *Identifying Hollywood's Audiences: Cultural Identity and the Movies*. London: BFI.

Chester, G. and Dickey, J. (eds) (1988) *Feminism and Censorship: The Current Debate*. Dorset: Prism Press.

Chibnall, S. (1977) *Law and Order News*. London: Tavistock.

Clark, D. (1990) '*Cagney and Lacey*: feminist strategies of detection', in M.E. Brown (ed.), *Television and Women's Culture: The Politics of the Popular*. London: Sage.

Clover, C. (1992) *Men, Women and Chain Saws: Gender in the Modern Horror Film*. London: BFI.

Cole, S. (1989) *Pornography and the Sex Crisis*. Toronto: Amanita Press.

Craft, N. (1992) 'The incredible case of the stack o' wheat prints', in J. Radford and D.E.H. Russell (eds), *Femicide: The Politics of Woman Killing*. Buckingham: Open University Press.

Creed, B. (1993) *The Monstrous Feminine: Film, Feminism, Psychoanalysis*. London: Routledge.

Cuklanz, L.M. (1995) 'Public expressions of "progress" in discourse of the Big Dan's rape', *Women and Language*, 17 (1): 1–11.

Cuklanz, L.M. (1996) *Rape on Trial: How the Mass Media Construct Legal Reform and Social Change*. Philadelphia, PA: University of Pennsylvania Press.

Cuklanz, L.M. (2000) *Rape on Prime Time: Television, Masculinity and Sexual Violence*. Philadelphia, PA: University of Pennsylvania Press.

Cumberbatch, G. (1987) *The Portrayal of Violence on British Television: A Content Analysis*. London: BBC.

Cumberbatch, G. and Howitt, D. (1989) *A Measure of Uncertainty: The Effects of the Mass Media*. London: John Libbey.

Cumberbatch, G., Wood, G. and Littlejohns, V. (2002) *Television: The Public's View 2000*. London: ITC.

D'Acci, J. (1994) *Defining Women: Television and the Case of* Cagney and Lacey. Chapel Hill, NC: University of North Carolina Press.

Danica, E. (1988) *Don't: A Woman's Word*. Dublin: Attic.

Dargis, M. (1994) 'Quentin Tarantino on *Pulp Fiction*', *Sight and Sound*, 4 (11): 16–19.

Daughtery, A.M. (2002) 'Just a girl: Buffy as icon', in R. Kaveney (ed.), *Reading the Vampire Slayer: An Unofficial Critical Companion to* Buffy *and* Angel. London: Tauris Parke.

Davies, J. and Smith, C.R. (1997) *Gender, Ethnicity and Sexuality in Contemporary American Film*. Edinburgh: Keele University Press.

de Lauretis, T. (1984) *Alice Doesn't: Feminism, Semiotics, Cinema*. London: Macmillan.

Dika, V. (1990) *Games of Terror:* Halloween, Friday the 13th, *and the Films of the Stalker Cycle*. Madison, NJ: Fairleigh Dickinson University Press.

Dines, G., Jensen, R. and Russo, A. (1998) *Pornography: The Production and Consumption of Inequality*. London: Routledge.

Doane, M.A. (1981) 'Woman's stake: filming the female body', in E.A. Kaplan (ed.) (2000), *Feminism and Film*. Oxford: Oxford University Press.

Doane, M.A. (1982) 'Film and the masquerade: theorising the female spectator', in M.A. Doane (ed.) (1991) *Femmes Fatales: Feminism, Film Theory, Psychoanalysis*. London: Routledge.

Doane, M.A. (1988–89) 'Masquerade reconsidered: further thoughts on the female spectator', in M.A. Doane (ed.) (1991) *Femmes Fatales: Feminism, Film Theory, Psychoanalysis*. London: Routledge.

Domingo, C. (1992) 'What the white man won't tell us: report from the Berkeley Clearinghouse on femicide', in J. Radford and D.E.H. Russell (eds), *Femicide: The Politics of Woman Killing*. Buckingham: Open University Press.

Doob, A. and MacDonald, G.E. (1979) 'Television viewing and fear of victimisation: is the relationship causal?', *Journal of Personality and Social Psychology*, 37 (2): 170–9.

Durham, A.M., Elrod, H.P. and Kinkade, P.T. (1995) 'Images of crime and justice: murder and the "true crime" genre', *Journal of Criminal Justice*, 23 (2): 143–52.

Dutta, M.B. (1999) 'Taming the victim: rape in soap opera', *Journal of Popular Film and Television*, 27 (1): 34–9.

Dworkin, A. (1981) *Pornography: Men Possessing Women*. London: Women's Press.

Dworkin, A. and MacKinnon, C. (1988) '*Pornography and civil rights: a new day for women's equality*, at www.nostatusquo.com/ACLU/dworkin/other/ordinance/newday/TOC.htm (accessed April, 2004).

Dyer, R. (1977) 'Stereotyping', in R. Dyer (ed.), *Gays in Film*. London: BFI.

Dyer, R. (1982) 'Don't look now', *Screen* 23 (3–4): 61–73.

Dyer, R. (1997a) *White*. London: Routledge.

Dyer, R. (1997b) 'Kill and kill again', *Sight and Sound*, 7 (9): 14–17.

Early, F. (2001) 'Staking her claim: *Buffy the Vampire Slayer* as transgressive woman warrior', *Journal of Popular Culture*, 35 (3): 11–27.

Ebert, R. (1981) 'Why audiences aren't safe anymore', *American Film*, 6 (5): 54–6.

Edwards, S. (1984) *Women on Trial*. Manchester: Manchester University Press.

Emerman, M. (1995) 'Only a reflection? Sexual violence on screen', *Metro*, 103: 72–5.

Estrich, S. (1987) *Real Rape*. Cambridge, MA: Harvard University Press.

Everywoman (1988) *Pornography and Sexual Violence: Evidence of the Links*. London: Everywoman.

Faludi, S. (1992) *Backlash: The Undeclared War Against Women*, rev. edn. London: Chatto & Windus.

Faludi, S. (2000) *Stiffed: The Betrayal of Modern Man*. London: Vintage.

Farley. M. (2003) 'Prostitution and the invisibility of harm', *Women and Therapy*, 26 (3–4): 247–80.

Federal Bureau of Investigation (2002) 'Uniform crime reports: crime in the US – 2001', Qunatico, VA: FBI, and at www.fbi.gov/ucr/01cius.htm (accessed April, 2004).

Filetti, J.S. (2001) 'From Lizzie Borden to Lorena Bobbitt: violent women and gendered justice', *Journal of American Studies*, 5 (3): 471–84.

Finn, G. (1989/90) 'Taking gender into account in the "theatre of terror": violence, media and the maintenance of male dominance', *Canadian Journal of Women and Law*, 3 (2): 375–94.

Foucault, M. (1972) *The Archaeology of Knowledge*, trans. S. Smith. London: Tavistock.

Francke, L. (1994) *Script Girls: Women Screenwriters in Hollywood*. London: BFI.

Fudge, R. (1999) 'The Buffy effect: or, a tale of cleavage and marketing', *Bitch: Feminist Response to Pop Culture*, 10, at www.bitchmagazine.com and click on 'archives/search', then scroll down list to title (accessed April, 2004).

Fuller, J. and Blackley, S. (1995) *Restricted Entry: Censorship on Trial* (edited by Nancy Pollak). Vancouver: Press Gang.

Gadd, D., Farrall, S., Dallimore, D. and Lombard, N. (2002) 'Domestic abuse against men in scotland', Scottish Executive, Edinburgh, and at www.scotland.gov.uk/cru/kd01/green/dvam-00.asp (accessed April, 2004).

Gaines, J. (1988) 'White privilege and looking relations: race and gender in feminist film theory', in E.A. Kaplan, (ed.) (2000), *Feminism and Film*. Oxford: Oxford University Press.

Gamble, S. (2001) 'Postfeminism', in S. Gamble (ed.), *The Routledge Companion to Feminism and Postfeminism*. London: Routledge.

Gamson, G.A. (1992) *Talking Politics*. Cambridge: Cambridge University Press.

Garber, M. (1995) *Vice Versa: Bisexuality and the Eroticism of Everyday Life*. London: Hamish Hamilton.

Gauntlett, D. (1995) *Moving Influences: Understanding Television's Influences and Effects*. London: John Libbey.

Gauntlett, D. (1997) 'Ten things wrong with the "effects model"', in R. Dickinson, R. Harindranath and O. Linne (eds), *Approaches to Audiences – A Reader*. London: Arnold.

Gavey, N. and Gow, V. (2001) '"Cry wolf", cried the wolf: constructing the issue of false rape allegations in New Zealand media texts', *Feminism and Psychology*, 11 (3): 341–60.

Geraghty, C. (1991) *Women and Soap Opera: A Study of Prime Time Soaps*. Oxford: Polity.

Gerbner, G., Gross, L., Jackson-Beeck, M., Jeffries-Fox, S. and Signorielli, N. (1978) 'Cultural indicators: violence profile no. 9', *Journal of Communication*, 28 (3): 176–207.

Gerbner, G., Gross, L., Morgan, M. and Signorielli, N. (1994) 'Growing up with television: the cultivation perspective', in J. Bryant and D. Zillman (eds), *Media Effects*. Hillsdale, NJ: Lawrence Erlbaum.

Gerbner, G., Gross, L., Signorielli, N., Morgan, M. and Jackson-Beeck, M. (1979) 'The demonstration of power: violence profile no. 10', *Journal of Communication*, 29 (3): 177–96.

Gibson, P.C. and Gibson, R. (eds) (1993) *Dirty Looks: Women, Pornography, Power*. London: BFI.

Giobbe, E. (1985) 'Surviving commercial sexual exploitation', in D.E.H. Russell (ed.) (1993), *Making Violence Sexy: Feminist Views on Pornography*. Buckingham: Open University Press.

Gledhill, C. (1978) '*Klute 1*: a contemporary *film noir* and feminist criticism', in E.A. Kaplan (ed.) (1998), *Women in* Film Noir, new edn. London: BFI.

Gray, A. (1992) *Video Playtime: The Gendering of a Leisure Technology*. London: Routledge.

Greer, C. (2003a) 'Sex crime and the media: press representations in Northern Ireland', in P. Mason (ed.), *Criminal Visions: Media Representations of Crime and Justice*, Cullompton: Willan.

Greer, C. (2003b) *Sex Crime and the Media: Sex Offending and the Press in a Divided Society*. Cullompton: Willan.

Gripsrud, J. (1995) *The* Dynasty *Years: Hollywood Television and Critical Media Studies*. New York: Routledge.

Grover, C. and Soothill, K. (1996a) 'A murderous "underclass": the press reporting of sexually motivated murder', *The Sociological Review*, 44 (3): 398–415.

Grover, C. and Soothill, K. (1996b) 'Ethnicity, the search for rapists and the press', *Ethnic and Racial Studies*, 19 (3): 567–84.

Grundmann, R. (1991) 'Hollywood sets the terms of the debate', *Cineaste*, 18 (4): 35–6.

Gunter, B. (1985) *Dimensions of Television Violence*. Aldershot: Gower.

Gunter, B. (1987) *Television and the Fear of Crime*. London: John Libbey.

Gunter, B. and Harrison, J. (1998) *Violence on Television: An Anlaysis of Amount, Nature, Location and Origin of Violence in British Programmes*. London: Routledge.

Haarman, L. (2001) 'Performing talk', in A. Tolson (ed.), *Television Talk Shows: Discourse, Performance, Spectacle*. Mahwah, NJ: Lawrence Erlbaum.

Hallam, J., with Marshment, M. (2000) *Realism and Popular Cinema*. Manchester: Manchester University Press.

Hardy, S. (1998) *The Reader, the Author, his Woman and her Lover: Soft-core Pornography and Heterosexual Men*. London: Cassell.

Hargreaves, T. (1996) 'Trying the *Brookside* two: domestic violence, soap opera, and real life', in A. Myers and S. Wight (eds), *No Angels: Women Who Commit Violence*. London: Pandora.

Hart, L. (1994) *Fatal Women: Lesbian Sexuality and the Mark of Aggression*. London: Routledge.

Harvey, S. (1978) 'Women's place: the absent family of *film noir*', in E.A. Kaplan (ed.) (1998), *Women in Film Noir*, new edn. London: BFI.

Haskell, M. (1974) *From Reverence to Rape: The Treatment of Women in the Movies*. Chicago, IL: University of Chicago Press.

Helford, E.R. (2002) '"My emotions give me power": the containment of girls' anger in *Buffy*', in R.V. Wilcox and D. Lavery (eds), *Fighting the Forces: What's at Stake in* Buffy the Vampire Slayer. Lanham, MD: Rowman & Littlefield.

Henderson, L.M. (2002) 'Social issue story lines in British soap opera'. Unpublished PhD thesis, University of Glasgow.

Henry, A. (1988) 'Does viewing pornography lead men to rape?', in G. Chester and J. Dickey (eds), *Feminism and Censorship: The Current Debate*. Dorset: Prism Press.

HM Crown Prosecution Service Inspectorate and HM Inspectorate of Constabulary (2002) 'A report on the joint inspection into the investigation and prosecution of cases involving allegations of rape'. London: Home Office, and at www.homeoffice.gov.uk/hmic/CPSI_HMIC_Rape_Thematic.pdf (accessed April, 2004).

Hill, A. (1997) *Shocking Entertainment: Viewer Responses to Violent Movies*. Luton: University of Luton Press.

Hill, A. (1999) 'Risky business: film violence as an interactive phenomenon', in M. Stokes and R. Maltby (eds), *Identifying Hollywood's Audiences: Cultural Identity and the Movies*. London: BFI.

Hirsch, P. (1980) 'The "scary world" of the nonviewer and other anomalies: a reanalysis of Gerbner et al.'s findings on cultivation analysis, part 1', *Communication Research*, 7 (4): 403–56.

Hirsch, P. (1981) 'On not learning from one's own mistakes: a reanalysis of Gerbner et al.'s findings on cultivation analysis, part 2', *Communication Research*, 8 (1): 3–38.

Hoberman, J. (1995) 'Victim victorious: well-fed yuppie Michael Douglas leads the charge for resentful white men', *Village Voice*, 7 March: 31–3.

Hobson, D. (1982) Crossroads: *The Drama of a Soap Opera*. London: Methuen.

Hollibaugh, A. (1996) 'Seducing women into "a lifestyle of vaginal fisting": lesbian sex gets *Virtually* dangerous', in D. Cornell (ed.) (2000), *Feminism and Pornography*. Oxford: Oxford University Press.

Hollway, W. (1981) '"I just wanted to kill a woman" Why? The Ripper and male sexuality', *Feminist Review*, 9: 33–40.

Holmlund, C. (1993a) 'Masculinity as multiple masquerade: the "mature" Stallone and the Stallone clone', in S. Cohan and I.R. Hark (eds), *Screening the Male: Exploring Masculinities in Hollywood Cinema*. London: Routledge.

Holmlund, C. (1993b) 'A decade of deadly dolls: Hollywood and the woman killer' in H. Birch (ed.), *Moving Targets: Women, Murder and Representation*. London: Virago.

hooks, b. (1992) 'The oppositional gaze: black female spectators', in b. hooks (ed.), *Black Looks: Race and Representation*. London: Turnaround.

hooks, b. (1995) 'Cool tool', *Artforum*, March: 63–4; 108–9.

Howe, A. (ed.) (1998) *Sexed Crime in the News*. Sydney: Federation Press.

Hughes, D. and Roche, C. (eds) (1999) *Making the Harm Visible: Global Sexual Exploitation of Women and Girls. Speaking Out and Providing Services*. Kingston, Rhode Island: Coalition Against Trafficking in Women.

Itzin, C. (1992a) 'The evidence of pornography related harm and a harm-based equality approach to legislating against pornography without censorship: a briefing paper'. Bradford: Research Unit on Violence, Abuse and Gender Relations.

Itzin, C. (1992b) 'Legislating against pornography without censorship', in C. Itzin (ed.), *Pornography, Women, Violence and Civil Liberties: A Radical New View*. Oxford: Oxford University Press.

Itzin, C. (1996) 'Pornography and the organisation of abuse', in P. Bibby (ed.), *Organised Abuse: The Current Debate*. Aldershot: Arena.

Jackson, D. (1995) *Destroying the Baby in Themselves: Why Did the Two Boys Kill James Bulger?* Nottingham: Mushroom & Five Leaves.

Jakubowski, M. and Braund, N. (eds) (1999) *The Mammoth Book of Jack the Ripper*. London: Robinson.

Jeffords, S. (1994) *Hard Bodies: Hollywood Masculinity in the Reagan Era*. New Brunswick, NJ: Rutgers University Press.

Jeffreys, S. (1997) *The Idea of Prostitution*. North Melbourne: Spinifex.

Jenkins, H. (1999) 'Testimony before the US senate Commerce Committee hearing on "marketing violence to children"', at http://commerce.senate.gov/hearings/0504jen. pdf (accessed April, 2004).

Jenkins, P. (1994) *Using Murder: The Social Construction of Serial Homicide*. New York: Aldine de Gruyter.

Jensen, R. (1998a) 'Using pornography', in G. Dines, R. Jensen and A. Russo (eds), *Pornography: The Production and Consumption of Inequality*. London: Routledge.

Jensen, R. (1998b) 'Introduction: pornographic dodges and distortions', in G. Dines, R. Jensen and A. Russo (eds), *Pornography: The Production and Consumption of Inequality*. London: Routledge.

Jhally, S. and Lewis, J. (1992) *Enlightened Racism*: The Cosby Show, *Audience and the Myth of the American Dream*. Oxford: Westview Press.

Johnson, E. and Schaefer, E. (1993) 'Soft core/hard gore: *Snuff* as a crisis in meaning', *Journal of Film and Video*, 45 (2–3): 40–59.

Jones, A. (1991) *Women Who Kill*, rev. edn. London: Victor Gollancz.

Justice for Women (n.d.) 'Battered women's syndrome: help or hindrance?', at www.jfw. org.uk (accessed April, 2004).

Kaplan, E.A. (ed.) (1998) *Women in Film Noir*, rev. edn. London: BFI.

Kappeler, S. (1995) *The Will to Violence: The Politics of Personal Behaviour*. London: Polity.

Karras, I. (2002) 'The third wave's final girl: *Buffy the Vampire Slayer*', *Thirdspace*, 1 (2), and at www.thirdspace.ca/articles/karras.htm (accessed April, 2004).

Kaye, B. (1995) 'The *femme fatale*', *Vox*, 52: 28–9.

Keesey, D. (2001) 'They kill for love: defining the erotic thriller as a film genre', *Cineaction*, 56: 44–53.

Kelleher, M.D. and Kelleher, C.L. (1998) *Murder Most Rare: The Female Serial Killer*. London: Bantam Doubleday Dell.

Kelly, L. (1988) *Surviving Sexual Violence*. Cambridge: Polity.

Kelly, L. (1991) 'Unspeakable acts', *Trouble and Strife*, 21: 13–20.

Kelly, L. (1992) 'Pornography and child sexual abuse', in C. Itzin (ed.), *Pornography, Women, Violence and Civil Liberties: A Radical New View*. Oxford: Oxford University Press.

Kelly, L. (1996a) 'Weasel words: paedophiles and the cycle of abuse', *Trouble and Strife*, 33: 44–9.

Kelly, L. (1996b) 'Feminist perspectives on violence by women', in M. Hester, L. Kelly and J. Radford (eds), *Women, Violence and Male Power*. Buckingham: Open University Press.

Kennedy, H. (1992) *Eve Was Framed: Women and British Justice*. London: Chatto & Windus.

Kim, L.S. (2001) ' "Sex and the single girl" in postfeminism: the *F* word on television', *Television and New Media*, 2 (4): 319–34.

Kimmel, M.S. (1993) 'Clarence, William, Iron Mike, Tailhook, Senator Packwood, Spur Posse, Magic ... and us', in E. Buchwald, P.R. Fletcher and M. Roth (eds), *Transforming a Rape Culture*. Minneapolis, MN: Milkweed.

King, A. (1993) 'Mystery and imagination: the case of pornography effects studies', in A. Assiter and A. Carol (eds), *Bad Girls and Dirty Pictures: The Challenge to Reclaim Feminism*. London: Pluto.

King, N. (1999) *Heroes in Hard Times: Cop Action Movies in the US*. Philadelphia, PA: Temple University Press.

Kitses, J. (2002) 'One man from now', *Sight and Sound*, 12 (4): 28–9.

Kitzinger, J. (1996) 'Media representations of child sexual abuse risks', *Child Abuse Review*, 5: 319–33.

Kitzinger, J. (1998) 'The gender-politics of news production: silenced voices and false memories', in C. Carter, G. Branston and S. Allan (eds), *News, Gender and Power*. London: Routledge.

Kitzinger, J. (1999a) 'Audience understandings of media messages about child sexual abuse: an exploration of audience reception and media influence'. Unpublished PhD thesis, University of Glasgow.

Kitzinger, J. (1999b) 'The ultimate neighbour from hell?: stranger danger and the media representation of "paedophilia" ', in B. Franklin (ed.), *Social Policy, the Media and Misrepresentation*. London: Routledge.

Kitzinger, J. (2000) 'Media templates: patterns of association and the (re)construction of meaning over time', *Media, Culture and Society*, 22: 61–84.

Kitzinger, J. (2001) 'Transformations of public and private knowledge: audience reception, feminism and the experience of childhood sexual abuse', *Feminist Media Studies*, 1 (1): 91–104.

Kozol, W. (1995) 'Fracturing domesticity: media, nationalism and the question of feminist influence', *Signs: A Journal of Women in Culture and Society*, 20 (31): 646–67.

Lamb, S. (ed.) (1999) *New Versions of Victims: Feminists Struggle With the Concept*. New York: New York University Press.

Lamb, S. and Keon, S. (1995) 'Blaming the perpetrator: language that distorts reality in newspaper articles on men battering women', *Psychology of Women Quarterly*, 19: 209–20.

Lees, S. (1992) 'Naggers, whores, and libbers: provoking men to kill', in J. Radford and D.E.H. Russell (eds), *Femicide: The Politics of Woman Killing*. Buckingham: Open University Press.

Lees, S. (1995) 'Media reporting of rape: the 1993 British "date rape" controversy'. in D. Kidd Hewitt and R. Osborne (eds), *Crime and the Media: The Postmodern Spectacle*. London: Pluto.

Lees, S. (2002) *Carnal Knowledge: Rape on Trial*, rev. edn. London: Women's Press.

Lehman, P. (1993) ' "Don't blame this on a girl": female rape revenge films', in S. Cohan and I.R. Hark (eds), *Screening the Male: Exploring Masculinities in Hollywood Cinema*. London: Routledge.

Leidholdt, D. (1999) 'Prostitution: a form of slavery', in D. Hughes and C. Roche (eds), *Making the Harm Visible: Global Sexual Exploitation of Women and Girls. Speaking Out and Providing Services*. Kingston, Rhode Island: Coalition Against Trafficking in Women.

Liebes, T. and Katz, E. (1990) *The Export of Meaning: Cross-cultural Readings of Dallas*. Oxford: Oxford University Press.

Linz, D. (1989) 'Exposure to sexually explicit materials and attitudes toward rape: a comparison of study results', *The Journal of Sex Research*, 26: 50–84.

Livingstone, S. and Lunt, P. (1994) *Talk on Television: Audience Participation and Public Debate*. London: Routledge.

Lloyd, A. (1995) *Doubly Deviant, Doubly Damned: Society's Treatment of Violent Women*. London: Penguin.

Longmore, P.K. (1985) 'Screening stereotypes: images of disabled people', *Social Policy*, 16 (1): 31–7.

Lotz, A.D. (2001) 'Postfeminist television criticism: rehabilitating critical terms and identifying postfeminist attributes', *Feminist Media Studies*, 1 (1): 105–21.

Lovelace, L. (1974) *Inside Linda Lovelace*. London: Heinrich Hanau.

Lovelace, L., with McGrady, M. (1981) *Ordeal: An Autobiography*. London: Star Books.

McCollum, H. (1998) 'What the papers say', *Trouble and Strife*, 37: 31–9.

McDonald, M.G. (1999) 'Unnecessary roughness: gender and racial politics in domestic violence media events', *Sociology of Sport Journal*, 16: 111–33.

McElroy, W. (n.d.) 'A feminist overview of pornography, ending in a defence thereof', at http://zetetics.com/mac/freeinqu.htm (accessed April, 2004).

MacKinnon, C. (1993) 'Turning rape into pornography: postmodern genocide', in A. Stiglmayer (ed.), *Mass Rape: The War Against Women in Bosnia-Herzegovina*. Lincoln, NE: University of Nebraska Press.

MacKinnon, C. (1995) 'Only words', extract in D. Cornell (ed.) (2000) *Feminism and Pornography*. Oxford: Oxford University Press.

MacKinnon, C. and Dworkin, A. (eds) (1997) *In Harm's Way: The Pornography Civil Rights Hearings*. Cambridge, MA: Harvard University Press.

McLaughlin, L. (1993) 'Chastity criminals in the age of electronic reproduction: re-viewing talk television and the public sphere', *Journal of Communication Inquiry*, 17 (1): 41–55.

MacNeill, S. (1991) 'Change the law (1)', *Trouble and Strife*, 22: 7–11.

McNeill, S. (1992) 'Woman killer as tragic hero', in J. Radford and D.E.H. Russell (eds), *Femicide: The Politics of Woman Killing*. Buckingham: Open University Press.

Manners, T. (1995) *Deadlier than the Male: Stories of Female Serial Killers*. London: Pan.

Marchiano, L. (1983) 'The myth about "Linda Lovelace"', in *Everywoman* (ed.) (1988), *Pornography and Sexual Violence: Evidence of the Links*. London: Everywoman.

Mathews, T.D. (1994) *Censored: What They Didn't Allow You to See, and Why: The Story of Film Censorship in Britain*. London: Chatto & Windus.

Mayne, J. (1988) '*L.A. Law* and prime-time feminism', in C. Brunsdon, J. D'Acci and L. Spigel (eds) (1997), *Feminist Television Criticism: A Reader*. Oxford: Oxford University Press.

Messner, M.A. and Solomon, W.S. (1993) 'Outside the frame: newspaper coverage of the Sugar Ray Leonard wife abuse story', *Sociology of Sport Journal*, 10: 119–34.

Meyers, M. (1994) 'News of battering', *Journal of Communication*, 44 (2): 47–63.

Meyers, M. (1997) *News Coverage of Violence Against Women: Engendering Blame*. London: Sage.

Miller, D. and Philo, G. (1999) 'The effective media', in G. Philo (ed.), *Message Received: Glasgow Media Group Research 1993–1998*. London: Longman.

Miller, J.P. (2003) '"The I in Team": Buffy and feminist ethics', in J. B. South (ed.), *Buffy the Vampire Slayer and Philosophy: Fear and Trembling in Sunnydale*. La Salle, IL: Open Court.

Mills, S. (1997) *Discourse*. London: Routledge.

Modleski, T. (1979) 'The search for tomorrow in today's soap operas: notes on a feminine narrative form', in C. Brunsdon, J. D'Acci and L. Spigel (eds) (1997), *Feminist Television Criticism: A Reader*. Oxford: Oxford University Press.

Modleski, T. (1984) *Loving with a Vengeance: Mass-produced Fantasies for Women*. London: Methuen.

Modleski, T. (1991) *Feminism Without Women: Culture and Criticism in a 'Postfeminist' Age*. London: Routledge.

Moorti, S. (2002) *Color of Rape: Gender and Race in Television's Public Spheres*. Albany, NY: State University of New York Press.

Morley, D. (1986) *Family Television: Cultural Power and Domestic Leisure*. London: Routledge.

Morris, A. and Wilczynski, A. (1993) 'Rocking the cradle: mothers who kill their children', in H. Birch (ed.), *Moving Targets: Women, Murder and Representation*. London: Virago.

Morris, J. (1991) *Pride Against Prejudice: Transforming Attitudes to Disability*. London: Women's Press.

Morrison, D.E., MacGregor, B., Svennevig, M. and Firmstone, J. (1999) *Defining Violence: The Search for Understanding*. Luton: University of Luton Press.

Morrison, T. (1997) 'Dead man golfing', in T. Morrison and C.B. Lacour (eds), *Birth of a Nation'hood: Gaze, Script, and Spectacle in the O.J. Simpson Case*. New York: Pantheon.

Morrison, T. and Lacour, C.B. (eds) (1997) *Birth of a Nation'hood: Gaze, Script, and Spectacle in the O.J. Simpson Case*. New York: Pantheon.

Morrissey, B. (2003) *When Women Kill: Questions of Agency and Subjectivity*. London: Routledge.

Moseley, R. and Read, J. (2002) '"Having it *Ally*": popular television (post-)feminism', *Feminist Media Studies*, 2 (2): 231–49.

Mulvey, L. (1975) 'Visual pleasure and narrative cinema', in E.A. Kaplan, (ed.) (2000), *Feminism and Film*. Oxford: Oxford University Press.

Mulvey, L. (1981) 'Afterthoughts on "Visual pleasure and narrative cinema" inspired by *Duel in the Sun*', in C. Penley (ed.) (1988), *Feminism and Film Theory*. London: BFI.

Myhill, A. and Allen, J. (2002) 'Rape and sexual assault of women: the extent and nature of the problem – findings from the British Crime Survey'. London: Home Office, and at www.homeoffice.gov.uk/rds/pdfs2/hors237.pdf (accessed April, 2004).

National Television Violence Study, vol. 1 (1997). London: Sage.

National Television Violence Study, vol. 2 (1998a). London: Sage.

National Television Violence Study, vol. 3 (1998b). London: Sage.

Nava, M. (1988) 'Cleveland and the press', *Feminist Review*, 28: 103–21.

Naylor, B. (2001a) 'Reporting violence in the British print media: gendered stories', *The Howard Law Journal*, 40 (2): 180–94.

Naylor, B. (2001b) 'The "Bad Mother" in media and legal texts', *Social Semiotics*, 11 (2): 155–76.

Neale, S. (1983) 'Masculinity as spectacle: reflections on men and mainstream cinema', in S. Cohan and I.A. Hark (eds), *Screening the Male*. London: Routledge.

Nelson, S. (1982) *Incest: Fact and Myth*. Edinburgh: Stramullion.

Newitz, A. and Sandell, J. (1994) 'Bisexuality and how to use it: toward a coalitional identity politics', *Bad Subjects*, 16, and at http://eserver.org/bs/16/Sandell.html (accessed April, 2004).

Newson, E. (1994) 'Video violence and the protection of children', *The Psychologist*, June: 272–4.

Norden, M. (1994) *The Cinema of Isolation: A History of Physical Disability in the Movies*. Piscataway, NJ: Rutgers University Press.

Oliver, M.B. and Armstrong, B. (1998) 'The color of crime: perceptions of Caucasians' and African Americans' involvement in crime', in M. Fishman and G. Cavender (eds), *Entertaining Crime: Television Reality Programs*. New York: Aldine de Gruyter.

Owen, S.A. (1999) '*Buffy the Vampire Slayer*: vampires, postmodernity and postfeminism', *Journal of Popular Film and Television*, 27 (2): 24–31.

Owens, T. (1993) 'Sex on my mind', in A. Assiter and A. Carol (eds), *Bad Girls and Dirty Pictures: The Challenge to Reclaim Feminism*. London: Pluto.

Paglia, C. (1993) *Sex, Art and American Culture*. London: Penguin.

Paik, H. and Comstock, G. (1994) 'The effects of television violence on antisocial behaviour: a meta-analysis', *Communication Research*, 21: 516–46.

Parks, L. (2003) 'Brave new *Buffy*: rethinking "TV violence"', in M. Jancovich and J. Lyons (eds), *Quality Popular Television: Cult TV, the Industry and Fans*. London: BFI.

Pender, P. (2002) '"I'm Buffy and you're … history": the postmodern politics of *Buffy*', in R.V. Wilcox and D. Lavery (eds), *Fighting the Forces: What's at Stake in* Buffy the Vampire Slayer. Lanham, MD: Rowman & Littlefield.

Petley, J. (2003) 'Video violence: how far can you go?', in P. Mason (ed.), *Criminal Visions: Media Representations of Crime and Justice*. Cullompton: Willan.

Pidduck, J. (1995) 'The 1990s Hollywood fatal femme: (dis)figuring feminism, family, irony, violence', *Cineaction*, 38: 64–72.

Place, J. (1978) 'Women in *film noir*', in E.A. Kaplan (ed.) (1998), *Women in* Film Noir, rev. edn. London: BFI.

Playden, Z-J. (2002) '"What you are, what's to come": feminism, citizenship and the divine', in R. Kaveney (ed.), *Reading the Vampire Slayer: An Unofficial Critical Companion to* Buffy *and* Angel. London: Tauris Parke.

Press, A. (1990) 'Class, gender and the female viewer: women's responses to *Dynasty*', in M.E. Brown (ed.), *Television and Women's Culture: The Politics of the Popular*. London: Sage.

Price, L. (1999) 'Making rape a war crime: the International Criminal Tribunal for the former Yugoslavia and its treatment of sexual violence'. Unpublished PhD thesis, Leeds Metropolitan University.

Price, L. (2001) 'Finding the man in the soldier-rapist: some reflections on comprehension and accountability', *Women's Studies International Forum*, 24 (2): 211–27.

Projansky, S. (2001) *Watching Rape: Film and Television in Postfeminist Culture*. New York: New York University Press.

Radford, J. and Russell, D.E.H. (eds) (1992) *Femicide: The Politics of Woman Killing*. Buckingham: Open University Press.

Radford, L. (1993) 'Pleading for time: justice for battered women who kill', in H. Birch (ed.), *Moving Targets: Women, Murder and Representation*. London: Virago.

Rapping, E. (1991) 'Feminism gets the Hollywood treatment', *Cineaste*, 18 (4): 30–2.

Rapping, E. (1992) *The Movie of the Week: Private Stories, Public Events*. Minneapolis, MN: University of Minnesota Press.

Rapping, E. (2000) 'The politics of representation: genre, gender violence and justice', *Genders*, 32, and at www.genders.org/g32/g32_rapping.html (accessed April, 2004).

Razack, S. (1994) 'What is to be gained by looking white people in the eye?: culture, race and gender in cases of sexual violence', *Signs: A Journal of Women in Culture and Society*, 19 (4): 894–923.

Read, J. (2000) *The New Avengers: Feminism, Femininity and the Rape Revenge Cycle*. Manchester: Manchester University Press.

Reiner, R., Livingstone, S. and Allen, J. (2003) 'From law and order to lynch mobs: crime news since the Second World War', in P. Mason (ed.), *Criminal Visions: Media Representations of Crime and Justice*. Cullompton: Willan.

Renzetti, C. (1999) 'The challenge to feminism posed by women's use of violence in intimate relationships', in S. Lamb (ed.), *New Versions of Victims: Feminists Struggle with the Concept*. New York: New York University Press.

Rich, B.R. (1992) 'Art house killers', in J. Arroyo (ed.) (2000), *Action/Spectacle Cinema: A Sight and Sound Reader*. London: BFI.

Roiphe, K. (1994) *The Morning After*. London: Hamish Hamilton.

Rosen, M. (1973) *Popcorn Venus: Women, Movies and the American Dream*. New York: Coward, McCann & Geoghegen.

Ross, B.L. (1997) '"It's merely designed for sexual arousal": interrogating the indefensibility of lesbian smut', in D. Cornell (ed.) (2000), *Feminism and Pornography*. Oxford: Oxford University Press.

Royalle, C. (1993) 'Porn in the USA', in D. Cornell (ed.) (2000), *Feminism and Pornography*. Oxford: Oxford University Press.

Rubin, G. (1993) 'Misguided, dangerous and wrong: an analysis of anti-pornography politics', in A. Assiter and A. Carol (eds), *Bad Girls and Dirty Pictures: The Challenge to Reclaim Feminism*. London: Pluto.

Rule, A. (1989) *The Stranger Beside Me*, rev. edn. London: Warner.

Russell, D.E.H. (1992) 'Pornography and rape: a causal model', in C. Itzin (ed.), *Pornography, Women, Violence and Civil Liberties: A Radical New View*. Oxford: Oxford University Press.

Russell, D.E.H. (1993) 'The experts cop out', in D.E.H. Russell (ed.), *Making Violence Sexy: Feminist Views on Pornography*. Buckingham: Open University Press.

Russo, V. (1981) *The Celluloid Closet: Homosexuality in the Movies*. New York: Harper & Row.

Ryan, M. and Kellner, D. (1988) *Camera Politica: The Politics and Ideology of Contemporary Hollywood Film*. Bloomington, IN: Indiana University Press.

Sander, I. (1997) 'How violent is TV violence?: an empirical investigation of factors influencing viewers' perceptions of TV violence', *European Journal of Communication*, 12 (1): 43–98.

Savage, S. (1996) 'Women who kill and the made-for-TV movie: the Betty Broderick story', in A. Myers and S. Wight (eds), *No Angels: Women Who Commit Violence*. London: Pandora.

Schlesinger, P., Dobash, R., Dobash, R. and Weaver, K. (1992) *Women Viewing Violence*. London: BFI.

Scholder, A. (ed.) (1993) *Critical Condition: Women on the Edge of Violence*. San Francisco, CA: City Lights Books.

Scottish Executive (2001a) 'Statistical bulletin CrJ/2001/9: homicide in Scotland 2000'. Edinburgh: Scottish Executive, and at www.scotland.gov.uk/stats/bulletins/00119-00.asp (accessed April, 2004).

Scottish Executive (2001b) 'Statistical bulletin CrJ/2001/7: criminal proceedings in Scottish courts, 2000'. Edinburgh: Scottish Executive, and at www.scotland.gov.uk/stats/bulletins/00117–00.asp (accessed April, 2004).

Segal, L. (1993) 'Does pornography cause violence?: the search for evidence', in P.C. Gibson and R. Gibson (eds), *Dirty Looks: Women, Pornography, Power*. London: BFI.

Segal, L. and McIntosh, M. (eds) (1992) *Sex Exposed: Sexuality and the Pornography Debate*. London: Virago.

Senn, C.Y. (1993) 'Research on women and pornography: the many faces of harm', in D.E.H. Russell (ed.), *Making Violence Sexy: Feminist Views on Pornography*. Buckingham: Open University Press.

Shattuc, J. (1997) *The Talking Cure: TV Talk Shows and Women*. London: Routledge.

Signorielli, N. and Gerbner, G. (1988) *Violence and Terror in the Mass Media: An Annotated Bibliography*. New York: Greenwood.

Silbert, M. and Pines, A. (1984) 'Pornography and the sexual abuse of women', *Sex Roles*, 10 (11/12): 857–69.

Silverman, J. and Wilson, D. (2002) *Innocence Betrayed: Paedophilia, the Media and Society*. Cambridge: Polity.

Silverman, K. (1980) 'Masochism and subjectivity', *Framework*, 12: 2–9.

Smelik, A. (1995) 'What meets the eye: feminist film studies', in R. Buikema and A. Smelik (eds), *Women's Studies and Culture: A Feminist Introduction*. London: Zed.

Smith, S.J., Wilson, B.J. and Kunkel, D. (1998) 'Violence in television programming overall: University of California, Santa Barbara study', in *National Television Violence Study*, vol. 3. London: Sage.

Smith, V. (1998) *Not Just Race, Not Just Gender: Black Feminist Readings*. London: Routledge.

Sommers, C.H. (1994) *Who Stole Feminism? How Women Have Betrayed Women*. New York: Simon & Schuster.

Soothill, K., Francis, B. and Ackerley, E. (1998) 'Paedophilia and paedophiles', *New Law Journal*, 148.

Soothill, K. and Soothill, D. (1993) 'Prosecuting the victim: a study of the reporting of barristers' comments in rape cases', *Howard Journal of Criminal Justice*, 32 (1): 12–24.

Soothill, K. and Walby, S. (1991) *Sex Crime in the News*. London: Routledge.

Squire, C. (1994) 'Empowering women? The *Oprah Winfrey Show*', in C. Brunsdon, J. D'Acci and L. Spigel (eds) (1997), *Feminist Television Criticism: A Reader*. Oxford: Oxford University Press.

Stables, K. (1998) 'The postmodern always rings twice: constructing the *femme fatale* in 1990s cinema', in E.A. Kaplan (ed.), *Women in* Film Noir, London: BFI.

Stacey, J. (1987) 'Desperately seeking difference', in E.A. Kaplan, (ed.) (2000), *Feminism and Film*. Oxford: Oxford University Press.

Stacey, J. (1994) *Star Gazing: Hollywood Cinema and Female Spectatorship*. London: Routledge.

Stahly, G.B. and Walker, L.E.A. (1997) 'What are nice feminists like you doing on the O.J. defense team?: personal ruminations on the "trial of the century"', *Journal of Social Issues*, 53 (3): 425–39.

Stanko, E. (2000) 'The day to count ...', at www.domesticviolencedata.org (accessed April, 2004).

Stanko, E. and Scully, A. (1996) 'Retelling the tale: the Emma Humphreys case', in A. Myers and S. Wight (eds), *No Angels: Women Who Commit Violence*. London: Pandora.

Steinem, G. (1983) 'The real Linda Lovelace', in D.E.H. Russell (ed.) (1993), *Making Violence Sexy: Feminist Views on Pornography*. Buckingham: Open University Press.

Stoltenberg, J. (1994) *What Makes Pornography Sexy?* Minneapolis, MA: Milkweed.

Strossen, N. (1995) *Defending Pornography: Free Speech, and the Fight for Women's Rights*. New York: Scribner.

Studlar, G. (1985) 'Masochism and the perverse pleasures of the cinema', in E.A. Kaplan (ed.) (2000), *Feminism and Film*. Oxford: Oxford University Press.

Sturken, M. (2000) *Thelma and Louise*. London: BFI.

Surette, R. (1998) *Media, Crime, and Criminal Justice: Images and Realities*, 2nd edn. Belmont, CA: Wadsworth.

Tasker, Y. (1993) *Spectacular Bodies: Gender, Genre and the Action Cinema*. London: Routledge.

Tasker, Y. (1998) *Working Girls: Gender and Sexuality in Popular Cinema*. London: Routledge.

Tasker, Y. (2002) *The Silence of the Lambs*. London: BFI.

Taubin, A. (1992) 'The boys who cried misogyny', *Village Voice*, 28 April: 36.

Taubin, A. (1993) 'Grabbing the knife: *The Silence of the Lambs* and the history of the serial killer movie', in P. Cook and P. Dodd (eds), *Women and Film: A Sight and Sound Reader*. London: Scarlett Press.

Tolson, A. (2001) 'Talking about talk: the academic debates', in A. Tolson (ed.), *Television Talk Shows: Discourse, Performance, Spectacle*. Mahwah, NJ: Lawrence Erlbaum.

Traube, E. (1992) *Dreaming Identities: Class, Gender, and Generation in 1980s Hollywood Movies*. Boulder, CO: Westview Press.

Tudor, A. (2002) 'From paranoia to postmodernism?: the horror movie in late modern society', in S. Neale (ed.), *Genre and Contemporary Hollywood*. London: BFI.

Vance, C.S. (ed.) (1984) *Pleasure and Danger: Exploring Female Sexuality*. London: Routledge & Kegan Paul.

Vint, S. (2002) 'Killing us softly?: a feminist search for the "real" Buffy', *Slayage: The Online International Journal of Buffy Studies*, 5, and at www.slayage.tv/ then click on 'Archives' and scroll down list of authors (accessed April, 2004).

Walkowitz, J. (1982) 'Jack the Ripper and the myth of male violence', *Feminist Studies*, 8 (3): 542–74.

Ward, E. (1984) *Father-Daughter Rape*. London: Women's Press.

Ward Jouve, N. (1986) *'The Street-Cleaner': The Yorkshire Ripper Case on Trial*. New York: Marion Boyars.

Ward Jouve, N. (1993) 'An eye for an eye: the case of the Papin sisters', in H. Birch (ed.), *Moving Targets: Women, Murder and Representation*. London: Virago.

Wartella, E., Witney, C., Lasorsa, D. et al. (1998) 'Television violence in "reality" programming: University of Texas, Austin study', in *National Television Violence Study*, vol. 2. London: Sage.

Watney, S. (1987) *Policing Desire: Pornography, AIDS, and the Media*. Minneapolis, MA: University of Minnesota Press.

Watts, C. (1995) 'Thinking *Disclosure* or, the structure of post-feminist cynicism', *Women: A Cultural Review*, 6 (3): 275–86.

Webster, D. (1989) ' "Whodunnit?" America did: *Rambo* and post-Hungerford rhetoric', *Cultural Studies*, 3 (2): 173–93.

Weiss, A. (1992) *Vampires and Violets: Lesbians in the Cinema*. London: Jonathon Cape.

Whatling, C. (1997) *Screen Dreams: Fantasising Lesbians in Film*. Manchester: Manchester University Press.

Whelehan, I. (2000) *Overloaded: Popular Culture and the Future of Feminism*. London: Women's Press.

Whitney, C., Wartella, E., LaSorsa, D., et al. (1997) 'Television violence in "reality" programming: University of Texas, Austin study', in *National Television Violence Study*, vol. 1. London: Sage.

Whitney, C., Wartella, E., Lasorsa, D., et al. (1998) 'Television violence in "reality" (non-fictional) programming: University of Texas, Austin study', in *National Television Violence Study*, vol. 3. London: Sage.

Wilcox, R.V. (2002) '"Who died and made her boss?": patterns of mortality in *Buffy*', in R.V. Wilcox and D. Lavery (eds.), *Fighting the Forces: What's at Stake in* Buffy the Vampire Slayer. Lanham, MD: Rowman & Littlefield.

Willemen, P. (1981) 'Anthony Mann: looking at the male', *Framework*, 15–17; 16–20.

Williams, C.T. (1992) *It's Time For My Story: Soap Opera Sources, Structure, and Response*. Westport, CT: Praeger.

Williams, D.E. (1994) 'Born to kill', *Film Focus*, 2: 12–18.

Williams, L. (1983) 'When the woman looks', in B.K. Grant (ed.) (1996), *The Dread of Difference: Gender and the Horror Film*. Austin, TX: University of Texas Press.

Williams, L. (1993) 'A provoking agent: the pornography and performance art of Annie Sprinkle', in P.C. Gibson and R. Gibson (eds), *Dirty Looks: Women, Pornography, Power*. London: BFI.

Williams, T. (1996) 'Trying to survive on the darker side: 1980s family horror', in B.K. Grant (ed.), *The Dread of Difference: Gender and the Horror Film*. Austin, TX: University of Texas Press.

Wilson, B.J., Kunkel, D., Linz, D., et al. (1997) 'Violence in television programming overall: University of California, Santa Barbara study', in *National Television Violence Study*, vol. 1. London: Sage.

Wilson, B.J., Kunkel, D., Linz, D., et al. (1998) 'Violence in television programming overall: University of California, Santa Barbara study', in *National Television Violence Study*, vol. 2. London: Sage.

Wilson, C., with Wilson, D. (1995) *A Plague of Murder: The Rise and Rise of Serial Killing in the Modern Age*. London: Robinson.

Wilton, T. (ed.) (1995) *Immortal Invisible: Lesbians and the Moving Image*. London: Routledge.

Wlodarz, J. (2001) 'Rape fantasies: hollywood and homophobia', in P. Lehman (ed.), *Masculinity: Bodies, Movies, Culture*. London: Routledge.

Wober, M. (1978) 'Televised violence and paranoid perception: the view from Great Britain', *Public Opinion Quarterly*, 42: 315–21.

Wolf, N. (1994) *Fire with Fire: The New Female Power and How to Use It*. New York: Fawcett Columbine.

Wood, H. (2001) ' "No, YOU rioted!": the pursuit of conflict in the management of "lay" and "expert" discourse on *Kilroy*', in A. Tolson (ed.), *Television Talk Shows: Discourse, Performance, Spectacle*. Mahwah, NJ: Lawrence Erlbaum.

Wood, R. (1986) *Hollywood from Vietnam to Reagan*. New York: Columbia University Press.

Wykes, M. (1995) 'Passion, murder and marriage: analysing the press discourse', in R.E. Dobash, R.P. Dobash and L. Noaks (eds), *Gender and Crime*. Cardiff: University of Wales Press.

Wykes, M. (2001) *News, Crime and Culture*. London: Pluto.

Zillman, D. and Weaver, J.B. (1997) 'Gender socialisation theory of reactions to horror', in J.B. Weaver and R. Tamborini (eds), *Horror Films: Current Research on Audience Preferences and Reactions*. Mahwah, NJ: Lawrence Erlbaum.

Index